JN419268

스파르타
TOEIC
실전
LC 1000제

TOEIC 실전1000제 LC

초판 1쇄 발행 2016년 6월 12일
초판 5쇄 발행 2019년 11월 25일

저 자   원정서
펴낸이   박성호
펴낸곳   잉글리쉬앤 (주)

편 집   박고우니
감 수   허창환
영 업   박상신, 정슬기

주소 서울 특별시 관악구 쑥고개로 67-1
대표전화 (02) 878-1945
출판등록 2002년 3월 3일 제 320-2002-00045호

ISBN 978-89-6715-079-2 13740

원쌤의 Q&A

Q1. 도대체 왜 안 들릴까?

안 들리는 이유는 '보이는 영어'를 가지고 들릴 것이라는 추측을 하고 공부를 시작했기 때문이다. 지금까지 중고등학교에서나 길거리 광고에서 영어의 알파벳을 한국어식으로 읽는 것은 '청취 공부'가 아니다. 들리게 하는 방법은 간단하다. '원어민의 영어 발음'을 듣는 공부를 꾸준히 하면 된다. 결국 청취 공부는 보는 공부와 달리 얼마나 많이 녹음을 듣느냐, 이해하기 어렵고 들리지 않는 발음을 글씨와 연결짓는 훈련을 얼마나 했느냐에 달려 있다.

Q2. 그냥 외워 버리면 될까요?

'듣는 공부'는 지겹고 눈에 보이지 않는다. 녹음을 듣고 따라하거나 해석이 안 되는 문장의 발음을 이해하는 것은 답답하다. 그래서 편법으로 '그냥 다 외워버리면 들리겠지'라고 생각하는 수험생들이 있다. 이 방법이야말로 가장 비효율적이고 시간 낭비이다. 위에서 말했듯이, '원어민의 발음'을 들어야 하는데, '나만의 발음, 나만의 영어'로 문장을 외워버리는 것은 아무 도움도 되지 않는 암기 훈련일 뿐이다. 이 무식한 방법은 토익 공부에 대한 의욕을 좌절시키므로 절대로 금기사항이다.

Q3. 들리면 답을 맞힐 수 있나요?

절대 그렇지 않다. 토익 시험뿐만 아니라, 모든 시험 과목에서 시험 출제 범위와 출제자의 의도를 파악하는 것이 가장 중요한 고득점 전략이다. 그렇기 때문에 토익 고득점을 위한 LC 공부는 아래와 같이 두 단계로 이해되어야 한다.

1. 정답을 맞히기 위한 공부: 유형 정리를 통한 정답과 오답 유형의 이해
2. 정답 부분의 이해 및 청취

들리기만 하면 LC 고득점이 가능할 거라고 생각하지만 그렇지 않다. 청취는 정답을 이해하고 맞히는 데 도움을 주는 것이지, 그 자체가 고득점을 보장하지는 않는다. 이는 어휘(Vocabulary)와 비슷하다. 어휘와 청취는 고득점에 꼭 필요하지만 무작정 단어를 외우고 청취 공부만 하는 것은 효율적으로 올라갈 수 있는 고득점을 굳이 돌아가는 것이다. 청취는 정답을 맞히고 '시험 유형'을 보완하는 하나의 도구로 생각하자.

Q4. 가장 효과적인 청취 방법은?

가장 효율적인 청취 방법은 학생의 레벨과 배경에 따라 다르다. 하지만 연음이 가장 강하고 녹음 속도가 빠른 Part 2의 질문과 정답(Question & Response)을 통해 소위 귀가 뚫리게 하는 것이 가능하다. 되도록 '스크립트를 보지 않고, 녹음을 듣고 따라읽기'를 통해 기본 청취의 단계를 넘을 수 있다. 원칙을 잊지 말자. '원어민의 녹음'을 얼마나 많이 듣고 연습했느냐가 청취의 비결이다. 400점 이상의 고득점을 획득한 학생은 본인이 틀린 부분만 반복 청취해서 약점을 보완할 수 있다. 하지만 목표는 청취가 아닌 LC 고득점이다. 청취를 연습하는 문장이 문제 안에서의 의미를 이해하는 유형 학습이 병행되어야 함을 잊지 말자.

레벨별 학습법

토익은 특별한 스킬과 체력을 요하는 수영, 골프 같은 스포츠와 같다. 체력과 기술이 부족한 상태에서 무작정 문제만 푸는 것은 힘든 것은 물론이고, 노력한만큼의 효과가 나타나지 않는다. **자신의 레벨과 약점을 확인하고 '가장 빠르고 효율적으로' 목적지에 다다를 수 있도록 훈련하자.** 〈스파르타 토익 LC 1000제〉는 400점 이상의 토익 고득점을 목표로, 495점 만점을 달성하기 위한 LC 집중 교재이다. 본인의 레벨을 확인하고 가장 알맞은 집중 훈련 방법을 찾도록 하자. 본 교재의 모의고사 또는 파트별 집중 문제집으로 사용함으로써 실전 감각과 고난도 문제에 대한 자신감을 얻을 수 있을 것이다.

토익 초보자의 고민
토익은 쉽다는데 어떻게 공부해야 할지 막막하다.
최대한 빠르게 고득점을 얻고 싶다!

LEVEL 1 토익 왕초보 (LC 330점 이상 목표)

▸ **무엇이 문제인가?**
토익은 소문만 듣고 아는 것이 전혀 없다.
도대체 무엇을 어떻게 공부해야 남들이 말하는 것처럼 빨리 고득점을 얻을 수 있을지 궁금하다.
토익뿐만 아니라 영어에 대한 자신감도 떨어지는 상황이라 더 불안하다.

▸ **학습 전략**
토익 파트별 유형 정리 ➡ 질문 유형별 구조 파악하기/ 정답 유형별 표현 암기하기
기초 청취 훈련 ➡ 스크립트 없이 영어 듣기 훈련/ 안 들리는 발음 듣기 훈련

▸ **본서 이용 방법**
초보는 토익 유형에 대한 이해와 자주 출제되는 유형의 문제를 안정감 있게 풀 수 있는 능력이 가장 중요하다. 〈스파르타 토익 700/800〉 교재를 통해 유형 분류와 기초 청취 부분을 학습하고 본 교재에 도전하자. 단기간 학습 플랜을 계획하고 있다면 실전 1000제를 병행하는 것도 가능하다. 시험 2주 전부터 〈스파르타 LC 1000제〉의 실전 1~5회 기출 레벨 문제를 Half Test 형태로 풀면서 실전 시험 대비 훈련을 하자.

LEVEL 2 토익을 시작해 봤다 (LC 380점 이상 목표)

▸ **무엇이 문제인가?**
간헐적인 공부로 이것저것 건드린 것은 많은데 머리 속에서 토익이란 시험과 유형이 정립되지 않았다.
토익의 7개 파트 중에서 무엇을 우선적으로 집중적으로 공부할지 고민 중이다.

▸ **학습 전략**
토익 파트별 유형 정리 & 유형별 문제 풀이 ➡ 배운 유형을 실전 문제를 통해 찾아내고 정답을 맞추는 훈련을 한다.
기초 청취(문장 구조별) 훈련 ➡ 단순히 안 들리는 어휘나 발음이 아닌, 문장 구조상에서의 안 들리는 구문을 정리한다.
(수동태, 완료형, 관계사절 등의 구조를 녹음으로 들을 수 있도록 한다.)

▸ **본서 이용 방법**
토익 초보는 유형에 대한 정리가 가장 시급하지만, 이제 시험장에서 실력을 발휘할 수 있도록 실전 문제 형태도 같이 병행해야 한다. 〈스파르타 토익 800 LC〉 교재를 통해 심화 유형 분류를 완성하고, 〈스파르타 토익 LC 1000제〉의 실전 1~5회 기출 레벨 100문제 또는 Half Test 형태로 풀면서 실전 시험 대비 훈련을 하자.

토익 중상급자의 고민
토익 공부를 좀 했으나 점수가 정체된다.
어떻게 하면 실수를 줄이고 집중력이 높일 수 있는지 알고 싶다.
토익 공부 EXIT PLAN을 알고 싶다!

 **토익 본격적으로 공부할 준비가 되었다 (LC 430점 이상 목표)**

▸ **무엇이 문제인가?**
토익에 대해 들어본 것도 많고 좀 알지만, 내가 문제를 풀면 생각보다 많이 틀린다.
다른 사람들에 비해 토익의 점수 향상 속도가 느린 것 같아서 불안하다.

▸ **학습 전략**
계속적인 정리와 이해만 가지고는 효율적으로 문제를 풀 수 없다. 이해는 그만, 문제를 풀어서 맞추자!
실전 형태에서 정답을 맞힐 수 있도록, 다수의 문제를 한꺼번에 푸는 훈련이 필요하다.
자신이 어떤 문제에 약하고 강한지를 파악하고, 오답 노트를 통해 취약 파트를 보완하자.

▸ **본서 이용 방법**
고득점 목표를 위해 만들어진 스파르타 실전 LC 1000제의 1단계 실전 레벨 모의고사로(Test 1~5)로 한 번에 100문제씩 풀면서
집중력을 키운다. 틀린 문제의 복습은 반복해서 문제 풀기: ① 문제 풀기, ② 다시 풀기, ③ 틀린 문제 다시 풀기의 형태로 해석
/해설을 보기 전까지 충분히 문제 풀기를 통해서 훈련을 한다. 전체 복습이 아닌 많이 틀린 문제만 뽑아서 집중적으로 풀고,
구문 해석과 청취 공부를 통해 한 유형씩 차례대로 완벽하게 마스터한다. ➡ 중간에 한 번씩 만점 목표 모의고사(Test 6~10)로
난이도를 올려 집중도를 확인한다.

 **토익 LC 만점 목표 (LC 495점 만점 목표)**

▸ **무엇이 문제인가?**
토익에 쏟아부은 시간이 얼마인데 왜 아직 안 될까 고민한다.
어려운 것은 없는 것 같은데, 해도 해도 실수가 줄지 않아 고민이다.
아는 것은 많은데도 현장 시험에서 실력을 보여주지 못하는 본인의 집중력에 실망할 때가 있다.

▸ **학습 전략**
고난도 문제가 등장해도 당황하지 않고 실수를 줄일 수 있는 전략을 짠다.
많은 문제를 풀어도 집중력이 떨어지지 않도록 훈련한다.
어려운 문제를 접해 보고 실전에서 당황하지 않고 풀 수 있도록 훈련한다.

▸ **본서 이용 방법**
LC 만점을 위해서는, 기출 레벨 문제를 반복해서 푸는 것으로는 충분하지 않다. 난이도 높은 문제를 풀어서 어떤 문제가 나오
더라도 집중할 수 있도록 하는 것이 필요하다. 난이도 높은 문제는 ① 빠른 속도, ② 난해한 동의 표현으로 나올 수 있다. 만점
목표 모의고사(Test 6~10)으로 난이도 높은 문제를 풀어 보고, 실제 토익시험 전에 실전 레벨 모의고사(Test 1~5)로 실수하지
않는 훈련을 한다.

Part 1 고득점 전략

원쌤의 고득점 Point! : 보이는 것이 다가 아니다!

- ✔ 동사와, 동사 시제를 마스터 한다.
- ✔ 지우기를 완성시켜 언제나 Best Answer를 고르자.

사진을 보고, 그 사진을 영어로 가장 잘 묘사한 표현을 고르는 것이 Part 1이다. 그러나 실전 토익에서는 그림을 잘 묘사한 것을 섣불리 고르려고 하다가는 오히려 실수하기 쉽다. 난이도가 점점 올라갈수록 사진에서 잘 보이는 어휘는 오답에 포함되는 경우가 많고, 사진을 보고 추측하기 힘든 표현이 정답이 되기 때문이다. 지우기 훈련을 통해서 특정 어휘가 마음에 들어도 틀린 부분이 있으면 지우고, 특별히 마음에 드는 어휘가 없으면 남는 정답지 중에서 Best Answer를 고르는 훈련을 하자.

(낮은 레벨)

Workers are painting outdoors. (O)
일꾼들은 야외에서 페인트칠하고 있다.

(고난도 레벨)

The house is boarded by the wall. (O)
집이 나무판으로 둘러싸여 있다.

There are paintings on the wall. (X)
벽에 그림들이 있다.

▶ 동사를 마스터하자! 행동/상태 동사 암기 & 능동/수동태, 진행/완료형 시제 청취력
능동형: 현재형(동사현재형), 진행형(be + ing형), 완료형(have + p.p.형)
수동형: 현재형(be + p.p.형), 수동태 진행형(be + being + p.p.형), 수동태 완료형(have been + p.p.형)
  ➡ 틀린 문제의 시제를 완벽하게 이해하고 사진과 매칭한다.

▶ 문장 구조를 이해하고 틀린 부분을 "골라내는" 훈련을 한다.
'주어+동사+목적어+부사구' 형태의 문장을 들으면서 틀린 부분이 있으면 전체 문장을 오답 처리 하고, 틀린 부분이 없거나 또는 해석이 안 되고 그림이 이해되지 않는 경우에는 지우지 않는다. 오답 처리를 하지 않은 지문 중에서 가장 좋은 것을 정답으로 골라낸다.
  ➡ 어떤 부분에서 틀렸는지 골라내는 훈련을 한다.

원쌤의 만점 Point! : 보이는 것이 다가 아니다!

- ✔ 고난도 풍경 별 어휘를 암기하자.
- ✔ 고난도 지우기 문제를 풀어 얼마나 정답이 "치사" 할 수 있는지 익혀 두자.

시험 현장에서 어려운 문제를 실수하지 않고 풀기 위해서는 평소에 그와 같은 레벨 또는 그 보다 높은 레벨의 문제를 많이 풀어서 고난도 문제가 나와도 당황하지 말아야 한다. Part 1 사진에서는 인물 사진이나 자주 접할 수 있는 일상생활 관련 사진 이외에 '특정 표현'이 등장하는 소위 고난도 유형의 사진들이 있다. 주로 공사 현장이나 선착장 야외 풍경 등의 사진으로, 자주 접해 보지 못한 표현들이 등장하므로 당황하지 않고 답을 고를 수 있도록 하자.

Mountains overlook the lake. (O)
산들이 물을 내려다 보고 있다. (물가에 산이 있다)

Trees are reflected on the water. (O)
나무들이 물에 반사되고 있다.

A boat is secured at a dock. (O)
배가 선착장에 고정되어 있다.

▶ **고난도 풍경 사진 (풍경) – 출제 빈도는 낮지만 꾸준한 최고 난이도 문제**
공사장: 외바퀴 손수레를 밀다(pushing a wheelbarrow), 흙을 파고 있다(digging the soil/dirt/earth)
선착장: 선착장에 배가 대어 있다(be tied/docked/anchored), 물위를 항해한다(be sailing/floating)
길/계단/다리 묘사: 길이 쭉 뻗다, 휘어지다, 연결된다(The path extends/leads to/curves/runs)
➡ **풍경 관련 어휘를 통해서 사진에서 잘 보이지 않는 정답 표현을 익힌다.**

▶ **고난도 사진 – 사진에서 잘 보이지 않는 구석, 천정, 바닥 등을 정답으로 만드는 문제**
하늘 묘사: 하늘에 구름(clouds in the sky), 연기가 하늘로 올라간다(smoke rising in the air)
바닥 묘사: 그림자를 드리우다(casting shadows), 길에 자동차 타이어 자국(tracks left on the ground)
안 보이는 소품 묘사: 벽에 콘센트가 꽂혀 있다(power cord has been plugged in)
➡ **사진에 안 보이는 부분으로 정답을 묘사하는 문제를 풀어, 실전에서 함정에 빠지지 않도록 훈련하자.**

Part 2 고득점 전략

원쌤의 고득점 Point! : 질문 듣기 & 지우기를 훈련하라!

- ✔ 의문문 앞에 3~4단어를 듣고 유형을 파악하자.
- ✔ "오답 지우기"를 완성시켜 언제나 Best Answer를 고르자.

청취력의 의존도가 높지만, 청취력만 가지고는 고득점을 받기 힘든 것이 Part 2이다. 난이도가 낮은 문제에서는 질문을 듣고, 내가 생각한 문장이 정답으로 등장하는 경우가 꽤 많다. 하지만, 점점 올라갈수록 추측하기 힘든 표현이 정답이 된다. 이런 경우에는 오히려 전형적인 오답을 통해서 정답을 고르는 것이 안전하다. 질문과 대답 세트를 많이 암기해두는 것을 기초로 해서, (A), (B), (C) 정답지에서 오답을 지우기 훈련을 통해서 특정 어휘가 마음에 들어도 틀린 부분이 있으면 지우고, 특별히 마음에 드는 어휘가 없으면 남은 선택지 중에서 Best Answer를 고르는 훈련을 하자.

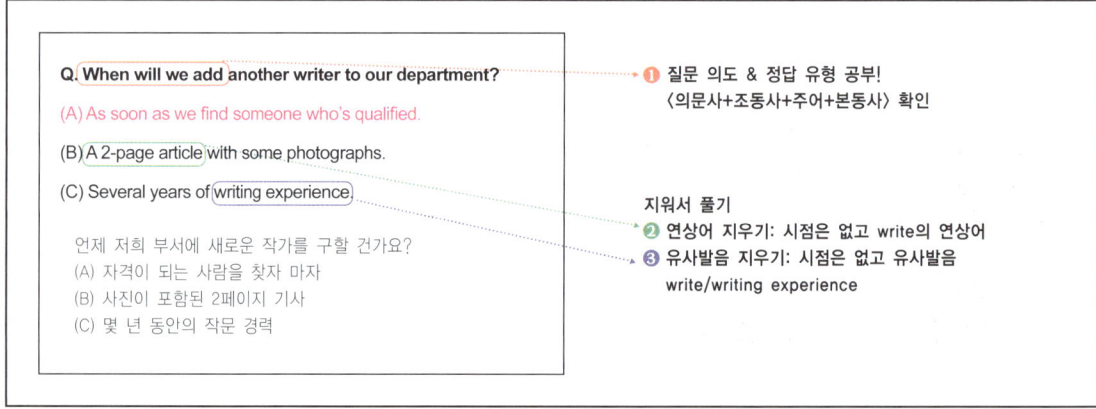

▶ 질문 파악과 정답 유형의 80% 이상을 좌우하는 첫 4단어를 마스터하라!

무엇보다도 질문을 듣고 해석하고 정답을 파악할 수 있으면 유리한 것은 사실이다. 첫 3~4단어로 의문문 유형/시제/주어를 한번에 파악할 수 있도록 하자. 토익 빈출 정답 표현으로 먼저 정답부터 암기한다.

의문사 의문문의 유형별 정답: 의문사 Who/Where/When/How/Why/Which/What 각각 파악
Yes-No 의문문의 유형별 정답: 선택/권유청유형/긍정/부정/부가/간접/평서문을 각각 파악

 ➖ 주로 실전의 앞쪽 문제(7번~ 25번)에서는 정답 유형으로, 뒤쪽 문제는(26~31번)에서는 지우기 문제가 자주 출제된다. 틀린 문제는 오답 노트를 작성해서 정답 유형, 오답 유형을 파악해 두자.

▶ 정답만큼 중요한 전형적인 오답을 익히자.

유사 발음이 등장하거나 연상어의 오답들은 토익에 익숙하지 않은 학생들이 오답 지우기로 가장 많이 사용하는 전략이다. 하지만, 맹목적인 오답 처리는 만점 전략과 맞지 않는다. 유사 발음이 하나도 등장하지 않은 문제 세트나, 정답지 3개가 전부 유사 발음이 등장하는 문제들도 있기 때문이다. 발음이 익숙하거나 연상되는 언어로 고르지 않는 것이 좀 더 안정적인 고득점 전략이다. 오답 노트에서 오답 유형 정리를 병행하면 자주 등장하는 함정도 알 수 있다.

 ➖ 유사 발음/연상어의 전형적인 오답 형태의 어휘/표현으로 정답을 하나씩 남기는 훈련을 하자.

원쌤의 만점 Point! : 매번 실수하는 "약점"을 없애라!

- Yes/No 의문문 최고의 인기스타 "평서문"을 정복하자.
- Yes/No 의문문에 Yes/No 빠진 상태로 대답하는 것을 훈련하자.

Part 2는 LC 전체에서 쉬운 문제와 어려운 문제의 난이도 폭이 제일 넓은 파트이다. 기본적으로 70%의 정답을 맞추는 것이 가능하다. 그 다음부터는 본인의 약점을 본격적으로 파악하고 보완하는 것이 필요하다. 최근에 출제 빈도가 꾸준히 늘고 있는 것은 평서문으로, 맨 앞만 듣고 해석이 안 되는 경우가 많고, 다양한 반응(response)이 정답이 되어 고난도 유형으로 뽑힌다. 스파르타 토익 LC 1000제는 평서문은 물론 고득점자가 약점으로 꼽는 Yes/No 없는 Yes/No 의문문 유형에 특별히 집중했다. 본인의 약점을 파악하고 보완할 수 있도록 하자.

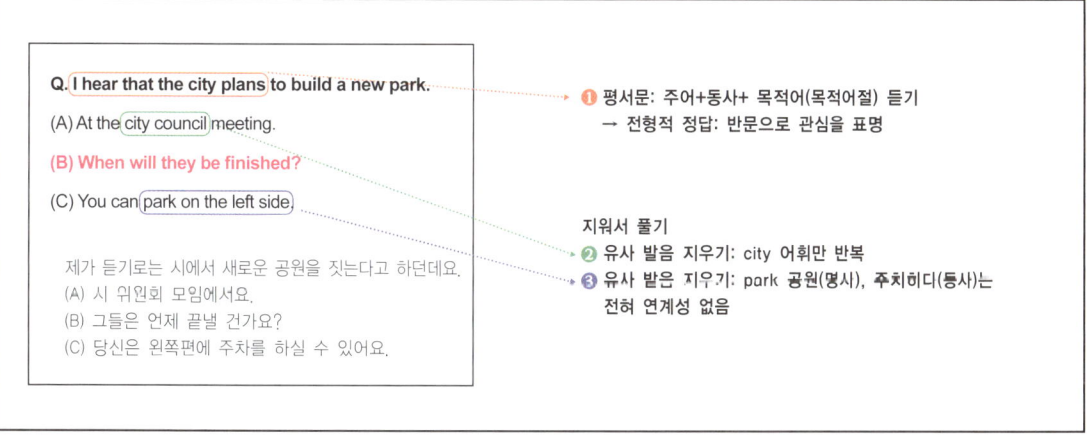

▶ 최대 약점 "평서문"에 세부 지식으로 반문, 조건을 제시하는 "전형적인 반응"을 익히자.

평서문도 유형별로 정리가 가능하다. ①문제점 ②좋은 소식 ③나쁜 소식 ④의견 ⑤FACT의 전달 등이다.
다른 유형과 마찬가지로, 각각의 평서문의 유형에 세부지식을 요청하는 전형적인 유형을 익히도록 하자.

ex) 9시에 회의한다 – 어디서/누가/무슨 준비물을 해야 하나 등의 진형직인 형태의 반응이다.

➥ 평서문의 유형별로 정답/오답을 정리하면 쉽게 넘어갈 수 있는 산이다.

▶ 최대 약점 2: Yes/No 없이 대답하는 고난도 정답

모든 시험 과목에서 고득점은 유형 분류가 기본적으로 깔려야 한다. 대부분의 학생들이 Yes/No 의문문의 유형 분류를 제대로 하지 않고 해석으로만 풀려다 보니 조금만 난이도가 올라가면 당황하게 된다. Yes/No 의문문에 양쪽으로 〈Yes + 긍정 내용〉〈No + 부정 내용〉으로 대답하는 훈련을 하면 Yes/No가 빠진 것도 정답을 맞히는 것이 가능하다.

ex) 내일 만날까? – (안 돼) 마이애미에 출장가는데. 결국 〈No + 바쁘다〉의 변형으로 볼 수 있다.

➥ Yes/No 의문문의 고난도 정답은 전형적인 유형의 변형이다. 오답 노트로 극복하자.

Part 3 고득점 전략

원쌤의 고득점 Point! : 읽은 만큼 들린다!! 완벽하게 준비하자!

- 녹음 전에 문제를 파악하고 기억하자!
- 기출 유형도 "미리 파악"하여 준비한다.

LC에서 가장 문항 수가 많고(39문제) 난이도가 높다는 파트이다. 하지만, 어렵게 출제된다기보다는 여전히 문제를 미리 읽고 파악한 후에 2~3사람의 긴 대화가 집중하기 힘들게 하는 것뿐이다. 정확하게 문제를 읽고 파악해 두면 본문의 흐름은 물론, 정답 예측까지 가능한 것이 Part 3/4이다. Part 3의 경우, 다수의 등장인물이 정신없이 대화하는 것 같지만, 본문을 다 듣고 summary하는 것이 아니라 각각의 문제에서 원하는 것만을 '정확하게 집어내는 것'이 목표라는 것을 잊지 말자.

Company	Location
Gourmet W	Newton
Sky View	Summerville
Tao Ling Food	Medford
Jessica's Cafe	Boston

68. What event is the company sponsoring?
(A) A race

69. What is the man concerned about?
(C) A limited budget

70. Look at the Graphic. Which company will the speakers choose?
(A) Gourmet W
(B) Sky View
(C) Tao Ling Food
(D) Jessica's Cafe

Questions 68 through 70 refer to the following conversation and a list.

M: Heather, I'm excited about the race our company is sponsoring. A lot of people will be running in it. So it'll be great publicity.

W: That reminds me. Have you looked over this list of catering firms we are considering to hire for the vent?

M: I can look at it now. Hmm – Skyview has the best options, but we need a company that's a little less expensive. Our budget is being reduced since last year's race.

W: Good point. Let's go for the one that is right here in Medford. They have a good reputation and their prices are reasonable.

M: 헤더, 우리 회사가 이번에 후원하고 있는 경주에 대해서 굉장히 기대돼요. 많은 사람들이 참가를 할 거고 아주 좋은 홍보가 될 거예요.

W: 그러니 생각나네요. 그 행사에 사용할 출장 요리업체 목록을 보셨나요?

M: 지금 보면 되죠. 스카이뷰가 선택 폭이 좋은데 조금 싼 업체가 필요해요. 우리 예산이 작년 경주 이후 줄었거든요.

W: 맞아요. 여기 메드포드 지역에 있는 곳으로 하죠. 그곳은 평판도 좋고 가격도 합리적이에요.

▶ 문제 3개를 읽고 기억하는 것은 기본이다. GQ/SQ 각각의 유형을 파악해 두고 준비한다.

정확하게 문제를 읽고 유형을 분류하고 "지문에서 어떻게 정답 단서를 줄까"를 예측하면서 듣는다.

표 관련 문제도 "문제&표"를 읽고 표의 어떤 부분이 녹음으로 들려줄지를 예측한다.

- 지문에서 정답의 단서를 포착해서 듣고, 문제 읽기를 훈련해서 정답을 맞춘다.

원쌤의 만점 Point! : 매번 실수하는 "약점"을 없애라!

- ✅ 독해형 문제의 긴 정답지 (A), (B), (C), (D)를 읽고 빠르게 요점을 파악할 수 있도록 훈련하자.
- ✅ 들은 단어를 "넓은 의미"의 동의 표현으로 바꾸어 고른다.

문제를 미리 읽고 파악한 후, 들으면서 동시에 풀어야 하는 파트에서는 다양하게 난이도를 조절할 수 있다. Part 3에서 문제를 어렵게 만들려면 ① 눈으로 읽는 부분인 문제 부분을 길고 난해하게 만들거나, ② 문제도 읽고 준비를 했는데도 불구하고 마치 정답이 없는 것과 같은 트릭으로 본문에서 나온 어휘로 동의 표현으로 바꾸어서 고르게 하는 경우이다. 특히, 초보는 읽는 속도가 느려 ①에서 많이 틀리고, 고득점자들은 ②의 동의 표현에 고민한다. 특히, ②의 경우에 소위 다 듣고 알아들었는데 고를 정답이 없는 경우가 생기는 것이다. 고난도 문제를 맞추기 위해서는 조금은 "어렵게" 본문과 타협해서 동의 표현을 고르는 훈련이 필요하다.

---

70. Why does the woman direct the man to the company's website?

(A) To make an online payment

(B) To get directions to the store

(C) To view available design options

(D) To revise an existing policy

W: If you visit our company website, you'll be able to search through the designs we do offer.

W: 당신의 저희 회사의 웹사이트를 방문하시면, 저희가 제공하는 디자인의 찾아보실 수 있을 겁니다.

▶ **독해형 문제의 유형을 파악하고 훈련한다.**

① 언급형(what is mentioned/said about the ~)

② 화자의 의도 파악 문제 (What does the woman mean when she says " "~)

③ 그 이외의 의문사 Why/What을 사용해서 목적/이유를 묻는 문제 (What made the speaker do ~)

긴 문장을 빨리 읽고 파악하지 못한다면 LC는 물론 Part 6, 7에서도 고득점을 받기 힘들다. 〈스파르타 투익 실전 1000제〉에 나온 긴 선택지를 처음 읽을 때 문장 구조의 주어/동사를 마킹하면서 빠르게 문제를 읽고 풀도록 하자. 오답노트 만들 때 해석이 안 되는 구문을 따로 익히는 훈련을 하자.

➡ **(A),(B),(C),(D)의 선택지들의 각각의 주요 포인트가 무엇인지를 파악하는 훈련을 하자.**

▶ **주어진 보기 중에 Best Answer인 동의 표현(Paraphrasing) 고르는 훈련을 한다.**

문제를 미리 읽고 본문에서 어떤 성우가 말할 것인지 위치를 파악했는데도 정답을 고르지 못했다는 것은 본문에 나온 어휘가 그대로 (A),(B),(C),(D)에 나오지 않았기 때문이다. LC의 경우에는 빈출 동의 표현을 암기하는 것만으로는 부족하다. 최상위의 동의 표현은 단순한 동의 표현이 아니라, 주어진 선택지 중에 가장 좋은 것을 골라야 하는 Best Answer이기 때문이다. 녹음을 듣고 정답을 작문하려고 하지 말고 주어진 것 중에 제일 좋은 것을 고르는 것에 익숙해지자.

➡ **자주 등장하는 동의 표현을 암기하고, 주어진 것 중에 가장 좋은 선택지를 고르는 훈련을 하자.**

Part 4 고득점 전략

원쌤의 고득점 Point! : 읽은 만큼 들린다!! 완벽하게 준비하자!

- ✅ 녹음 전에 문제를 파악하고 기억하자!
- ✅ 주제별 유형/어휘를 익혀서 "정답"을 좀 더 쉽게 맞힌다.

복수의 등장인물이 정신없이 대화하는 Part 3에 비해, Part 4는 언제나 1명의 화자(speaker)가 주어진 주제에 대해서 일정한 방향으로 발표를 이끌어 나가게 된다. 회화의 연장선에 있는 Part 3와 달리, Part 4는 사람들 앞에서의 발표(speech)로 문어체적인 딱딱한 면이 있기에 소위 기습 공격같은 문제는 자주 등장하지 않는다. 다소 생소한 문어체 표현의 벽만 넘으면 오히려 Part 3보다 정답을 맞히는 것이 쉽다.

Program	
Presenter	**Time**
Dr. Randolph	9:30 a.m.
Ms. Nelson	11:00 a.m.
Break	12:00~1:30 p.m.
Workshops	2:00 p.m.

98. What is the purpose of this announcement?
(C) To provide a schedule overview

99. Look at the graphic. Which program has the incorrect information?
(A) Dr. Randolph's
(B) Ms. Nelson's
(C) Lunch break
(D) Workshops

100. Where can the listeners find information on local restaurants?
(C) In the conference program

Thank you for coming to the opening day of public speaking seminar. As you can see in your program, we have an exciting day ready for you today. But before we start, I have a brief announcement about the schedule. Dr. Steve Randolph' speech on image training will be at 10 o'clock instead of 9:30 due to some technical difficulties in the meeting room B. But, I'm sure his speech will worth the wait. There will be a break for lunch at 12:00 noon as scheduled. For your convenience, we've provided a list of local restaurants on the back page of the program, or you can visit the downstairs cafeteria. In the afternoon, we will break into groups and you can either take intensive workshops around 2 o'clock, or visit the exhibition halls. I hope you enjoy the best of what we have prepared for you.

연설 기술 세미나의 첫 날에 와주셔서 감사합니다. 여러분의 프로그램을 보시면 저희가 여러분을 위해서 재미있는 하루를 준비해 놓은 것을 아실 겁니다. 하지만 저희가 시작하기 전에 일정표에 대해서 간단히 안내드릴 것이 있습니다. 9시반에 이미지 트레이닝에 대한 스티브 랜돌프 박사의 연설이 기술적인 문제로 30분 지연되어 9시반이 아닌 10시에 시작하겠습니다. 그 분의 발표는 기다릴 값어치가 있을 겁니다. 일정대로 12시에는 점심 시간이 있을 예정이고요. 여러분의 편의를 위해서 프로그램 뒤편에 근처의 식당 목록을 드렸습니다. 또한, 간단한 식사를 위해서는 아래층의 구내 식당을 이용하실 수 있습니다. 오후에는 그룹으로 나누어서 심화 워크숍을 들으시거나 전시홀을 방문하실 수 있습니다. 저희가 여러분을 위해 준비한 것들을 최대한 즐기시기 바랍니다.

▶ 문제 3개를 읽고 기억하는 것은 기본이다. 문제 3개와 표를 통해서 TOPIC 별 추측이 가능하다.

정확하게 문제를 읽고 유형을 분류하고 "지문에서 어떻게 정답 힌트를 줄까"를 예측하면서 듣는다. 특히 Part 4는 TOPIC별로 같은 문제/표현이 정답이 되는 경우가 많다. 표 관련 문제도 "문제&표"를 읽고 표의 어떤 부분을 녹음으로 들려줄지를 예측한다.

━ 지문에서 정답을 들어낼 수 있는 문제 읽기를 훈련해서 정답을 맞힌다.

원쌤의 만점 Point! : 어려운 주제(Topic)를 마스터하라!

✅ 90번대 이후로 출제되는 고난이도 주제(TOPIC)를 훈련하라.
✅ 독해형 문제의 긴 선택지 (A), (B), (C), (D)를 읽고 빠르게 요점을 파악할 수 있도록 훈련하자.

문제를 미리 읽고 파악하고, 들으면서 동시에 풀어야 하는 파트이다. 물론 간단히 녹음을 빠르게 할 수도 있겠지만, Part 3에서 문제를 어렵게 만들려면 ① 눈으로 읽는 부분인 문제 부분을 길고 난해하게 만들거나, ② 문제도 읽고 준비를 했는데도 불구하고 마치 정답이 없는 것과 같은 트릭으로 본문에서 나온 어휘로 동의 표현으로 바꾸어서 고르게 하는 경우이다. 특히, 초보는 읽는 속도가 느려서 ①에서 많이 틀리고, 고득점자들은 ②의 동의 표현에 고민한다. 특히, ②의 경우에 소위 다 듣고 알아들었는데 고를 정답이 없는 경우가 생기는 것이다. 고난도 문제를 맞히기 위해서는 조금은 "어렵게" 본문과 타협해서 동의 표현을 고르는 훈련이 필요하다.

---

98. Where do the speakers most likely work?

(A) A food processing plant

(B) A financial services corporation

(C) A corporate law firm

(D) A video production company

I have a few words to say about our meeting with the representatives from Wong's Foods next week. Let's remember that Wong's Foods is our video production's biggest client. It is critical that we get the contract.

다음 주에 있을 웡푸드 사 직원들과의 회의에 대해 몇 마디 드리고 싶습니다. 웡푸드는 우리 비디오 생산의 가장 큰 고객이라는 것을 다시 한번 알려 드리고 싶습니다. 우리가 계약을 따는 것은 정말 중요합니다.

▶ 뉴스 관련 주제는 자주 등장하는 Project를 이해하자.
  ① Business News: 기업체의 CEO가 준 정보를 기업 인수/합병/신상품/공장신설 등의 중요한 결정에 대한 내용을 기자(reporter)나 방송국의 아나운서(announcer)가 전달한다.
  ② Local News: 시장(mayor)과 시 위원회(city council)가 지역 공동체의 활성화를 위해서 다양한 건설/문화 Project를 제안하고 승인하는 내용이 등장한다.

어휘나 표현이 딱딱하고 까다롭지만 Part 6나 7에서도 고난이도 문제로 출제될 수 있는 내용으로, 고득점으로 가기 위해 빈드시 익혀야 될 내용이나.
  ➡ **지역 공동체(local community)와 한 사업체의 비즈니스 활동 관련 주제를 마스터하자.**

▶ 업무 배정(project assignment)은 고객사(client)와 하청/공급업체(agency/supplier) 관계를 이해하자.
  ① Staff Meeting: 특정 기업체의 특정 부서의 특정인에게 일(Project)를 배정하는 내용에 익숙해지자. 특히 다양한 업체의 부서별 업무의 특징을 파악하면 정답을 맞히는 데 도움이 될 것이다.

주제는 계약(Contract)일 수 있으나 계약을 하는 쌍방(both parties)의 상관 관계를 이해하는 것이 추론 문제 등에서 도움이 될 것이다. 이 주제도 Part 6와 7에 자주 등장하는 내용이다.
  ➡ **특정 업체(business)의 업무(Contract-Project-Task)를 이해할 수 있도록 비즈니스 상식을 키우자.**

원쌤의 "Reality Check"

언제! 어디서! 얼마나 틀렸는지 눈 뜨고 확인하자!! ◉◉

시험 날짜: _____월 _____일

시험 장소: _____ (이어폰 ☐ 스피커 ☐)

시험 시작 시간: _____시 _____분

시험 종료 시간: _____시 _____분

파트별 점수 분석(맞은 숫자)

Part 1	
Part 2	
Part 3	
Part 4	
총 맞은 개수	

239페이지에 있는 점수 환산표를 확인해 주세요.

TEST

01

LISTENING TEST

In the Listening test, you will be asked to demonstrate how well you understand spoken English. The entire Listening test will last approximately 45 minutes. There are four parts, and directions are given for each part. You must mark your answers on the separate answer sheet.
Do not write your answers in your test book.

PART 1

Directions: For each question in this part, you will hear four statements about a picture in your test book. When you hear the statements, you must select the one statement that best describes what you see in the picture. Then find the number of the question on your answer sheet and mark your answer. The statements will not be printed in your test book and will be spoken only one time.

Sample Answer

Statement (B), "They're shaking hands," is the best description of the picture, so you should select answer (B) and mark it on your answer sheet.

1.

2.

Go on to the next page

3.

4.

5.

6.

Go on to the next page

PART 2

Directions: You will hear a question or statement and three responses spoken in English. They will not be printed in your test book and will be spoken only one time. Select the best response to the question or statement and mark the letter (A), (B), or (C) on your answer sheet.

7. Mark your answer on your answer sheet.

8. Mark your answer on your answer sheet.

9. Mark your answer on your answer sheet.

10. Mark your answer on your answer sheet.

11. Mark your answer on your answer sheet.

12. Mark your answer on your answer sheet.

13. Mark your answer on your answer sheet.

14. Mark your answer on your answer sheet.

15. Mark your answer on your answer sheet.

16. Mark your answer on your answer sheet.

17. Mark your answer on your answer sheet.

18. Mark your answer on your answer sheet.

19. Mark your answer on your answer sheet.

20. Mark your answer on your answer sheet.

21. Mark your answer on your answer sheet.

22. Mark your answer on your answer sheet.

23. Mark your answer on your answer sheet.

24. Mark your answer on your answer sheet.

25. Mark your answer on your answer sheet.

26. Mark your answer on your answer sheet.

27. Mark your answer on your answer sheet.

28. Mark your answer on your answer sheet.

29. Mark your answer on your answer sheet.

30. Mark your answer on your answer sheet.

31. Mark your answer on your answer sheet.

PART 3

Directions: You will hear some conversations between two or more people. You will be asked to answer three questions about what the speakers say in each conversation. Select the best response to each question and mark the letter (A), (B), (C), or (D) on your answer sheet. The conversations will not be printed in your test book and will be spoken only one time.

32. Where are the speakers?

(A) In an office
(B) At a restaurant
(C) At the airport
(D) In the parade

33. Why is the traffic jam expected?

(A) Many people are going on a picnic.
(B) Construction is ongoing.
(C) There will be a street parade.
(D) There was an accident on the street.

34. What time will the speakers leave?

(A) At 5 p.m.
(B) At 6 p.m.
(C) At 7 p.m.
(D) At 9 p.m.

35. What is the purpose of the call?

(A) To promote a new service
(B) To make a complaint
(C) To inform a customer of unpaid bills
(D) To confirm a schedule

36. According to the woman, what was the problem?

(A) She was not aware of the new services.
(B) She could not meet the deadline.
(C) She was unfairly treated by a staff member.
(D) She may have forgotten to notify some change.

37. What will the man probably do next?

(A) Call a colleague
(B) Provide her with a discount
(C) Explain the procedure
(D) Update some information

38. Where do the speakers most likely work?

(A) At a bank
(B) At a supermarket
(C) At an employment firm
(D) At a business school

39. What does the man say he wants to do?

(A) Register for a management class
(B) Work as a cashier
(C) Hire a new loan officer
(D) Open a new account

40. What do the women say they will send the man tomorrow?

(A) Handouts from a presentation
(B) Brochures for financial services
(C) An application for the new position
(D) A list of some names

41. Where is the conversation probably taking place?

(A) In a restaurant
(B) In the office
(C) On the street
(D) At the park

42. What does the man say about the restaurant?

(A) It was too expensive.
(B) It was as good as its reputation.
(C) It was below his expectations.
(D) It was far away from the office.

43. What will the speakers probably do?

(A) Go out to eat
(B) Leave for the day
(C) Take a walk
(D) Order some food

Go on to the next page

44. Where does the woman work?

   (A) At a theater
   (B) At a dental clinic
   (C) At a travel agency
   (D) At a restaurant

45. How long did it take for the man to make a reservation?

   (A) Three hours
   (B) One week
   (C) Two weeks
   (D) Three weeks

46. What does the man say he will do?

   (A) Cancel his appointment with his client
   (B) Look for some reviews
   (C) Book another time
   (D) Finish the work early

47. What is the conversation mainly about?

   (A) A vacation trip
   (B) Office supply purchase
   (C) Changes in personnel
   (D) Software installation

48. What does the woman mean when she says, "I knew that he would be promoted soon"?

   (A) She was notified about the news before.
   (B) She is very close to Mr. Russell.
   (C) She wants to get promoted, too.
   (D) She thinks Mr. Russell has worked hard.

49. What will the woman do next?

   (A) Call Mr. Russell
   (B) Talk to a former colleague
   (C) Interview an applicant
   (D) Make a reservation

50. Why did the woman invite the man?

   (A) To request a refund
   (B) To sign a business contract
   (C) To obtain more information
   (D) To rent some equipment

51. What kind of company does the woman work for?

   (A) A shipping company
   (B) A heavy equipment company
   (C) A real estate agency
   (D) A law firm

52. What is the woman most likely to do next?

   (A) Give a lecture
   (B) Prepare for shipment
   (C) Answer the questions
   (D) Sign a contract

53. Where most likely are the speakers?

   (A) At a bus stop
   (B) In an auto repair shop
   (C) In an office
   (D) On the road

54. According to the woman, when does she expect to be back?

   (A) By 5 p.m.
   (B) By 6 p.m.
   (C) By 6:30 p.m.
   (D) By 8 p.m.

55. What does the woman ask the man to do?

   (A) Order more parts
   (B) Drop her keys off
   (C) Close the shop later than usual
   (D) Notify any change

56. Who is the man calling?

(A) A business owner
(B) A job applicant
(C) A photographer
(D) A journalist

57. Why does the woman say, "It's a relief to hear the news"?

(A) She's been sick for the last few days.
(B) She had applied for this company before.
(C) She is working for a newspaper company.
(D) She was worried she might not get the job.

58. According to the man, why does the woman have to see him?

(A) To complete some documents
(B) To submit a certification
(C) To celebrate an anniversary
(D) To start working

---

59. What problem are the speakers mainly discussing?

(A) A flight has been canceled.
(B) Tickets are all sold out.
(C) The registration has not been completed.
(D) Hotel rooms are unavailable.

60. What solution does the woman suggest?

(A) Reserving rooms in another area
(B) Postponing a business trip
(C) Calling a travel agent
(D) Taking public transportation

61. What does the man imply when he says, "That makes sense"?

(A) They may be late for the conference.
(B) They may not exceed the budget.
(C) They may have missed the deadline.
(D) The rooms may be too small for the group.

---

62. What problem does the woman have?

(A) Her presentation materials are inaccessible.
(B) There are a number of mistakes in her report.
(C) The technical support team is out of the office all day.
(D) The meeting is canceled due to the inclement weather.

63. When was the technician supposed to arrive?

(A) This morning
(B) This afternoon
(C) Tomorrow morning
(D) Tomorrow afternoon

64. What will the man do next?

(A) Make a call
(B) Help her presentation
(C) Contact her client
(D) Repair her computer

Go on to the next page

Travel Itinerary in Thailand

Customer: Helena Kim

Dates	Days	Location
July 1st	2 days	Bangkok
July 3rd	3 days	Phuket
July 6th	Lunch	Chiangmai

65. What do the speakers want to do?

(A) Plan a party for customers
(B) Conduct a training session for employees
(C) Mail out some information to participants
(D) Show their appreciation to sponsors

66. What did the organization send out last year?

(A) Thank you cards
(B) Money orders
(C) Picture frames
(D) Monogrammed cups

67. Look at the graphic. What number shows where the gift shop is located?

(A) 1
(B) 2
(C) 3
(D) 4

68. What is the conversation mainly about?

(A) Taking a vacation
(B) Winning a prize
(C) Testing a program
(D) Booking a flight

69. Look at the graphic. In which location has the woman decided to stay longer?

(A) At Bangkok
(B) At Phuket
(C) At Chiangmai
(D) At home

70. What does the woman say was the problem with her vacation?

(A) Her flight was delayed.
(B) She got too much sun.
(C) Her schedule was too tight.
(D) One of her friends got sick.

PART 4

Directions: You will hear some talks given by a single speaker. You will be asked to answer three questions about what the speaker says in each talk. Select the best response to each question and mark the letter (A), (B), (C), or (D) on your answer sheet. The talks will not be printed in your test book and will be spoken only one time.

71. When is the report being broadcasted?

    (A) In the morning
    (B) At noon
    (C) In the afternoon
    (D) At midnight

72. What is causing the traffic delay?

    (A) Road construction
    (B) Electric repairs
    (C) Bad weather
    (D) An accident in a highway

73. What will people hear next?

    (A) An interview with the guest
    (B) An emergency weather report
    (C) A presidential election
    (D) An advertisement

74. What is the purpose of the message?

    (A) To explain a change in the invoice
    (B) To ask for the mailing address
    (C) To respond to a customer complaint
    (D) To report a problem with the order

75. Why has the product been discontinued?

    (A) The style was out of date.
    (B) The color was not popular.
    (C) The quality was below expectation.
    (D) The manufacturer has been changed.

76. What does the speaker suggest the customers do?

    (A) Speak with a manager
    (B) Cancel the order
    (C) Wait for the new model
    (D) Visit the store

77. Who most likely is the speaker?

    (A) A well-known reporter
    (B) A radio host
    (C) A technical staff
    (D) A political commentator

78. Why has the schedule changed?

    (A) The election was delayed.
    (B) The live performance was cancelled.
    (C) A studio is not available at the moment.
    (D) Some equipment is not working.

79. What has Barbara Fisher recently done?

    (A) She joined a political party.
    (B) She wrote a book.
    (C) She moved to a suburb.
    (D) She received a prestigious award.

80. What is the problem with the fax message?

    (A) It is blurring.
    (B) It is incomplete.
    (C) It has been damaged.
    (D) It's been sent to a wrong place.

81. What has the speaker requested?

    (A) Give him a call
    (B) Fix the fax machine
    (C) Confirm the appointment time
    (D) Send the information again

82. What is Peter asked to do?

    (A) Contact Ms. Thompson for help
    (B) Deliver the item soon
    (C) Check the order form again
    (D) Place the coversheet on top of the document

Go on to the next page

83. Who probably is making this announcement?

(A) A local farmer
(B) A museum administrator
(C) A tour leader
(D) A store manager

84. What can be said about tulips?

(A) They are annual plants.
(B) They are from tropical regions.
(C) They have strange names.
(D) They are the most popular flowers.

85. What does the speaker mean when she says, "I'm going to walk you through"?

(A) The tour will begin soon.
(B) They'll move to another location.
(C) She'll distribute some materials.
(D) She'll give more information about the flowers.

86. Who most likely are the listeners?

(A) Potential customers
(B) New employees
(C) Maintenance staff
(D) Job applicants

87. According to the speaker, what contributes to the company's good reputation?

(A) Affordable prices
(B) Scenic neighborhood
(C) Convenient location
(D) Capable staff

88. What will the speaker give the listeners after the video?

(A) Individual presentations
(B) A questionnaire
(C) Viewing of the property
(D) Sample products

89. What is the report mainly about?

(A) A city park
(B) A new city hall
(C) Exercising equipment
(D) A public swimming pool

90. Who is Elizabeth Greenfield?

(A) A news reporter
(B) A building architect
(C) A city official
(D) An event coordinator

91. What does the man imply when he says, "She expressed enthusiasm"?

(A) She was eager to go to the park.
(B) She is excited about the new project.
(C) She wants to have a bigger family.
(D) She is happy to be reelected as a mayor.

Sales Receipt
Cinemark Theater Online

Two adults	$18.00
Tax	$1.26
Members discount	$2.00
Total	$17.26

Visit us again soon at www.cinemarthateronline.org.com
(Keep this receipt for free popcorns or other special discounts. Check out with your local theater for details)

92. What is the speaker doing?

(A) Introducing an actress of a movie
(B) Explaining precautions before viewing
(C) Selling tickets for an event
(D) Cleaning up the area for the audience

93. What are the listeners asked to do?

(A) Use a mobile phone
(B) Take some notes
(C) Put the receipt in the bag
(D) Discard the trash in the can

94. Look at the graphic. What special gift will be available to a customer with this receipt?

(A) Price discount
(B) Popcorns
(C) Free programs
(D) Autographs by celebrities

Check list for Inspection

- record keeping process	Excellent
- machine maintenance	Good
- Safety training for new employees	Needs improvement
- Aisle blockage	Needs improvement

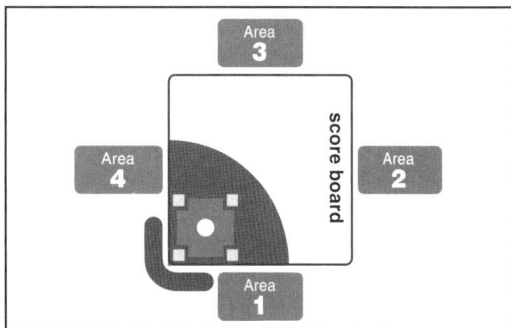

95. What will the inspectors do first?

(A) Meet with the supervisors
(B) File a complaint to the authority
(C) Check the updated records
(D) Set up a follow-up meeting

96. Why will the listeners meet next week?

(A) To meet with inspectors
(B) To discuss some results
(C) To learn about the procedures
(D) To train new employees

97. Look at the graphic. Which area should the managers be notified about?

(A) Record keeping procedures
(B) Regular machine maintenance
(C) Safety training for new employees
(D) Aisle cleaning and maintenance

98. What has the speaker finished inspecting?

(A) Street lamps
(B) First aid kits
(C) Electricity lines
(D) Building's exits

99. Look at the graphic. Where does the man suggest signs to be checked?

(A) Area 1
(B) Area 2
(C) Area 3
(D) Area 4

100. What will the speaker send in his e-mail?

(A) An estimate for the repair job
(B) Suggestions for better conditions
(C) A manual for emergency evacuation
(D) Locations of problematic areas

Go on to the next page

원쌤의 "Reality Check"

언제! 어디서! 얼마나 틀렸는지 눈 뜨고 확인하자!! ◉◉

시험 날짜: _____월 _____일

시험 장소: _____ (이어폰 ☐ 스피커 ☐)

시험 시작 시간: _____시 _____분

시험 종료 시간: _____시 _____분

파트별 점수 분석(맞은 숫자)

Part 1	
Part 2	
Part 3	
Part 4	
총 맞은 개수	

239페이지에 있는 점수 환산표를 확인해 주세요.

TEST

02

LISTENING TEST

In the Listening test, you will be asked to demonstrate how well you understand spoken English. The entire Listening test will last approximately 45 minutes. There are four parts, and directions are given for each part. You must mark your answers on the separate answer sheet.
Do not write your answers in your test book.

PART 1

Directions: For each question in this part, you will hear four statements about a picture in your test book. When you hear the statements, you must select the one statement that best describes what you see in the picture. Then find the number of the question on your answer sheet and mark your answer. The statements will not be printed in your test book and will be spoken only one time.

Sample Answer

Statement (B), "They're shaking hands," is the best description of the picture, so you should select answer (B) and mark it on your answer sheet.

1.

2.

Go on to the next page

3.

4.

5.

6.

Go on to the next page →

PART 2

Directions: You will hear a question or statement and three responses spoken in English. They will not be printed in your test book and will be spoken only one time. Select the best response to the question or statement and mark the letter (A), (B), or (C) on your answer sheet.

7. Mark your answer on your answer sheet.

8. Mark your answer on your answer sheet.

9. Mark your answer on your answer sheet.

10. Mark your answer on your answer sheet.

11. Mark your answer on your answer sheet.

12. Mark your answer on your answer sheet.

13. Mark your answer on your answer sheet.

14. Mark your answer on your answer sheet.

15. Mark your answer on your answer sheet.

16. Mark your answer on your answer sheet.

17. Mark your answer on your answer sheet.

18. Mark your answer on your answer sheet.

19. Mark your answer on your answer sheet.

20. Mark your answer on your answer sheet.

21. Mark your answer on your answer sheet.

22. Mark your answer on your answer sheet.

23. Mark your answer on your answer sheet.

24. Mark your answer on your answer sheet.

25. Mark your answer on your answer sheet.

26. Mark your answer on your answer sheet.

27. Mark your answer on your answer sheet.

28. Mark your answer on your answer sheet.

29. Mark your answer on your answer sheet.

30. Mark your answer on your answer sheet.

31. Mark your answer on your answer sheet.

PART 3

Directions: You will hear some conversations between two or more people. You will be asked to answer three questions about what the speakers say in each conversation. Select the best response to each question and mark the letter (A), (B), (C), or (D) on your answer sheet. The conversations will not be printed in your test book and will be spoken only one time.

32. What is the woman's problem?

    (A) She was overcharged.
    (B) Her room is too small.
    (C) Facility is not working properly.
    (D) She checked in too late.

33. How long has the woman stayed in her room?

    (A) One day
    (B) Two days
    (C) Three days
    (D) Five days

34. What does the man offer?

    (A) Move to another hotel
    (B) Give her a refund
    (C) Change the room
    (D) Investigate the problem himself

35. Who is the woman?

    (A) A school teacher
    (B) A sales clerk
    (C) A librarian
    (D) A songwriter

36. What problem does the woman mention?

    (A) All classes have been filled up.
    (B) A musical instrument cannot be returned.
    (C) Only advanced level books are available.
    (D) Inexpensive guitars are difficult to tune.

37. What does the woman suggest the man do?

    (A) Sign up for lessons
    (B) Attend a guitar concert
    (C) Purchase some books
    (D) Visit the store again later

38. Why is the man at the store?

    (A) To see the manager
    (B) To meet with his brother
    (C) To apply for the card
    (D) To purchase a present

39. What special offer is currently available?

    (A) A discount card
    (B) Extended warranty
    (C) Personalized gift wrapping
    (D) Free delivery

40. What will the man most likely do next?

    (A) Speak to the manager
    (B) Join the fitness club
    (C) Sign up for the card
    (D) Apply for the position

41. According to the woman, what will happen next week?

    (A) She will be transferred.
    (B) A colleague will visit.
    (C) A sale will begin.
    (D) A new show will be introduced.

42. What does the woman ask about?

    (A) City tours
    (D) Broadway shows
    (C) Flight schedules
    (D) Contact information

43. What does the man suggest the woman do?

    (A) Find out where the hotel is
    (B) Call the manager right away
    (C) Reserve the city tours
    (D) Check the ticket availability

Go on to the next page

44. What is the couple planning to do?

(A) Remodel a kitchen
(B) Open a restaurant
(C) Build a new house
(D) Hire a real estate agent

45. What is available only until the end of the month?

(A) A free gift with a purchase
(B) An extended warranty
(C) Free installation service
(D) A fifteen percent discount

46. What does the store manager offer to do?

(A) Place an order
(B) Give a promotional catalog
(C) Set up a home visit
(D) Contact customer service

---

47. What are the speakers discussing?

(A) Getting a surgery
(B) Moving into a new place
(C) Filling a prescription.
(D) Renovating an apartment

48. What happened to the woman last month?

(A) She changed the doctor.
(B) Her condition got worse.
(C) She found a new roommate.
(D) She moved to a new apartment.

49. What information will the woman give the receptionist?

(A) A telephone number
(B) Discount coupons
(C) The name of an employee
(D) The location of the pharmacy

---

50. What is the woman's problem?

(A) She missed her flight.
(B) She lost her ticket.
(C) She wants a direct flight.
(D) She couldn't find her luggage.

51. What is the woman's final destination?

(A) New York
(B) Los Angeles
(C) San Francisco
(D) Miami

52. What does the man mean when he says, "You're fine"?

(A) He likes the woman's appearance.
(B) She is going to miss the flight.
(C) He will take the woman to the gate.
(D) She doesn't have to pay for the charge.

---

53. What position is the woman interviewing for?

(A) An electrician
(B) A service representative
(C) A sales manager
(D) A school administrator

54. What is said about Sanwa Electronics?

(A) It makes quality electronic appliances.
(B) The products are sold in many countries.
(C) It was established in the year 2007.
(D) It gives out awards to employees.

55. Why does the woman say she wants to change jobs?

(A) She will be attending classes.
(B) She wants to make more money.
(C) She wants to work closer to home.
(D) She would like to have more responsibilities.

---

56. What problem did the woman have?

(A) She was too nervous to talk aloud.
(B) Some equipment malfunctioned.
(C) Some of her slides weren't ready.
(D) Some of the board members didn't show up.

57. What did the woman do to solve the problem?

(A) She postponed the presentation.
(B) She asked for a new projector.
(C) She took a break in the middle.
(D) She made some extra copies.

58. Why does the woman say, "I'm feeling exhausted"?

(A) Because she didn't sleep well last night.
(B) Because there was a natural disaster.
(C) Because she worked hard for the presentation.
(D) Because the copy machine was broken.

---

59. According to the speakers, what will happen this weekend?

(A) Workers will be relocated.
(B) New furniture will be delivered.
(C) A painting will be purchased.
(D) An office will be painted.

60. What is the woman asked to do?

(A) Choose a paint color
(B) Remove items from the desk
(C) Open the windows
(D) Contact the delivery person

61. What has the man requested that the workers do?

(A) Use a specific type of product
(B) Place all the furniture back in its places
(C) Finish the work in time
(D) Use some fans to dry off the paint

Advance Single 1st ●

| From | **Richmond Station** |
| To | **London Terminals** |

Valid on 10-May-10   **Adult 1st Class**

Valid only on the following services

10-May-10   7:30   : Coach H Seat 15

Not refundable.

                    12345-1234-1234-00-01-00

62. Why is the woman concerned?

(A) She is late for her appointment.
(B) She couldn't get a loan from a bank.
(C) The weather has not been nice.
(D) The train got delayed.

63. Look at the graphic. When is likely the new departure time for the man's train?

(A) 7:30 a.m.
(B) 8:00 a.m.
(C) 8:30 a.m.
(D) 9:00 a.m.

64. Where does the man work?

(A) At a weather agency
(B) At a bank
(C) At a training center
(D) At a repair shop

Go on to the next page

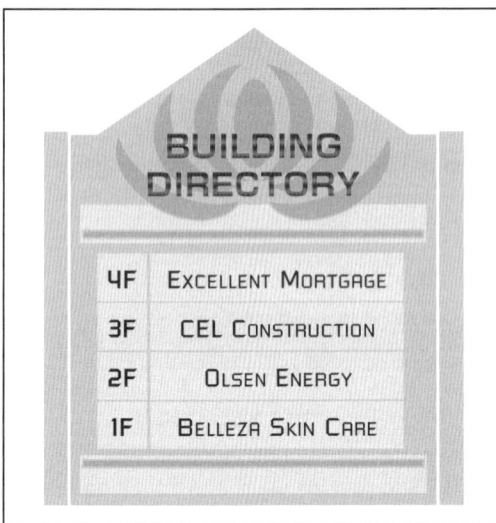

BUILDING DIRECTORY

4F	EXCELLENT MORTGAGE
3F	CEL CONSTRUCTION
2F	OLSEN ENERGY
1F	BELLEZA SKIN CARE

Options	Price
Printing	$3.00
Sewing	$5.00
Customized color/pattern	$7.00
Customized Embroidery	$10.00

Prices of basic T-shits and hats are extra.

65. Who most likely are the speakers?

(A) Interior designers
(B) Appliance store clerks
(C) Maintenance crew
(D) Office receptionists

66. Look at the graphic. Where is the man currently working?

(A) On the first floor
(B) On the second floor
(C) On the third floor
(D) On the fourth floor

67. What are the speakers probably going to do next?

(A) Move a table
(B) Install a new lighting fixture
(C) Fix the machine
(D) Make a conference call

68. What information does the woman provide?

(A) Discount on larger orders
(B) Designing tips for company logos
(C) Sales strategy to treat customers
(D) Availability of different styles and options

69. What is the man concerned about?

(A) When the order will be complete
(B) Where the order will be delivered to
(C) Who he should contact for more information
(D) What kind of payment options he has

70. Look at the graphic. How much will the man's order cost?

(A) $300.00
(B) $500.00
(C) $700.00
(D) $1000.00

PART 4

Directions: You will hear some talks given by a single speaker. You will be asked to answer three questions about what the speaker says in each talk. Select the best response to each question and mark the letter (A), (B), (C), or (D) on your answer sheet. The talks will not be printed in your test book and will be spoken only one time.

71. Why is the speaker calling?

(A) To inquire about employment opportunity
(B) To find more about packaged tours
(C) To book a business trip
(D) To request a price discount

72. How did the speaker learn about the agency?

(A) From a newspaper
(B) From a website
(C) From an acquaintance
(D) From a family member

73. What will the speaker do on Saturday?

(A) Visiting his family
(B) Take a history class
(C) Return from work
(D) Leave for a trip

74. What is offered in this advertisement?

(A) A sale on office equipment
(B) An extended warranty on mattress
(C) Reduced prices on a refrigerator
(D) A service contract for appliances

75. Why does the man say, "call us day or night, 7 days a week"?

(A) To sell new appliances to customers
(B) To emphasize the company's service
(C) To encourage to log in their website
(D) To explain the refund policy

76. How long is the special offer good for?

(A) For one day
(B) For seven days
(C) For ten days
(D) For fifteen days

77. What type of merchandise does the factory produce?

(A) Ceramic ware
(B) Electronics
(C) Packaged food
(D) Office supplies

78. Why is the factory getting new equipment?

(A) To manufacture different products
(B) To replace broken machinery
(C) To cut down the production cost
(D) To increase production

79. According to the speaker, how will the employees receive training?

(A) The will take online courses.
(B) They will take turns.
(C) They will receive certificates afterwards.
(D) Someone from the main office will teach them.

80. What department does the speaker work for?

(A) Human resources
(B) Accounting
(C) Banking
(D) Purchasing

81. What does the woman imply when she says, "receipts don't match the amounts"?

(A) There has been a scheduling conflict.
(B) The restaurant complained about the process.
(C) The discount amount has not been applied.
(D) Information on receipts is inaccurate.

82. What does the speaker ask the listener to do?

(A) Make their payment
(B) Talk to his supervisor
(C) Visit her office soon
(D) Contact her through the phone

Go on to the next page

83. Who is the speaker?

(A) A real estate agent
(B) A local resident
(C) A service representative
(D) A building manager

84. What does the speaker say her first task will be?

(A) Communicating well with tenants
(B) Getting in touch with the city council
(C) Passing the annual inspection
(D) Installing new safety equipment

85. What are the listeners asked to do?

(A) Introduce themselves to each other
(B) Give their feedbacks to her
(C) Call her if there is an emergency
(D) Make a decision on a certain issue

86. What are the listeners asked to do?

(A) Join a nonprofit organization
(B) Take care of your garden better
(C) Donate some money
(D) Plant trees for a cause

87. Who provided the article that the speaker is distributing?

(A) A company officer
(B) A newspaper reporter
(C) A government official
(D) A charity organization

88. What type of information about trees does the article contain?

(A) Where they should send the donation
(B) How to protect trees for better environment
(C) How to volunteer for the on-going projects
(D) Which environmental agency to contact

89. Who is Michael Santos?

(A) A marketing expert
(B) A design staff
(C) A corporate executive
(D) A newspaper reporter

90. What did Michal Santos announce?

(A) Introduction of a new line of products
(B) The construction of a new factory
(C) A change in product features
(D) Increased production of a popular product

91. What does the man imply when he mention, "DW-3000 will be the only car model produced in Australia"?

(A) Additional safety precautions will be taken in the factory.
(B) They're going to expand to Australian auto market.
(C) They will focus on meeting the demand of one product model.
(D) They're going to close down some manufacturing facilities.

92. What is the purpose of the event?

(A) To solicit more sponsors
(B) To inform schedule changes
(C) To advertisement a particular company
(D) To publicize job openings

93. Who is one of the sponsors of the event?

(A) A employment agency
(B) A radio station
(C) A web-designing firm
(D) A non-profit organization

94. According to the speaker, what can be found on the website?

(A) Steps to register in a fair
(B) Recommendations from the hiring manger
(C) History of the city's events being held
(D) A list of participating organizations

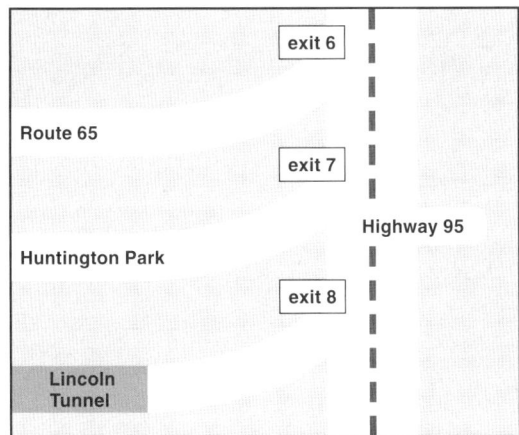

Route 65

Highway 95

Huntington Park

exit 6

exit 7

exit 8

Lincoln Tunnel

95. What is the problem with the tunnel?

(A) The repair work is being conducted.
(B) There has been an accident.
(C) The entrance has been blocked.
(D) The road is being repaved.

96. Look at the graphic. Which exit are the motorists advised to take?

(A) Exit 6
(B) Exit 7
(C) Exit 8
(D) Stay on Highway 95

97. What will the listeners most likely hear next?

(A) News on road conditions
(B) Weather updates
(C) An interview with the police
(D) An advertisement

Super Store   E-Coupons

50% Off

Look for **Super Save Vegetables** in the store
Expires May 15th

98. What is the announcement about?

(A) A new store promotion
(B) A going-out-of-business sale
(C) A change in payment method
(D) Recent customer complaints

99. Who most likely are the listeners?

(A) Marketing researchers
(B) Store employees
(C) Supermarket customers
(D) Website designers

100. Look at the graphic. What day is the coupon valid on?

(A) Monday
(B) Wednesday
(C) Weekends
(D) Any of the weekdays

Go on to the next page

원쌤의 "Reality Check"

언제! 어디서! 얼마나 틀렸는지 눈 뜨고 확인하자!! ◎◎

시험 날짜: _____월 _____일

시험 장소: _____ (이어폰 ☐   스피커 ☐)

시험 시작 시간: _____시 _____분

시험 종료 시간: _____시 _____분

파트별 점수 분석(맞은 숫자)

Part 1	
Part 2	
Part 3	
Part 4	
총 맞은 개수	

239페이지에 있는 점수 환산표를 확인해 주세요.

TEST

03

LISTENING TEST

In the Listening test, you will be asked to demonstrate how well you understand spoken English.
The entire Listening test will last approximately 45 minutes. There are four parts, and directions are
given for each part. You must mark your answers on the separate answer sheet.
Do not write your answers in your test book.

PART 1

Directions: For each question in this part, you will hear four statements about a picture in your test
book. When you hear the statements, you must select the one statement that best describes what
you see in the picture. Then find the number of the question on your answer sheet and mark your
answer. The statements will not be printed in your test book and will be spoken only one time.

Sample Answer

Statement (B), "They're shaking hands," is the best description of the picture, so you should select
answer (B) and mark it on your answer sheet.

1.

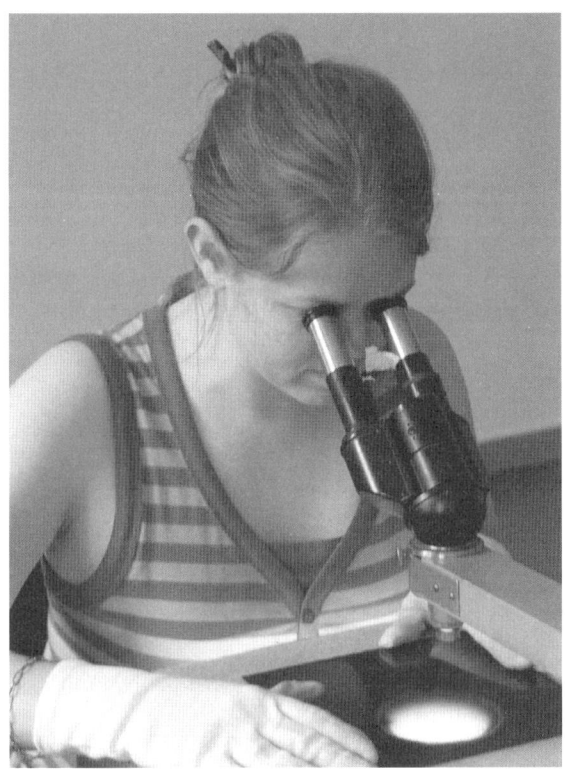

2.

Go on to the next page

3.

4.

5.

6.

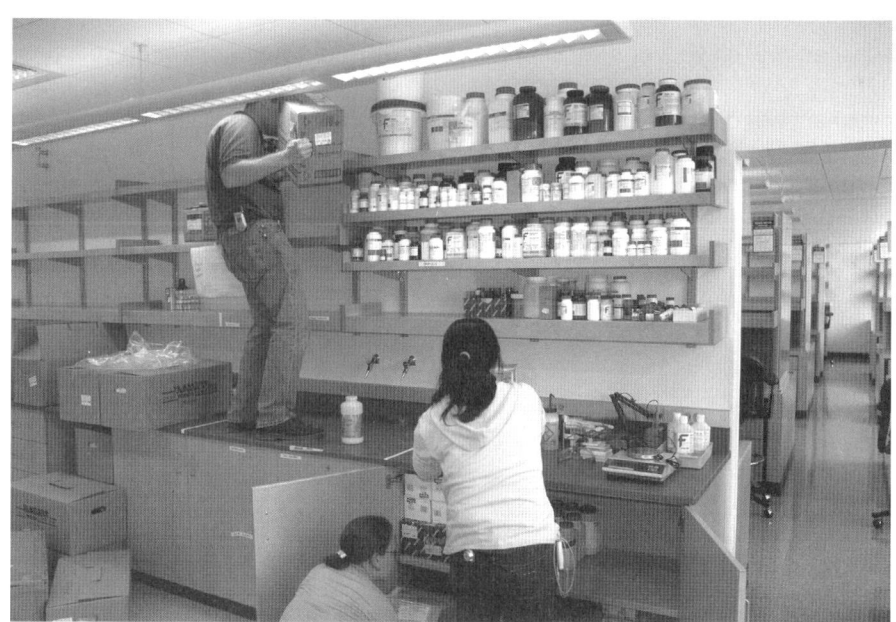

Go on to the next page

PART 2

Directions: You will hear a question or statement and three responses spoken in English. They will not be printed in your test book and will be spoken only one time. Select the best response to the question or statement and mark the letter (A), (B), or (C) on your answer sheet.

7. Mark your answer on your answer sheet.

8. Mark your answer on your answer sheet.

9. Mark your answer on your answer sheet.

10. Mark your answer on your answer sheet.

11. Mark your answer on your answer sheet.

12. Mark your answer on your answer sheet.

13. Mark your answer on your answer sheet.

14. Mark your answer on your answer sheet.

15. Mark your answer on your answer sheet.

16. Mark your answer on your answer sheet.

17. Mark your answer on your answer sheet.

18. Mark your answer on your answer sheet.

19. Mark your answer on your answer sheet.

20. Mark your answer on your answer sheet.

21. Mark your answer on your answer sheet.

22. Mark your answer on your answer sheet.

23. Mark your answer on your answer sheet.

24. Mark your answer on your answer sheet.

25. Mark your answer on your answer sheet.

26. Mark your answer on your answer sheet.

27. Mark your answer on your answer sheet.

28. Mark your answer on your answer sheet.

29. Mark your answer on your answer sheet.

30. Mark your answer on your answer sheet.

31. Mark your answer on your answer sheet.

PART 3

Directions: You will hear some conversations between two or more people. You will be asked to answer three questions about what the speakers say in each conversation. Select the best response to each question and mark the letter (A), (B), (C), or (D) on your answer sheet. The conversations will not be printed in your test book and will be spoken only one time.

32. What does the man ask Cindy to do?
(A) Reschedule a client meeting
(B) Arrange the company banquet
(C) Train her assistants
(D) Work on a building design

33. Why does the man want Cindy to do the work?
(A) Because she can save more money than other employees.
(B) Because the deadline is approaching quickly.
(C) Because she had won the award for the excellent design.
(D) Because she has worked for the client before.

34. What will the man likely do next?
(A) Sign the contract
(B) Hire Maria instead of Cindy
(C) Notify another employee about the change
(D) Meet with a new client

35. What is the woman calling about?
(A) A damaged product
(B) A late shipment
(C) Travel arrangements
(D) Computer problems

36. What does the woman want the man to do?
(A) Confirm a reservation
(B) Send some replacement parts
(C) Refund a purchase
(D) Return a phone call

37. According to the man, what will the woman receive by e-mail?
(A) A cost estimate
(B) A product brochure
(C) A revised invoice
(D) A shipping label

38. What does the woman ask for?
(A) A ride to a place
(B) Help with a report
(C) Directions to the office
(D) Mr. Yamamoto's itinerary

39. Where does the man need to go in the afternoon?
(A) To the woman's house
(B) To Tokyo branch
(C) To the airport
(D) To the bus station

40. What does the man offer to do?
(A) Meet her at the airport
(B) Work over time tonight
(C) Change the schedule
(D) Give some information

41. How did the woman learn about the movie?
(A) By reading a review
(B) By talking to a friend
(C) By listening to the radio
(D) By checking the internet

42. What does the man mean he says, "I was so disappointed"?
(A) She didn't like the movie.
(B) The actors didn't do a good job.
(C) The theater was too crowded.
(D) Tickets were unavailable.

43. What does the woman suggest the man do?
(A) Wait until the DVD version comes out
(B) Arrive early to avoid the crowd
(C) Find another place to watch the movie
(D) Change his seat to another one

Go on to the next page

⟶

44. What are the speakers discussing?

(A) A job candidate
(B) A newly won contract
(C) Company expansion
(D) A travel arrangement

45. What has Steven Johnson done before?

(A) He had applied for this company before.
(B) He's been exercising a lot.
(C) He made a reservation at a restaurant.
(D) He won a big contract with a foreign company.

46. When will the speakers meet Mr. Johnson?

(A) Today
(B) Tomorrow
(C) Next week
(D) In two weeks

47. What is the woman's problem?

(A) She forgot her password.
(B) She cannot use the e-mail system.
(C) She forgot to meet an accountant.
(D) She lost her Identification card.

48. Who has the woman been trying to contact?

(A) A computer manufacturer
(B) A technical support staff
(C) A customer service representative
(D) A building security

49. What does the man offer to do?

(A) Visit the security office
(B) Change the password
(C) Give her a direction to an office
(D) Find a telephone number

50. Where most likely does the man work?

(A) At a post office
(B) At an Internet company
(C) At a print shop
(D) At a travel agency

51. What has changed about the event?

(A) Its starting time
(B) Its location
(C) The number of guests
(D) The room size

52. What does the man ask the woman to do?

(A) Revise her order online
(B) Confirm her telephone number
(C) Call another vendor
(D) Rent an equipment for the event

53. What does the woman say she just read?

(A) A training manual
(B) A book review
(C) A company newsletter
(D) An annual report

54. According to the man, what happens at the weekly meetings?

(A) Individual projections are given.
(B) A manager reviews sales figures.
(C) Products are demonstrated.
(D) Employees discuss the strategies.

55. What does the woman imply when she says, "ask other managers to follow Mandy's example"?

(A) Mandy broke the record of highest sales.
(B) Mandy did a great job of leading her team.
(C) Other managers don't like Mandy very much.
(D) Mandy was just promoted to a manager.

56. Why is the woman calling?

(A) To place an order
(B) To return a product
(C) To inquire about a product
(D) To confirm an appointment

57. Who most likely is the man?

(A) A sales representative
(B) A medical personnel
(C) A physician
(D) A machine operator

58. What does the man offer to do?

(A) Send some samples through mail
(B) Give some discounts on a new product
(C) Process an urgent order
(D) Give a product demonstration

---

59. What is the man having difficulty doing?

(A) Contacting the technical support
(B) Getting permission from a supervisor
(C) Winning a contract from a client
(D) Accessing some information

60. Who does the man say he has requested help from?

(A) A software programmer
(B) The technology department
(C) An overseas manager
(D) The accounting department

61. What does the woman say she will do?

(A) Revise some document
(B) Prepare a sales presentation
(C) Post a memo on the board
(D) Send an e-mail

---

62. What are the speakers mainly discussing?

(A) Updating software
(B) Lack of staff
(C) Medical surgeries
(D) Laboratory equipment

63. What is the man surprised at?

(A) A deadline has been extended.
(B) More teachers were hired.
(C) A purchase has been approved.
(D) Tuition has been increased.

64. What does the man mean when he says, "it would be much easier"?

(A) Students these days are much smarter than before.
(B) New equipment will be very helpful in teaching students.
(C) Medical advances in the industry have been amazing.
(D) Hospital staff has to be trained to provide better services.

Go on to the next page

Product List

Name	Material	Price
MT215	Marble	$10.00
MT320	Marble	$12.50
CA101	Ceramic	$5.00
CA201	Ceramic	$7.00

65. What is the store planning to do?

(A) Introduce a new product
(B) Manufacture new tiles
(C) Survey customers
(D) Lower the product prices

66. What is the woman concerned about?

(A) The packaging might be weak.
(B) The environmentalist might complain.
(C) A product will not sell well.
(D) Customers will call the authority.

67. Look at the graphic. Which model will the speakers likely order?

(A) MT215
(B) MT320
(C) CA101
(D) CA201

You're cordially invited to the Drama Society's
production of

All is well That Ends well

starring Ryley Anderson

Stafford Theater at 7:00
1320 Main Street
Stafford, MO

68. Why is the woman calling?

(A) To ask about the admission fee
(B) To book a performance space
(C) To correct an error
(D) To ask for directions

69. Look at the graphic. What information on the invitation is no longer accurate?

(A) The name of the play
(B) The starring actress
(C) The name of the theater
(D) The time of the performance

70. What does the man say will happen next?

(A) Play tickets will be given away.
(B) An announcement will be made.
(C) A traffic report will be given.
(D) An official apology will be made.

PART 4

Directions: You will hear some talks given by a single speaker. You will be asked to answer three questions about what the speaker says in each talk. Select the best response to each question and mark the letter (A), (B), (C), or (D) on your answer sheet. The talks will not be printed in your test book and will be spoken only one time.

71. What does the speaker suggest about today's weather?

(A) It will rain all day.
(B) It will be unusually warm.
(C) It will change later today.
(D) It will be similar to last year's.

72. What will likely happen next week?

(A) The weather report will be at a different time.
(B) The summer will begin sooner.
(C) There will be sunnier days.
(D) The temperature will decrease.

73. When will the next weather report take place?

(A) In twenty minutes
(B) In half an hour
(C) In an hour
(D) In a day

74. What type of business is being advertised?

(A) Museum
(B) Art supplies
(C) On-line education
(D) Office equipment

75. What will the contest winners receive?

(A) Free products
(B) Back-state passes
(C) Tickets to a concert
(D) Cash prizes

76. According to the advertisement, what is found on the website?

(A) Procedure for registration
(B) Directions to different locations
(C) Schedules for an event
(D) Lists of products on sale

77. What department does the speaker work for?

(A) Graphic designing team
(B) Sales team
(C) Advertisement department
(D) Human resources division

78. What does the speaker need help with?

(A) Promoting new products
(B) Training new employees
(C) Scheduling works for the next 6 months
(D) Meeting the supervisor for consultation

79. What is scheduled to happen next month?

(A) They will move to a new location.
(B) The new employees will start working.
(C) A new product will be available.
(D) An advertising campaign will be changed.

80. What is the purpose of the talk?

(A) To create jobs for new employees
(B) To determine the number of positions
(C) To explain the interview process
(D) To make a lunch appointment

81. Who will conduct the first round of interviews?

(A) A personnel manager
(B) A personnel director
(C) A committee of volunteers
(D) A company president

82. What will happen next?

(A) They will apply for the job.
(B) The will receive some information.
(C) They will meet the president.
(D) They will meet the new employees.

Go on to the next page

83. What type of work is scheduled?

(A) Software upgrades
(B) Weekend getaway trips
(C) Electronic maintenance
(D) Telephone system installation

84. What are the employees asked to do?

(A) Contact the security office
(B) Upgrade your software
(C) E-mail the necessary information
(D) Shut down some equipment

85. What does the man imply when he says, "sorry to cause you trouble"?

(A) He's justifying the company procedure.
(B) He made a mistake when doing some electrical job.
(C) He's complimenting employees for their good work.
(D) He is angry because something bad had happened during the construction.

---

86. What is the main purpose of the talk?

(A) To announce a job opening
(B) To discuss the opening of an overseas branch
(C) To welcome a new employee
(D) To introduce a new company procedure

87. What is said about Rachel Park?

(A) She accepted an award from the company.
(B) She speaks several different languages.
(C) She used to work at a competitor.
(D) She plans to move to an Asian country.

88. What will happen after the meeting?

(A) New products will be released.
(B) Job description will be posted.
(C) They will take a break for a while.
(D) Food and beverages will be served.

---

89. What is the purpose of the call?

(A) To request an application
(B) To confirm a delivery
(C) To schedule an interview
(D) To place an order

90. What does the woman imply when she said, "to finally meet you in person"?

(A) He had applied for this company before.
(B) She hasn't seen him face to face.
(C) She wants to meet him and his family.
(D) She is happy that he accepted the position.

91. What does the speaker ask Mr. Mitchell to do?

(A) Reserve a hotel room
(B) Provide reference information
(C) Take personal belongings with him
(D) Return a telephone call

Delivery Schedules

Customer: Brooks Industries

Date	Order	Charge
Aug 5th		Corporate Card
Aug 12th	Steel Pipe: 1ton Copper Wire: 2 spools	
Aug 21st		Bank Transfer
Aug 27th		

92. What is the speaker calling about?

(A) To report a mistake
(B) To schedule a delivery
(C) To place an order
(D) To receive a refund

93. Look at the graphic. Which date of the charge should be corrected?

(A) August 5th
(B) August 12th
(C) August 21st
(D) August 27th

94. What does the speaker request?

(A) A formal letter of apology
(B) A written confirmation
(C) A price list of each item
(D) A corrected bill

Singapore Airlines		BORADING PASS	
Passenger **Laura Finch**	Date **28 May**	Origin Destination **Boston → Chicago**	
Flight **SL902**	Class **E**	Seat **56C**	Departure Time / Gate **9:45 P.M. / 15B**

** Please insert into the machine at the gate **

95. What is the reason for the announcement?

(A) A ticket has been recovered from the airport.
(B) The flight has been cancelled.
(C) Some important information has to be updated.
(D) The gate agent is not available at the moment.

96. Look at the graphic. What information is incorrectly printed?

(A) 15B
(B) 9:45 P.M.
(C) 56C
(D) SL902

97. What should listeners have to do if they have a question?

(A) Wait until the boarding is completed
(B) Proceed to the main terminal
(C) Visit the information booth
(D) Use a designated telephone

Orientation Schedule

Time	Program
9:30 a.m.	Introduction
10:00 a.m.	Company policy & procedure
12:00~1:30 p.m.	Lunch Break
2:00 p.m.	Meet the colleagues
3:00 p.m.	Group activities

98. Who most likely are the listeners?

(A) Electronic engineers
(B) Laboratory technicians
(C) Department store employees
(D) Sales representatives

99. What have the listeners already been given?

(A) Employee ID badges
(B) Company manuals
(C) Social security codes
(D) Personal pin numbers

100. Look at the graphic. What will be the last program on the schedule?

(A) Program introduction
(B) Company policy & procedure
(C) Meet the colleagues
(D) Group activities

Go on to the next page

원쌤의 "Reality Check"

언제! 어디서! 얼마나 틀렸는지 눈 뜨고 확인하자!!
◉◉

시험 날짜: _____월 _____일

시험 장소: _____ (이어폰 ☐ 스피커 ☐)

시험 시작 시간: _____시 _____분

시험 종료 시간: _____시 _____분

파트별 점수 분석(맞은 숫자)

Part 1	
Part 2	
Part 3	
Part 4	
총 맞은 개수	

239페이지에 있는 점수 환산표를 확인해 주세요.

TEST

04

LISTENING TEST

In the Listening test, you will be asked to demonstrate how well you understand spoken English.
The entire Listening test will last approximately 45 minutes. There are four parts, and directions are
given for each part. You must mark your answers on the separate answer sheet.
Do not write your answers in your test book.

PART 1

Directions: For each question in this part, you will hear four statements about a picture in your test
book. When you hear the statements, you must select the one statement that best describes what
you see in the picture. Then find the number of the question on your answer sheet and mark your
answer. The statements will not be printed in your test book and will be spoken only one time.

Sample Answer

Ⓐ ● Ⓒ Ⓓ

Statement (B), "They're shaking hands," is the best description of the picture, so you should select
answer (B) and mark it on your answer sheet.

1.

2.

Go on to the next page

3.

4.

5.

6.

Go on to the next page

PART 2

Directions: You will hear a question or statement and three responses spoken in English. They will not be printed in your test book and will be spoken only one time. Select the best response to the question or statement and mark the letter (A), (B), or (C) on your answer sheet.

7. Mark your answer on your answer sheet.

8. Mark your answer on your answer sheet.

9. Mark your answer on your answer sheet.

10. Mark your answer on your answer sheet.

11. Mark your answer on your answer sheet.

12. Mark your answer on your answer sheet.

13. Mark your answer on your answer sheet.

14. Mark your answer on your answer sheet.

15. Mark your answer on your answer sheet.

16. Mark your answer on your answer sheet.

17. Mark your answer on your answer sheet.

18. Mark your answer on your answer sheet.

19. Mark your answer on your answer sheet.

20. Mark your answer on your answer sheet.

21. Mark your answer on your answer sheet.

22. Mark your answer on your answer sheet.

23. Mark your answer on your answer sheet.

24. Mark your answer on your answer sheet.

25. Mark your answer on your answer sheet.

26. Mark your answer on your answer sheet.

27. Mark your answer on your answer sheet.

28. Mark your answer on your answer sheet.

29. Mark your answer on your answer sheet.

30. Mark your answer on your answer sheet.

31. Mark your answer on your answer sheet.

PART 3

Directions: You will hear some conversations between two or more people. You will be asked to answer three questions about what the speakers say in each conversation. Select the best response to each question and mark the letter (A), (B), (C), or (D) on your answer sheet. The conversations will not be printed in your test book and will be spoken only one time.

32. Who is the woman talking to?

(A) A receptionist
(B) A traffic officer
(C) A doctor
(D) A bus driver

33. Where does the woman want to go?

(A) To a bus terminal
(B) To a doctor's office
(C) To a florist's shop
(D) To a shopping center

34. What does the man tell the woman to do?

(A) Take a different bus
(B) Get off the bus right away
(C) Look at the map
(D) Come back again

35. What did the man do today?

(A) He started a new job.
(B) He registered for a class.
(C) He met an instructor.
(D) He made some purchase online.

36. What does the man want to purchase?

(A) A textbook
(B) A painting
(C) Some art supplies
(D) Some postage stamps

37. What does the woman say she will do?

(A) Teach a class
(B) Drive the man to the museum
(C) Postpone the event to until next week
(D) Forward an e-mail

38. Where are the speakers?

(A) At a farm
(B) At a restaurant
(C) At a supermarket
(D) At a product fair

39. What does the man ask about?

(A) The price of a dessert
(B) Where about of a person
(C) Availability of seats left
(D) The location of a product

40. What does the woman recommend?

(A) Speak with the manager
(B) Check the directions to the farm
(C) Buy a kind of food
(D) Look at the menu again

41. Why does the woman want to meet with the man?

(A) To schedule an interview
(B) To offer a job in Sydney
(C) To discuss a performance review
(D) To meet the new supervisor

42. Why does the woman reschedule the meeting?

(A) She needs to visit her family.
(B) She needs to see her doctor.
(C) She has to work overtime.
(D) She has to visit another branch.

43. What time will the meeting take place?

(A) At lunch time
(B) At one o'clock
(C) At two o'clock
(D) At four o'clock

Go on to the next page

44. Who most likely is the man?

   (A) A hotel receptionist
   (B) A tour guide
   (C) A convenience store clerk
   (D) A police officer

45. What does the man offer to do?

   (A) Update an itinerary
   (B) Check a price
   (C) Provide a local map
   (D) Have an item delivered

46. What does the man notify the woman about?

   (A) A closing time
   (B) An additional fee
   (C) A road closure
   (D) A departure date

---

47. What problem does the woman mention?

   (A) The weather has not been good.
   (B) The competitor launched a new product.
   (C) Sales are below their expectation.
   (D) They need to expand the market.

48. How does the woman suggest they address the problem?

   (A) By increasing advertisement
   (B) By hiring more staff
   (C) By reducing prices
   (D) By extending business hours

49. What does the man offer to do?

   (A) Contact the manager
   (B) Investigate the competitor
   (C) Develop a new product
   (D) Review some data

---

50. What are the speakers discussing?

   (A) Applying for a job
   (B) Missing an appointment
   (C) Getting a loan
   (D) Upcoming deadline

51. When does the man have the appointment?

   (A) Monday
   (B) Wednesday
   (C) Thursday
   (D) Friday

52. Why does the woman say, "We have everything here at the bank"?

   (A) She will open a bank account for him.
   (B) He doesn't have to worry about closing time.
   (C) He wants to change his appointment.
   (D) He can finish the process at the bank.

---

53. Who most likely are the speakers?

   (A) Fitness instructors
   (B) Website designers
   (C) Clothing store owners
   (D) Costume designers

54. What will the speakers like to have more time to do?

   (A) Review applications
   (B) Investigate fashion trends
   (C) Design clothing
   (D) Build a new website

55. What does the woman say she plans to do?

   (A) Fix a window display
   (B) Contact a supplier
   (C) Train new employees
   (D) Post some advertisement

---

56. Who most likely are the speakers?

(A) Board members
(B) Department managers
(C) Designing staff
(D) Receptionists

57. Why do they have to see the supervisor?

(A) To discuss future projects
(B) To share their opinions
(C) To be introduced at the meeting
(D) To improve the service quality

58. What does the woman imply when she says, "How about we see each other first thing tomorrow"?

(A) The boss wants to change the building design.
(B) They're not going to be busy all day.
(C) They don't have enough time before the deadline.
(D) She's not available in the afternoon.

---

59. Why is the man interviewing Ms. Swift?

(A) She started her own company.
(B) She grew vegetables in her garden.
(C) She is an event coordinator.
(D) She volunteered for the interview.

60. What product is being discussed?

(A) Organic food
(B) Trade magazine
(C) New recipe
(D) Moisturizing cream

61. According to Ms. Swift, what happened after the trade fair?

(A) She expended to overseas.
(B) She opened up a store.
(C) Sales have increased drastically.
(D) Customers have been calling her.

Package Rates	
Regular mail	$12.00
Registered mail	$18.00
Express mail	extra $10.00
Irregular sizes	extra $12.00

62. What are the speakers talking about?

(A) Giving a delivery address
(B) Sending a gift to a family member
(C) Buying some stamps at the post office
(D) Traveling to New York

63. Look at the graphic. How much would the man have to pay?

(A) 10 dollars
(B) 12 dollars
(C) 18 dollars
(D) 22 dollars

64. What will the man probably do next?

(A) Buy some gifts
(B) Wait for two more days
(C) Put the items in the box
(D) Complete some paperwork

Go on to the next page

Conference Room #3

September 2nd Monday

Time	Department	Person in charge
10:00 a.m.	Weekly meeting	Maintenance supervisor
12:00 p.m.	Lunch Break	
1:00 p.m.	New product Development	ext. 5 – Ms. Hwang
3:00 p.m.	Accounting	ext. 16 – Ms. Peterson

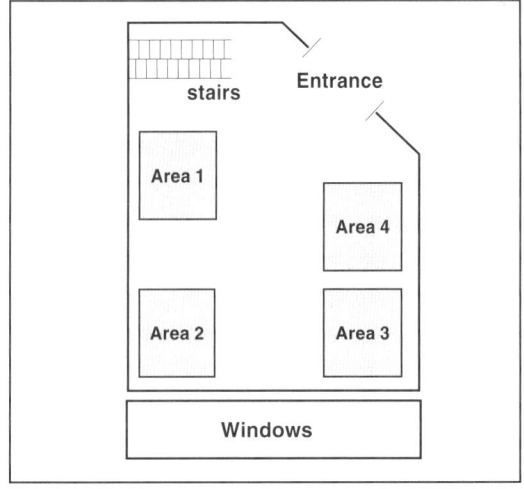

65. What are the speakers talking about?

(A) The confusion of meeting schedule
(B) The cost of accounting software
(C) The contents for the next report
(D) The location of a sales presentation

66. How do the speakers resolve the issues?

(A) By contacting the receptionist
(B) By searching the online help link
(C) By reducing the time for the meeting
(D) By looking at some information on the board

67. Look at the graphic. What team does the man work for?

(A) Maintenance department
(B) New product development team
(C) Accounting department
(D) Facility Department

68. Why is the man concerned?

(A) There is not enough office space.
(B) They need to hire more people.
(C) They have to publish more magazines.
(D) He's being transferred to an office upstairs.

69. What does the woman recommend to do?

(A) Hire part time staff
(B) Move some employees
(C) Work after hours
(D) Train the new employees

70. Look at the graphic. Which area will the new employee be seated?

(A) Area 1
(B) Area 2
(C) Area 3
(D) Area 4

PART 4

Directions: You will hear some talks given by a single speaker. You will be asked to answer three questions about what the speaker says in each talk. Select the best response to each question and mark the letter (A), (B), (C), or (D) on your answer sheet. The talks will not be printed in your test book and will be spoken only one time.

71. Who is Edgar Wolfe?
(A) A regional manager
(B) A city official
(C) A news announcer
(D) A local doctor

72. What did the Lincoln Hospital announce?
(A) It will hire more medical personnel.
(B) It will be updating its official website.
(C) It will be adding another location.
(D) It will be installing state-of-the-art equipment.

73. How long has the Lincoln Hospital been operating?
(A) For seven years
(B) For ten years
(C) For fifteen years
(D) For twenty years

74. What type of class does the center offer?
(A) Career development
(B) Language courses
(C) Creative writings
(D) Computer classes

75. What is mentioned about the location of the center?
(A) It has many locations in the city.
(B) It has recently moved to a new place.
(C) It is next to the city park.
(D) It is near the public transportation.

76. What does the speaker say is available at no cost?
(A) Free use of photocopiers
(B) An introductory class
(C) A meeting with a staff
(D) A textbook

77. What type of business is being advertised?
(A) A grocery store
(B) An electronic appliance
(C) A home improvement store
(D) A restaurant chain

78. How is the company different from its competitors?
(A) It opens 24 hours.
(B) It has the lowest prices.
(C) It offers free delivery.
(D) It has a large selection of goods.

79. Why does the woman say, "what are you waiting for"?
(A) To find out discounted products
(B) To order a special product
(C) To encourage to visit the store
(D) To be on time for a special occasion

80. Who most likely is the speaker?
(A) A company president
(B) A marketing director
(C) A department head
(D) A sales clerk

81. What does the man mean when he says, "this product will rewrite the history?"
(A) Many people participated in its development.
(B) The product will be a great success.
(C) The product has a traditional design.
(D) The product is easier to operate.

82. What will Sean Taylor discuss?
(A) A quality control standard
(B) An advertisement strategy
(C) A cost estimate for the new project
(D) An upcoming reception party

Go on to the next page

83. What is the purpose of the speech?

   (A) To explain a new policy
   (B) To introduce a new employee
   (C) To give an award
   (D) To select a committee member

84. Who is Ms. Tang?

   (A) An executive at an accounting firm
   (B) A property manager in a building
   (C) A government official
   (D) An award winning architect

85. What does the speaker say about the downtown area?

   (A) It was completely demolished 20 years ago.
   (B) Historical sites have been restored.
   (C) It needs further investment from the citizens.
   (D) It will accept new immigrants and settlers.

86. What is the subject of the talk?

   (A) A fitness program
   (B) Sports equipment
   (C) A technical workshop
   (D) A sales competition

87. How can you add points?

   (A) By working overtime
   (B) By smoking less
   (C) By walking as a group
   (D) By keeping a good record

88. What will the winning team receive?

   (A) Cash prizes
   (B) Gift certificates
   (C) Free airline tickets
   (D) A medal of honor

89. What is the purpose of this message?

   (A) To report the international growth
   (B) To reschedule a telephone conference
   (C) To confirm the attendance of a meeting
   (D) To discuss the details of an e-mail message

90. What did Mr. Gerald's assistant tell Mr. Welch?

   (A) Mr. Gerald's plans are uncertain.
   (B) Mr. Gerald is away on a business trip.
   (C) Mr. Gerald will not participate in the meeting.
   (D) Mr. Gerald has already reserved a seat.

91. What does the man mean when he says, "just in case"?

   (A) He just talked with the secretary.
   (B) He will contact Mr. Gerald in person.
   (C) He will send extra information for Mr. Gerald.
   (D) He wants to purchase new suitcases for this trip.

92. What kind of event are the listeners attending?

   (A) A new employee orientation
   (B) An international job fair
   (C) A corporate board meeting
   (D) A banking conference

93. According to the speaker, what will be different from last year?

   (A) Some programs are available for free.
   (B) Pre-registration is needed.
   (C) Internet access is available.
   (D) Interpretation service can be provided.

94. What will the listeners probably do next?

   (A) Hear from an industry expert
   (B) Sign up for an event
   (C) Receive a registration form
   (D) Attend the welcoming reception

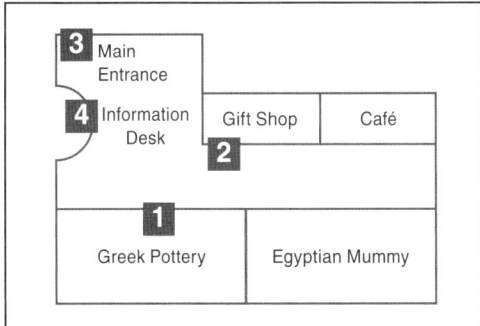

| Carton Catering |||
| Customer: Chris Mitchell |||
Item		Quantity
Tuna Sandwiches		8
BLT Sandwiches		12
Beverages		20
Fruit cups		15

95. Who probably is the speaker?

(A) A museum administration
(B) A tour leader
(C) A painter
(D) A sale person

96. What are the listeners encouraged to see?

(A) Greek pottery
(B) The collection of cassette players
(C) Paintings at the gift shop
(D) Floor maps at the information desk

97. Look at the graphic. Where should listeners meet at 3:00?

(A) 1
(B) 2
(C) 3
(D) 4

98. Why is the woman calling?

(A) To cancel an order
(B) To promote a new product
(C) To find out about the picnic location
(D) To confirm some information

99. Look at the graphic. What quantity on the original order form is no longer accurate?

(A) 20
(B) 8
(C) 12
(D) 15

100. What is the listener asked to do?

(A) Open the store late today
(B) Call the department head
(C) Visit the store as soon as possible
(D) Check out the website

Go on to the next page

원쌤의 "Reality Check"

언제! 어디서! 얼마나 틀렸는지 눈 뜨고 확인하자!! ◉◉

시험 날짜: _____월 _____일

시험 장소: _____ (이어폰 ☐ 스피커 ☐)

시험 시작 시간: _____시 _____분

시험 종료 시간: _____시 _____분

파트별 점수 분석(맞은 숫자)

Part 1	
Part 2	
Part 3	
Part 4	
총 맞은 개수	

239페이지에 있는 점수 환산표를 확인해 주세요.

TEST

05

LISTENING TEST

In the Listening test, you will be asked to demonstrate how well you understand spoken English. The entire Listening test will last approximately 45 minutes. There are four parts, and directions are given for each part. You must mark your answers on the separate answer sheet.
Do not write your answers in your test book.

PART 1

Directions: For each question in this part, you will hear four statements about a picture in your test book. When you hear the statements, you must select the one statement that best describes what you see in the picture. Then find the number of the question on your answer sheet and mark your answer. The statements will not be printed in your test book and will be spoken only one time.

Sample Answer

Statement (B), "They're shaking hands," is the best description of the picture, so you should select answer (B) and mark it on your answer sheet.

1.

2.

Go on to the next page

3.

4.

5.

6.

Go on to the next page

PART 2

Directions: You will hear a question or statement and three responses spoken in English. They will not be printed in your test book and will be spoken only one time. Select the best response to the question or statement and mark the letter (A), (B), or (C) on your answer sheet.

7. Mark your answer on your answer sheet.

8. Mark your answer on your answer sheet.

9. Mark your answer on your answer sheet.

10. Mark your answer on your answer sheet.

11. Mark your answer on your answer sheet.

12. Mark your answer on your answer sheet.

13. Mark your answer on your answer sheet.

14. Mark your answer on your answer sheet.

15. Mark your answer on your answer sheet.

16. Mark your answer on your answer sheet.

17. Mark your answer on your answer sheet.

18. Mark your answer on your answer sheet.

19. Mark your answer on your answer sheet.

20. Mark your answer on your answer sheet.

21. Mark your answer on your answer sheet.

22. Mark your answer on your answer sheet.

23. Mark your answer on your answer sheet.

24. Mark your answer on your answer sheet.

25. Mark your answer on your answer sheet.

26. Mark your answer on your answer sheet.

27. Mark your answer on your answer sheet.

28. Mark your answer on your answer sheet.

29. Mark your answer on your answer sheet.

30. Mark your answer on your answer sheet.

31. Mark your answer on your answer sheet.

PART 3

Directions: You will hear some conversations between two or more people. You will be asked to answer three questions about what the speakers say in each conversation. Select the best response to each question and mark the letter (A), (B), (C), or (D) on your answer sheet. The conversations will not be printed in your test book and will be spoken only one time.

32. What are the speakers mainly discussing?

(A) Receiving landscaping service
(B) Repainting the house
(C) Repairing the damaged area
(D) Selling real property

33. What does the man say he can do tomorrow?

(A) Delay the payment
(B) Visit a site
(C) Listen to the forecast
(D) Meet with the architect

34. What does the woman request the man do?

(A) Send a price estimate
(B) Make a quick decision
(C) Update the construction schedule
(D) Correct the bill

35. What is the purpose of the call?

(A) To request directions
(B) To ask about an item
(C) To place an order
(D) To change an appointment

36. What does the woman offer to do?

(A) Replace a damaged product
(B) Change their hours
(C) Close early today
(D) Check the status of an order

37. What time does the business close today?

(A) At 4:00
(B) At 4:30
(C) At 5:00
(D) At 5:30

38. Where are the speakers?

(A) In a shoe store
(B) On a mountain
(C) At a paint shop
(D) At a dry cleaner

39. Why does the man say, "I don't really care for these bright colors"?

(A) The sun-shine is too bright in outdoor hiking.
(B) Lighter colors tend to get dirty easily.
(C) He wants to see different colors.
(D) He wants to receive some extra discounts.

40. What does the woman offer to do?

(A) Look for a product
(B) Call another store
(C) Place a special order
(D) Change the sizes

41. Where do the speakers most likely work?

(A) At an employment agency
(B) At a manufacturing facility
(C) At an electronic store
(D) At a trade expo

42. What is the subject of the training class?

(A) Proper procedures for safety
(B) Qualifications for line workers
(C) Efficient project management
(D) Practical application of software

43. What does the woman imply when she says, "This should be very useful"?

(A) She needs to get a degree in engineering.
(B) They are trying to hire more assembly workers.
(C) The robotic devices will increase the productivity of the factory.
(D) The training will help her operate some machinery.

Go on to the next page

44. What has Rick already done this week?

(A) Send some e-mails
(B) Deliver some merchandise
(C) Called the customer
(D) Compliant about customer service

45. According to the man, what was the problem?

(A) A sales agent was out of town.
(B) The product was sent to a wrong place.
(C) Some of the information was missing.
(D) The customer complained about the late delivery.

46. What will the man probably do next?

(A) Order a different product
(B) Stop by at Ms. Looney's house
(C) Clean up the space
(D) Talk to someone in charge

47. What are the speakers mainly discussing?

(A) Ordering new office equipment
(B) Handouts for the meeting
(C) Changes in the meeting location
(D) Woman's performance at the company

48. What was the woman's problem?

(A) A presentation was delayed.
(B) An order was not processed.
(C) A machine is not working.
(D) There is a lack of supplies during the meeting.

49. What will the woman do next?

(A) Copy some documents
(B) Contact her clients
(C) Order more snacks
(D) Invite a few more guests

50. Who is Mr. Richardson?

(A) A magazine editor
(B) A geologist
(C) An art donor
(D) A public relations employee

51. What is Mr. Richardson doing right now?

(A) Showing the museum around to visitors
(B) Filling out some paperwork
(C) Giving a lecture to his students
(D) Meeting with some local artists

52. What is the woman asked to do?

(A) Explore the museum on her own
(B) Receive a visitor's pass
(C) Go to the exhibit room
(D) Wait in his office

53. According to the woman, what will take place in Hamburg?

(A) A bicycle competition
(B) A film festival
(C) A professional conference
(D) A museum opening

54. Why is the man going to Hamburg?

(A) To meet with some clients
(B) To purchase some real estate
(C) To attend a family celebration
(D) To be trained for a competition

55. What does the woman recommend?

(A) Buy a monthly pass
(B) Take a later train
(C) Rent a bicycle
(D) Pay less for the same ticket

56. What are the speakers discussing?

(A) A budget report
(B) A financial spreadsheet
(C) A computer technician
(D) A business loan

57. What seems to be the problem?

(A) The new version hasn't come out yet.
(B) The woman is not good at calculation.
(C) Some numbers don't add up correctly.
(D) An accountant gave the wrong data.

58. What does the man imply when he says, "I'll look at it myself"?

(A) He likes to work alone.
(B) He had the same problem.
(C) He knows enough to help the woman.
(D) He is not in his office right now.

59. What is the purpose of the woman's visit?

(A) To make travel arrangement
(B) To pick up a package
(C) To distribute some coupons
(D) To promote a business

60. What does the man inquire about?

(A) Information about the cuisine
(B) A company's location
(C) Payment options
(D) Business hours

61. What is the man planning to do?

(A) Try different clothes
(B) Register for a cooking class
(C) Eat at a new restaurant
(D) Look for online menus

62. What does the man need some help with?

(A) Hire a new employee
(B) Copy some reports
(C) Extend the deadline
(D) Find some data

63. Why is the woman unable to help the man?

(A) She needs to be somewhere.
(B) She has to finish her report.
(C) She is selling some products.
(D) She is meeting with Peter.

64. What does the woman suggest the man do?

(A) Change the competition date
(B) Find someone to replace him
(C) Contact an assistant for help
(D) Leave the office early today

TEST 05

Go on to the next page

GRAND OPERA HOUSE

Sincerity Jazz Band
Saturday, August 7th

VIP Ticket

65. What does the woman plan to do on the weekend?

(A) Attend a conference
(B) Watch a performance
(C) Meet with family member
(D) Buy a ticket for an opera

66. What is the woman's problem?

(A) She lost her ticket.
(B) She doesn't care for arts.
(C) She has no ride.
(D) She has to work.

67. Look at the graphic. When will the woman plan to arrive at the opera house?

(A) At 6:00 p.m.
(B) At 7:00 p.m.
(C) At 8:00 p.m.
(D) At 9:00 p.m.

Itinerary

Time	Schedule	Location
10:00 a.m.	Remodeling Project	Conference ROOM 2
12:00 p.m.	Consultation	Mr. Carlos' office
1:00 p.m.	Lunch	Restaurant NOVA
3:00 p.m.	Q&A	Company Lobby
3:30 p.m.	wrap-up	Return flight to SF

68. What is the purpose of the client's visit?

(A) To hire more staff for the project
(B) To plan a luncheon meeting
(C) To schedule a conference
(D) To discuss the building remodeling

69. Why has the man waited to make a reservation?

(A) He has to revise some reports.
(B) He was working for some other projects.
(C) He did not know how many guests are coming.
(D) He wasn't sure what food to order.

70. Look at the graphic. Which scheduled time has the incorrect location?

(A) 10 a.m.
(B) 12 p.m.
(C) 1 p.m.
(D) 3 p.m.

PART 4

Directions: You will hear some talks given by a single speaker. You will be asked to answer three questions about what the speaker says in each talk. Select the best response to each question and mark the letter (A), (B), (C), or (D) on your answer sheet. The talks will not be printed in your test book and will be spoken only one time.

71. What do they sell?

(A) Office furniture
(B) Bedding sheets
(C) Filing folders
(D) Electronic appliance

72. What does the speaker encourage people to do?

(A) Take a holiday break
(B) Redecorate the office
(C) Enter a contest for an office remodeling
(D) Save money for the future

73. How long will the sale last?

(A) One day
(B) Two days
(C) Three days
(D) Seven days

74. What is the purpose of the message?

(A) To place an advertisement
(B) To transfer to another department
(C) To ask for catering service
(D) To recommend a picnic place

75. What has been planned for March?

(A) A farewell dinner
(B) A sales promotion
(C) A company event
(D) A birthday party

76. What is the listener asked to do?

(A) Meet with the chef in person
(B) Call family members
(C) Come up with the new menu
(D) Contact the following number

77. Where most likely is the announcement being made?

(A) In a recording studio
(B) In an orchestra concert
(C) At a bus terminal
(D) At a radio station

78. Why has there been a schedule change?

(A) The stage needs to be cleaned up.
(B) The instrument needs to be shipped.
(C) A special guest has arrived late.
(D) Seating arrangement is taking longer.

79. According to the speaker, what did Martin Russo do?

(A) He played the violin.
(B) He used to live in Russia.
(C) He conducted some interviews.
(D) He wrote an article.

80. What is the purpose of this message?

(A) To inform a maintenance job
(B) To train how to use new software
(C) To purchase new equipment
(D) To hire more technicians

81. What will happen to personal files?

(A) They have to be copied beforehand.
(B) They have to be moved to a different place.
(C) They got some viruses.
(D) They won't be affected.

82. What should you do if you have a laptop?

(A) Copy your files to a desktop
(B) Replace it with a new one
(C) Visit the technical support team
(D) Leave home early on Friday

Go on to the next page

83. What is the speaker introducing?

    (A) A healthy menu for everyone
    (B) A tour of the factory
    (C) A mountain hiking trip
    (D) A safety inspection

84. Why did the speaker mention Blue Mountain?

    (A) Because it is where he lives.
    (B) Because it has beautiful scenery.
    (C) Because it has rather steep slopes.
    (D) Because it is the water source.

85. What does the man imply when he says, "more enjoyable and safe"?

    (A) The tour is interesting and enjoyable.
    (B) They invest a lot on factory safety.
    (C) They produce health conscious products.
    (D) They have to hurry to get to the show not to be late.

86. What is the purpose of the message?

    (A) To sell a new product
    (B) To advertise discounted prices
    (C) To request detailed information
    (D) To tell the contract term is almost finished

87. What will happen at the end of September?

    (A) The ownership of domains is finished.
    (B) They will launch a new product.
    (C) They will send out some information.
    (D) They will move it to a new place.

88. What is the listener asked to do as soon as possible?

    (A) Bring in the old contract
    (B) Pay $200 in advance
    (C) Contact the company
    (D) Purchase one more domain

89. Why does the woman say, "Our newspaper is planning to run an article"?

    (A) She wants him to participate in a race. sponsored by the newspaper company.
    (B) She wants to deliver some newspaper to his restaurant.
    (C) She wants him to edit some manuscript.
    (D) She wants to put his story on the paper.

90. What is the purpose of the message?

    (A) To change an appointment
    (B) To provide fresh ingredients
    (C) To request an interview
    (D) To apply for the open position

91. What does speaker say about Mr. Taylor?

    (A) He has little experience.
    (B) He is in charge of the restaurant.
    (C) He is publishing a new book.
    (D) He has changed his job recently.

Weekly Schedules		
	Date	**Subject**
1	Oct 2nd	Business Strategy
2	Oct 9th	Finance for managers
3	Oct 16th	Managing quality
4	Oct 23rd	Managing operations
5	Oct 30th	IT and e-business
6	Nov 6th	Global environment

92. What is the main subject of the course?

    (A) Writing persuasive articles
    (B) Business management
    (C) Presentation skills
    (D) Obtaining a job in IT industry

93. Look at the graphic. Which class subject has been revised to a different one?

    (A) Business Strategy
    (B) Finance for managers
    (C) IT and e-business
    (D) Global environment

94. What does the speaker consider to be the most valuable part of this class?

    (A) Various newspaper articles
    (B) Lectures and presentation during the seminar
    (C) Weekly homework assignment
    (D) Class discussion with other people

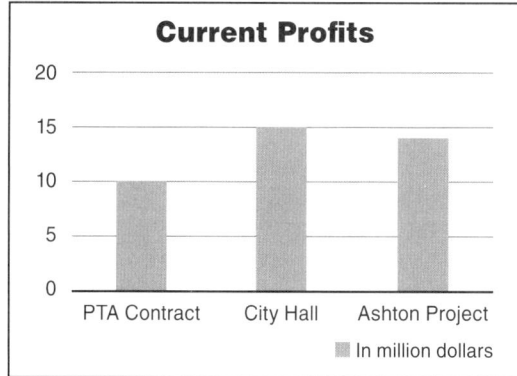

Current Profits

20	
15	
10	
5	
0	

PTA Contract   City Hall   Ashton Project

▦ In million dollars

Rate of Increase

Boston	30%
Quincy	25%
Cambridge	20%
Worcester	7%

95. What is the purpose of this message?

(A) To hire a new employee
(B) To set up an interview time
(C) To get more information
(D) To offer a job at her company

96. What does the speaker want to do know about Mr. Patrick Nelson?

(A) His professional experience
(B) His relations with managers
(C) His educational background
(D) His appearance

97. Look at the graphic. What project is Mr. Nelson involved in?

(A) Sam Electronics
(B) PTA Contract
(C) City Hall
(D) Ashton Project

98. According to the speaker, what will happen next week?

(A) The discounted prices will be available.
(B) The demand for electricity will decrease.
(C) The weather will finally get warmer.
(D) The cost of electricity will increase.

99. Look at the graphic. Residents of which region are NOT recommended to purchase new equipment?

(A) Boston
(B) Quincy
(C) Cambridge
(D) Worcester

100. What does the speaker recommend that listeners do?

(A) Contact the energy provider in your community
(B) Take the plugs out of unused outlets
(C) Use a traditional way of cooling method
(D) Keep watching the news for further information

Go on to the next page

TEST 05

원쌤의 "Reality Check"

언제! 어디서! 얼마나 틀렸는지 눈 뜨고 확인하자!! ◉◉

시험 날짜: _____월 _____일

시험 장소: _____ (이어폰 ☐ 스피커 ☐)

시험 시작 시간: _____시 _____분

시험 종료 시간: _____시 _____분

파트별 점수 분석(맞은 숫자)

Part 1	
Part 2	
Part 3	
Part 4	
총 맞은 개수	

239페이지에 있는 점수 환산표를 확인해 주세요.

TEST

06

LISTENING TEST

In the Listening test, you will be asked to demonstrate how well you understand spoken English. The entire Listening test will last approximately 45 minutes. There are four parts, and directions are given for each part. You must mark your answers on the separate answer sheet.
Do not write your answers in your test book.

PART 1

Directions: For each question in this part, you will hear four statements about a picture in your test book. When you hear the statements, you must select the one statement that best describes what you see in the picture. Then find the number of the question on your answer sheet and mark your answer. The statements will not be printed in your test book and will be spoken only one time.

Sample Answer

Statement (B), "They're shaking hands," is the best description of the picture, so you should select answer (B) and mark it on your answer sheet.

1.

2.

Go on to the next page

3.

4.

5.

6.

Go on to the next page

PART 2

Directions: You will hear a question or statement and three responses spoken in English. They will not be printed in your test book and will be spoken only one time. Select the best response to the question or statement and mark the letter (A), (B), or (C) on your answer sheet.

7. Mark your answer on your answer sheet.

8. Mark your answer on your answer sheet.

9. Mark your answer on your answer sheet.

10. Mark your answer on your answer sheet.

11. Mark your answer on your answer sheet.

12. Mark your answer on your answer sheet.

13. Mark your answer on your answer sheet.

14. Mark your answer on your answer sheet.

15. Mark your answer on your answer sheet.

16. Mark your answer on your answer sheet.

17. Mark your answer on your answer sheet.

18. Mark your answer on your answer sheet.

19. Mark your answer on your answer sheet.

20. Mark your answer on your answer sheet.

21. Mark your answer on your answer sheet.

22. Mark your answer on your answer sheet.

23. Mark your answer on your answer sheet.

24. Mark your answer on your answer sheet.

25. Mark your answer on your answer sheet.

26. Mark your answer on your answer sheet.

27. Mark your answer on your answer sheet.

28. Mark your answer on your answer sheet.

29. Mark your answer on your answer sheet.

30. Mark your answer on your answer sheet.

31. Mark your answer on your answer sheet.

PART 3

Directions: You will hear some conversations between two or more people. You will be asked to answer three questions about what the speakers say in each conversation. Select the best response to each question and mark the letter (A), (B), (C), or (D) on your answer sheet. The conversations will not be printed in your test book and will be spoken only one time.

32. What are the speakers discussing?
    (A) Staying at a hotel
    (B) Reserving a flight
    (C) A special exhibit
    (D) Entertaining a visitor

33. What does the woman NOT suggest?
    (A) A museum
    (B) A theater
    (C) A restaurant
    (D) A scenic place

34. What will the woman do next?
    (A) Reserve tickets for the event
    (B) Make a list of activities
    (C) Contact Mr. Hwang
    (D) Talk with the travel agency

35. Why is the man calling the restaurant?
    (A) To ask if her client is there.
    (B) To reserve a table by the window
    (C) To ask about a missing item.
    (D) To request a special menu

36. What does the woman ask the man to do?
    (A) Provide a description
    (B) Confirm a credit card number
    (C) Supply a guest list
    (D) Choose a date for the event

37. According to the woman, what will happen in one hour?
    (A) A manager will call back.
    (B) An announcement will be made.
    (C) A transaction will be approved.
    (D) A business will close

38. What does the woman mean when she says, "we are two people shorter than usual"?
    (A) Some of the employees are not as tall as the others.
    (B) They have fewer employees working these days.
    (C) The hours of operation have been shortened.
    (D) They don't have enough money on their budget.

39. What did they get yesterday?
    (A) A promotion
    (B) A pay raise
    (C) A transfer
    (D) A contract

40. What does the man suggest as a solution?
    (A) Contacting an employment agency
    (B) Putting an advertisement in the paper
    (C) Working overtime until the project is finished
    (D) Getting help from another department

41. What are the speakers discussing?
    (A) Volunteering in the community
    (B) Changing the work shifts
    (C) Organizing a sports team
    (D) Buying baseball game tickets

42. What does the man imply when he says, "I could definitely get more exercise"?
    (A) He wants to other players in the team.
    (B) He'd like to join the sport team.
    (C) He'd rather to play other sports.
    (D) He'd like to join a gym near the office.

43. What does the woman suggest?
    (A) Gathering on the weekend
    (B) Finding a sponsor
    (C) Waiting for a special offer
    (D) Participating in a competition

Go on to the next page

44. Who most likely is the woman?

(A) A newspaper reporter
(B) A city official
(C) A technical support agent
(D) A television producer

45. What is the woman's problem?

(A) She is too busy these days.
(B) Steve's gone on a business trip.
(C) The printer needs the story sooner.
(D) She has not been able to schedule
a meeting.

46. What does the man decide to do?

(A) Let go of the woman
(B) Talk to the mayor himself
(C) Print a different story
(D) Delay the printing job for Sunday

47. What is the man's problem?

(A) He cannot make copies.
(B) The phone connection is weak.
(C) The power is out in the whole building.
(D) He needs to save money for the future.

48. According to the woman, what is special
about the equipment?

(A) It is powerful for its size.
(B) It reduces energy use.
(C) It updates software automatically.
(D) It is environmentally friendly.

49. How did the woman learn to operate the
equipment?

(A) She took classes.
(B) She watched a video.
(C) She read it from an instruction.
(D) Someone told her.

50. Why is the woman at the supermarket
today?

(A) To meet the owner
(B) To conduct a survey
(C) To set up a display
(D) To buy some food

51. What did the owner change about the
supermarket last year?

(A) The location
(B) The hours
(C) The names
(D) The manager

52. What do the men say they like about the
supermarket?

(A) The low prices
(B) The store design
(C) The wide selection of products
(D) The friendly customer service

53. Where do the speakers most likely work?

(A) At a newspaper company
(B) At a hotel
(C) At an interior designer's office
(D) At a furniture store

54. What does the woman suggest?

(A) Inviting more people
(B) Buying more lamps
(C) Cleaning the facility
(D) Borrowing money from a bank

55. What does the man say their next step
should be?

(A) To request extra payment
(B) To make an appointment
(C) To visit the regional office
(D) To write the proposal

56. What does the woman want to order?

(A) A telephone system
(B) Desks and chairs
(C) Training manuals
(D) Business cards

57. According to the man, what is the problem with Office-Max?

(A) Its prices are expensive.
(B) It's not as fast as the others.
(C) Its products are poor quality.
(D) Its location is inconvenient.

58. What does the woman mean when she says, "That'll be fine"?

(A) She'll order from the suggested company.
(B) She thinks three weeks' training is too long.
(C) She'll use a different supplier.
(D) She'll call other places for an estimate.

59. What is the woman's occupation?

(A) An assistant librarian
(B) A facility manager
(C) An architect
(D) A film director

60. What does the man say the woman has to do?

(A) Stay open late tonight
(B) Select a different location
(C) Receive a written permission
(D) Get a library card

61. What does the man offer to do for the woman?

(A) Get a permission before they close today
(B) Ask someone to call her
(C) Meet with her on Monday
(D) Give her a phone number

62. What does the woman say about Derek Simmons?

(A) He applied for several positions.
(B) He doesn't like his current position.
(C) He has more experience than required.
(D) He wants to live abroad.

63. According to the woman, what is happening in the Paris office?

(A) They are hiring more staff.
(B) They are expanding its facility.
(C) They are relocating to a new location.
(D) They're opening up a shopping center.

64. What will the man probably do next?

(A) Review a resume
(B) Call the manager in Paris
(C) Speak to an applicant
(D) Arrange an interview

TEST 06

Go on to the next page

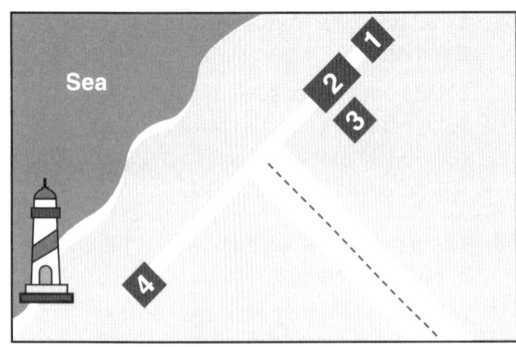

Schedules		
Please take any one of three sessions.		
#	Dates	Location
1	Aug 10th	Headquarters
2	Aug 17th	Garner Factory
3	Sept 1st	Babcock Branch

65. Who most likely is the woman?

(A) A tour guide
(B) A store cashier
(C) A property manager
(D) A newspaper editor

66. What does the man ask about?

(A) The cost of renting
(B) The size of the house
(C) The availability of extra beds
(D) The proximity to the city market

67. Look at the graphic. Which location will the man probably take?

(A) 1
(B) 2
(C) 3
(D) 4

68. What does the man want the woman to do?

(A) Apply for a job
(B) Conduct a safety inspection
(C) Deliver some equipment
(D) Attend a training session

69. What is the woman doing this week?

(A) Interviewing some applicants
(B) Supervising an installation
(C) Training new employees
(D) Taking some time off from work

70. Look at the graphic. On which date will the woman take the required course?

(A) August 10th
(B) August 17th
(C) August 25th
(D) September 1st

PART 4

Directions: You will hear some talks given by a single speaker. You will be asked to answer three questions about what the speaker says in each talk. Select the best response to each question and mark the letter (A), (B), (C), or (D) on your answer sheet. The talks will not be printed in your test book and will be spoken only one time.

71. Who is the caller?

(A) A receptionist
(B) A doctor
(C) A pharmacist
(D) A patient

72. What is the purpose of the call?

(A) To make a reservation
(B) To change the prescription
(C) To inquire about a patient
(D) To remind of an appointment

73. What is the listener asked to do?

(A) Arrive a few minutes early
(B) Report an address change
(C) Bring some paperwork
(D) Change the appointment to another time

74. What is the speaker promoting?

(A) Extended hours
(B) Music classes
(C) Newly published books
(D) An innovative new instrument

75. What will happen next month?

(A) Lessons will begin.
(B) A new location will open.
(C) A performance will be held.
(D) A guest player will be invited.

76. What is located next to the advertised business?

(A) A sports arena
(B) A famous bookstore
(C) A large sculpture
(D) A public facility

77. What is this announcement about?

(A) An upcoming inspection
(B) Relocation to a new place
(C) An updated website
(D) A maintenance job

78. What do employees have to do?

(A) Install the new software
(B) Contact technical support staff
(C) Check the homepages on their computer
(D) Be punctual in the morning at the worksite

79. Why should employees contact Becky?

(A) To register for the online seminar
(B) To talk to the management via Internet
(C) To complain about the poor connection
(D) To submit possible announcements

80. According to the speaker, what can you see during the tour?

(A) Other travelers
(B) Rare trees and plants
(C) Traditional architecture
(D) Some sea animals

81. What does the speaker imply when she says, "once-in-a-lifetime chance"?

(A) It will be the biggest sale of the year.
(B) They will have a great time during the tour.
(C) There will be a chance to see the natives.
(D) The guest speaker is usually hard to meet.

82. Who will the listeners meet later on?

(A) An industry expert
(B) A seafood chef
(C) A sales person
(D) A hotel manager

Go on to the next page

TEST 06

83. How does the speaker want to improve the company headquarters?

(A) Painting offices with diverse colors
(B) Using land around the building wisely
(C) Giving better trainings to employees
(D) Displaying more artworks

84. What has Ms. Dunmore agreed to do?

(A) Visit the company's other locations
(B) Lend some artworks
(C) Lead training classes
(D) Decorate private houses

85. What will Ms. Dunmore speak about?

(A) The inspiration for her work
(B) How she got started in her business
(C) Where she met the speaker
(D) Her favorite art pieces

86. What is the message mainly about?

(A) Arranging an international conference
(B) Cancelling a hotel reservation
(C) Inviting people over to his house
(D) Making a travel arrangement

87. What does the speaker mean when he says, "needs some polishing"?

(A) He needs some help to reserve a hotel room.
(B) He wants to fix his car right away.
(C) He cannot speak the language fluently.
(D) He wants to visit the Spain soon.

88. What information does the speaker request?

(A) How to use certain equipment
(B) The company's travel policy
(C) Possible locations for an event
(D) The price of a new product

89. What is the news mainly about?
(A) A possible merger deal in the computer industry
(B) Development of a new product
(C) A company's sales figures
(D) A technical training session

90. How can customers try the new product for free?
(A) By visiting a nearby store
(B) By mailing out the request from
(C) By submitting an online form
(D) By purchasing another product

91. According to Mr. Martinez, what will most likely happen by the end of the year?
(A) Company sales will increase.
(B) Additional employees will be hired.
(C) New facility will be added to the existing one.
(D) Company cost will be reduced.

BUSINESS HOURS

Monday - Friday
9:00 a.m. - 6:00 p.m.

Saturday: 10:00 a.m. - 5:00 p.m.

---

92. What does the store sell?
(A) Shipping materials
(B) Electronic equipment
(C) Cakes and baking items
(D) Stationery products

93. What does the business do for its customers?
(A) It holds a special promotional event.
(B) It orders out of stock items.
(C) It opens on Sundays.
(D) It gives out special prices.

94. Look at the graphic. What time will the store open until on Saturdays from this week?
(A) At 9:00 a.m.
(B) At 10:00 a.m.
(C) At 5:00 p.m.
(D) At 6:00 p.m.

Schedules for May

	Departure time	Sunset Road	Morrow Street	Cypress	Hartsville
Hartsville Express	10:00		10:50	11:50	12:30
Morrison Local	10:10	10:30	11:00	12:00	12:40
Hampton Local	11:00	11:30	12:00		13:40

95. Who most likely is the speaker?

(A) A flight attendant
(B) A ticket agent
(C) A train conductor
(D) A travel guide

96. Look at the graphic. What should passengers going for Cypress do?

(A) Take the Hartsville Express
(B) Take the Morrison Local train
(C) Change trains at Sunset Road
(D) Go to track number 11

97. Where are the passengers advised to put oversized bags?

(A) Next to the doors
(B) In the baggage cars
(C) On the seats next to yours
(D) In the aisles

Regular Price List

Easy Learn Corporation

Word for Word	$30.00
Make up a Story	$60.00
Pro Photoshop	$80.00

98. Where are the listeners?

(A) At a PTA meeting
(B) At a sales training workshop
(C) At a teachers' conference
(D) In a studio for a radio program

99. What is being described?

(A) Graduation requirements
(B) New computer equipment
(C) A new software program
(D) A family counseling

100. Look at the graphic. How much will participants to today's event have to pay for "Make up a Story"?

(A) 20 dollars
(B) 30 dollars
(C) 40 dollars
(D) 60 dollars

Go on to the next page

TEST 06

원쌤의 "Reality Check"

언제! 어디서! 얼마나 틀렸는지 눈 뜨고 확인하자!! ◉◉

시험 날짜: _____월 _____일

시험 장소: _____ (이어폰 ☐ 스피커 ☐)

시험 시작 시간: _____시 _____분

시험 종료 시간: _____시 _____분

파트별 점수 분석(맞은 숫자)

Part 1	
Part 2	
Part 3	
Part 4	
총 맞은 개수	

239페이지에 있는 점수 환산표를 확인해 주세요.

TEST

07

LISTENING TEST

In the Listening test, you will be asked to demonstrate how well you understand spoken English. The entire Listening test will last approximately 45 minutes. There are four parts, and directions are given for each part. You must mark your answers on the separate answer sheet.
Do not write your answers in your test book.

PART 1

Directions: For each question in this part, you will hear four statements about a picture in your test book. When you hear the statements, you must select the one statement that best describes what you see in the picture. Then find the number of the question on your answer sheet and mark your answer. The statements will not be printed in your test book and will be spoken only one time.

Sample Answer

Statement (B), "They're shaking hands," is the best description of the picture, so you should select answer (B) and mark it on your answer sheet.

1.

2.

Go on to the next page

3.

4.

5.

6.

Go on to the next page

PART 2

Directions: You will hear a question or statement and three responses spoken in English. They will not be printed in your test book and will be spoken only one time. Select the best response to the question or statement and mark the letter (A), (B), or (C) on your answer sheet.

7. Mark your answer on your answer sheet.

8. Mark your answer on your answer sheet.

9. Mark your answer on your answer sheet.

10. Mark your answer on your answer sheet.

11. Mark your answer on your answer sheet.

12. Mark your answer on your answer sheet.

13. Mark your answer on your answer sheet.

14. Mark your answer on your answer sheet.

15. Mark your answer on your answer sheet.

16. Mark your answer on your answer sheet.

17. Mark your answer on your answer sheet.

18. Mark your answer on your answer sheet.

19. Mark your answer on your answer sheet.

20. Mark your answer on your answer sheet.

21. Mark your answer on your answer sheet.

22. Mark your answer on your answer sheet.

23. Mark your answer on your answer sheet.

24. Mark your answer on your answer sheet.

25. Mark your answer on your answer sheet.

26. Mark your answer on your answer sheet.

27. Mark your answer on your answer sheet.

28. Mark your answer on your answer sheet.

29. Mark your answer on your answer sheet.

30. Mark your answer on your answer sheet.

31. Mark your answer on your answer sheet.

PART 3

Directions: You will hear some conversations between two or more people. You will be asked to answer three questions about what the speakers say in each conversation. Select the best response to each question and mark the letter (A), (B), (C), or (D) on your answer sheet. The conversations will not be printed in your test book and will be spoken only one time.

32. Where does the conversation probably take place?

(A) At a farm
(B) At a restaurant
(C) At a grocery store
(D) At a post office

33. What does the woman say about the shipment?

(A) It has been delayed.
(B) It is imported from a foreign country.
(C) It has been small.
(D) It has been damaged.

34. What is the man making?

(A) A multi-grain bread
(B) A vegetable soup
(C) A fruit pie
(D) A mixed salad

---

35. Why is Mr. Takeshi out of the office?

(A) He's on a business trip.
(B) He's on a vacation.
(C) He's working in a hospital.
(D) He was in a car accident.

36. How long will Mr. Takeshi be away from work?

(A) One week
(B) Two weeks
(C) Three weeks
(D) One month

37. What does the woman suggest doing?

(A) Visiting him at his house
(B) Paying him some money
(C) Delivering him some documents
(D) Seeing him at the hospital

38. Who most likely is the man?
(A) A potential client
(B) A new employee
(C) A technical consultant
(D) A pharmacist

39. What did the woman send in advance?
(A) A meeting agenda
(B) Directions to the company
(C) Her account information
(D) Some paperwork

40. What is the man asked to show?
(A) Photo identification
(B) A revised contract
(C) A confirmation e-mail
(D) A work portfolio

---

41. What are the speakers discussing?
(A) A play
(B) A novel
(C) A lecture
(D) A concert

42. What do the speakers say about Emily Johnson?
(A) She played different roles in a movie.
(B) She published a new book.
(C) She has won prizes before.
(D) She likes many actors.

43. What do the speakers agree with?
(A) They're going to watch the movie together.
(B) They're waiting for a new novel by Emily Johnson.
(C) They both liked the story by Emily Johnson.
(D) They don't want the story to be made as a movie.

Go on to the next page

44. What are the speakers doing?

   (A) Delivering computers
   (B) Installing software
   (C) Assembling office furniture
   (D) Preparing musical instruments

45. What does the woman suggest?

   (A) Starting early tomorrow
   (B) Taking a break
   (C) Meeting with her brother
   (D) Working late tonight

46. What does the man plan to do in the evening?

   (A) Visit his brother from out of town
   (B) Go to a company banquet
   (C) Check out the inventory in the warehouse
   (D) Attend a musical performance

47. What are the speakers discussing?

   (A) Booking a flight
   (B) Signing up for a lecture
   (C) Shipping some items
   (D) Updating a website

48. What is the problem?

   (A) A phone number is not listed in the directory.
   (B) A website is not working properly.
   (C) The marketing team has few staff members.
   (D) An e-mail address is incorrect.

49. What does the man offer to do?

   (A) Register for the seminar
   (B) Have the pamphlet delivered
   (C) Call some clients
   (D) Send the woman some information

50. What is the woman's problem?

   (A) Her printer was jammed.
   (B) The service was too slow at a restaurant.
   (C) The online connection needs to be updated.
   (D) Her computer doesn't work properly.

51. What is NOT the reason the man recommend High-Tech Electronics?

   (A) They have wide selections.
   (B) Their prices are reasonable.
   (C) They deliver for free.
   (D) Their employees are kind and willing to help.

52. What does the woman mean when she says, "I need to do some research"?

   (A) She majored in science research before.
   (B) She needs to find some discount information.
   (C) She wants to learn more about computer software.
   (D) She needs more information before making a purchase.

53. Where do the speakers most likely work?

   (A) In a warehouse
   (B) In a shopping center
   (C) At a real estate agency
   (D) At a moving company

54. What is the cause of the problem?

   (A) A store closed earlier than usual.
   (B) A shipping date was delayed.
   (C) A package was heavier than expected.
   (D) A customer complaint was filed.

55. What does the woman say she will do?

   (A) Call the customer about the delay
   (B) Label some boxes
   (C) Check the database for information
   (D) Talk to a supervisor

56. Where does the man work?

(A) A manufacturing facility
(B) An airline company
(C) A shipping company
(D) A travel agency

57. What does the man mean when he says, "you'll find our rates are all very competitive"?

(A) They are the fastest growing company.
(B) They're providing faster services.
(C) They can accommodate large orders.
(D) Their prices are lower than other companies'.

58. What will the speakers probably do next?

(A) Deliver some merchandise
(B) Look for more suppliers
(C) Arrange shipping schedules
(D) Discuss a business contract

---

59. Why is the man concerned?

(A) He's trying something new.
(B) He has to talk to the company president.
(C) He forgot about an appointment.
(D) He forgot to send a reply.

60. What does the man ask the woman to do?

(A) Help with a telephone call
(B) Check some calculations
(C) Make a reservation
(D) Prepare some report

61. Why is the man going to check his e-mail again?

(A) It needs to be printed out.
(B) It needs to be replied soon.
(C) It was sent to a wrong person.
(D) It contains some information.

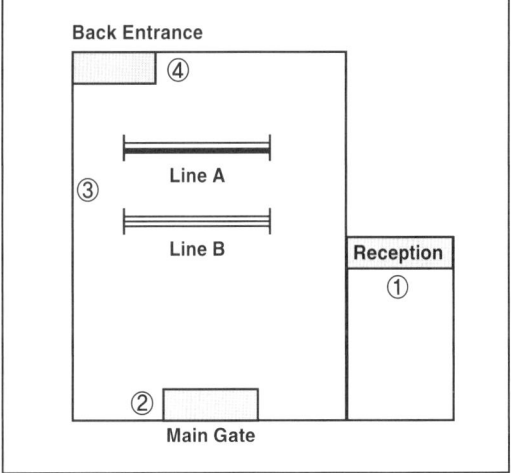

62. Where do the speakers work?

(A) At a production facility
(B) At a medical clinic
(C) At a restaurant
(D) At a government agency

63. Look at the graphic. Which location should the document be posted?

(A) 1
(B) 2
(C) 3
(D) 4

64. According to the man, what will occur on Friday?

(A) A facility will shut down.
(B) New employees will start.
(C) A permit will expire.
(D) An inspector will visit.

Go on to the next page

Nutrition Facts

serving size 1 cup(230mg)
Serving Per Container 1

Calories:	160
Protein	10 grams
Fat	5 grams
Sugar	2 grams
Sodium	160 milligrams

65. Why is the woman looking for a certain product?

(A) She wants to open up a grocery store.
(B) She's allergic to a particular ingredient.
(C) She wants to change her diet to a healthier one.
(D) She's looking for a specific brand of food.

66. Look at the graphic. Which of the ingredients does the woman express concern about?

(A) Protein
(B) Fat
(C) Sugar
(D) Sodium

67. What does the man suggest that the woman do?

(A) Try one of new products
(B) Consult her doctor first
(C) Go to another store
(D) Purchase a different one

Properties on Mason Boulevard

* Please press unit number for viewing photographs.

Unit number	Location	Rent
1	1200 Mason Boulevard	$1,200
2	Park Drive	$1,500
3	Saint Paul Street	$2,000
4	Longwood Station	$1,400

68. What does the woman want to rent?

(A) A storage space
(B) An office unit
(C) Some furniture
(D) A direction to a place

69. What can be inferred about her business?

(A) She's opening a new store.
(B) She's borrowing money from a bank.
(C) She's moving into a new location.
(D) She's importing products from overseas.

70. Look at the graphic. Which unit will the woman likely see today?

(A) Unit 1
(B) Unit 2
(C) Unit 3
(D) Unit 4

PART 4

Directions: You will hear some talks given by a single speaker. You will be asked to answer three questions about what the speaker says in each talk. Select the best response to each question and mark the letter (A), (B), (C), or (D) on your answer sheet. The talks will not be printed in your test book and will be spoken only one time.

71. What type of business does Tim Sanders probably work for?
    (A) A flooring company
    (B) A cleaning service company
    (C) An accounting firm
    (D) A moving company

72. What information does the speaker want?
    (A) The cost of a job
    (B) The location of a business
    (C) The time of completion date
    (D) The availability of a product

73. What did the speaker's colleagues say about the business?
    (A) It is conveniently located.
    (B) It only takes large scale orders.
    (C) It does high-quality job.
    (D) It gives discounts for new customers.

74. What did Mr. Phillips request?
    (A) Contact number of the doctor
    (B) An appointment to see a doctor
    (C) Information about prescription cost
    (D) Delivery of some medicine

75. Why is there a delay?
    (A) A medication is out of stock.
    (B) An address was incomplete.
    (C) An autograph was missing.
    (D) A doctor was out of office.

76. Why does the man say, "Some information should be verified"?
    (A) They need to receive the payment information.
    (B) They have to fix the fax machine.
    (C) They have to check the prescription again.
    (D) They have to find out the correct address.

77. Where does this talk take place?
    (A) On a mountain
    (B) In Vancouver
    (C) Near the boarders
    (D) On a bus

78. According to the speaker, what will the listeners do later in the day?
    (A) Climb the mountain trail
    (B) Visit the local stores
    (C) Cross the international border
    (D) Transfer to trains in Canada

79. What does the speaker ask the listeners to do?
    (A) Take out their tickets
    (B) Check out some documents
    (C) Have some snack
    (D) Look at the maps

80. What does the woman imply when she says, "Now, you can have it all"?
    (A) People can buy the product today.
    (B) The exercise can help you balance your life.
    (C) The yoga will help you lose weight.
    (D) People can meet the expert they've been waiting for.

81. What has recently been available for customers?
    (A) Autographed books
    (B) Discount coupons
    (C) Tickets to a live performance
    (D) An online course

82. What do you have to do to get more information about the business?
    (A) Visit the website
    (B) Contact the store manager
    (C) Stop by at the nearest location
    (D) Call the following number

TEST 07

Go on to the next page

83. What is the report about?

(A) Local history
(B) Gardening tips
(C) A new national park
(D) The discovery of rare plants

84. According to the speaker, what does Sun Valley have?

(A) Historic architecture
(B) Natural caves
(C) Unusual animals
(D) Unique plants

85. What do some people expect will happen?

(A) New plants and trees will be studied.
(B) The local traffic will be increased.
(C) The business in the area will be benefited from the decision.
(D) Some environment could be damaged.

---

86. What is the purpose of the message?

(A) To receive customer feedback
(B) To complain about the product quality
(C) To inform customers about upcoming holidays
(D) To give information on office operations

87. What should listeners do if they need immediate help?

(A) Contact another number
(B) Leave a message after the tone
(C) Visit the emergency location
(D) Call again the next morning

88. What information should the listener provide?

(A) A registration number
(B) A name and a number
(C) The name of the store
(D) An insurance policy

---

89. Who most likely is the speaker?

(A) An engineer
(B) A sales agent
(C) An accounting officer
(D) A graphic designer

90. What is the talk mainly about?

(A) Boosting product sales
(B) Designing a package
(C) Drawing a new building plan
(D) Developing an advertising campaign

91. What does the man imply when he says, "I'm looking forward to hearing some fresh ideas"?

(A) Employees should save some money.
(B) Employees should purchase fresh ingredients.
(C) Employees should produce new lamps.
(D) Employees should come up with new designs.

---

92. What is the purpose of the talk?

(A) To introduce a new product
(B) To announce a change in the deadline
(C) To explain new company procedures
(D) To accept applications for a sales job

93. What is the speaker responsible for?

(A) Developing the company's website
(B) Answering customer questions
(C) Promoting company's new products
(D) Consulting with company executives

94. What should the listeners do if they have time available?

(A) Call him immediately
(B) Fill out the request form
(C) Check the website for any errors
(D) Request additional work

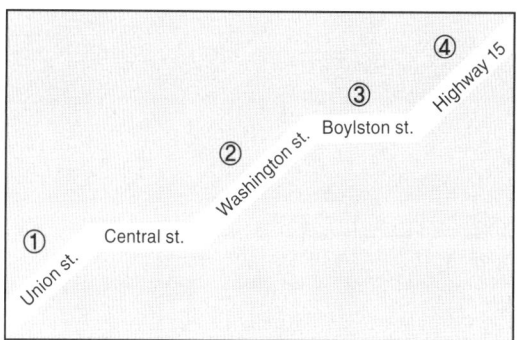

95. What is this announcement about?

(A) An upcoming event
(B) A travel destination
(C) A design competition
(D) Rush hour traffic

96. Look at the graphic. Where will the participants finish their race?

(A) 1
(B) 2
(C) 3
(D) 4

97. What should people with questions do?

(A) Visit the office
(B) Call the marathon manager
(C) Send an e-mail to BAA's office
(D) Contact the relevant agency

Conference Rooms

Program	Room #
Keynote speech	Banquet hall
New Age Software	Conference Room B
Latest industry trend	Conference room C
Welcome dinner	Dining hall

98. Where most likely is the announcement being made?

(A) At a musical performance
(B) At a professional conference
(C) At a software demonstration
(D) At a retirement banquet

99. Look at the graphic. Which room is no longer used at today's programs?

(A) Banquet hall
(B) Conference Room B
(C) Conference Room C
(D) Dining hall

100. Where can you buy tickets for tomorrow night's event?

(A) In the banquet hall
(B) At the book signing
(C) At the product demonstration
(D) At the registration desk

Go on to the next page

TEST 07

원쌤의 "Reality Check"

언제! 어디서! 얼마나 틀렸는지 눈 뜨고 확인하자!! ◎◎

시험 날짜: _____월 _____일

시험 장소: _____ (이어폰 □ 스피커 □)

시험 시작 시간: _____시 _____분

시험 종료 시간: _____시 _____분

파트별 점수 분석(맞은 숫자)

Part 1	
Part 2	
Part 3	
Part 4	
총 맞은 개수	

239페이지에 있는 점수 환산표를 확인해 주세요.

TEST

08

LISTENING TEST

In the Listening test, you will be asked to demonstrate how well you understand spoken English. The entire Listening test will last approximately 45 minutes. There are four parts, and directions are given for each part. You must mark your answers on the separate answer sheet.
Do not write your answers in your test book.

PART 1

Directions: For each question in this part, you will hear four statements about a picture in your test book. When you hear the statements, you must select the one statement that best describes what you see in the picture. Then find the number of the question on your answer sheet and mark your answer. The statements will not be printed in your test book and will be spoken only one time.

Sample Answer

Statement (B), "They're shaking hands," is the best description of the picture, so you should select answer (B) and mark it on your answer sheet.

1.

2.

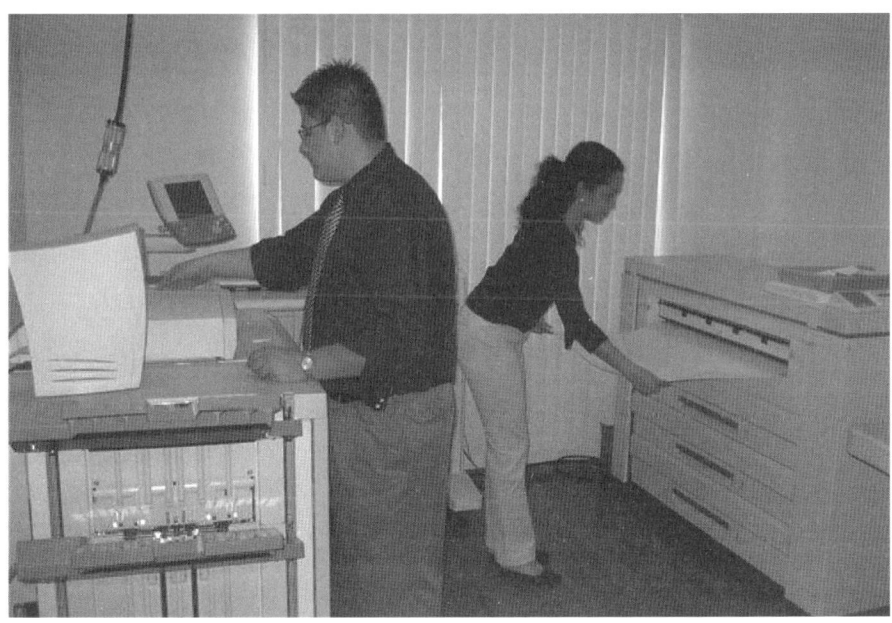

Go on to the next page

TEST 08

3.

4.

5.

6.

Go on to the next page

TEST 08

PART 2

Directions: You will hear a question or statement and three responses spoken in English. They will not be printed in your test book and will be spoken only one time. Select the best response to the question or statement and mark the letter (A), (B), or (C) on your answer sheet.

7. Mark your answer on your answer sheet.

8. Mark your answer on your answer sheet.

9. Mark your answer on your answer sheet.

10. Mark your answer on your answer sheet.

11. Mark your answer on your answer sheet.

12. Mark your answer on your answer sheet.

13. Mark your answer on your answer sheet.

14. Mark your answer on your answer sheet.

15. Mark your answer on your answer sheet.

16. Mark your answer on your answer sheet.

17. Mark your answer on your answer sheet.

18. Mark your answer on your answer sheet.

19. Mark your answer on your answer sheet.

20. Mark your answer on your answer sheet.

21. Mark your answer on your answer sheet.

22. Mark your answer on your answer sheet.

23. Mark your answer on your answer sheet.

24. Mark your answer on your answer sheet.

25. Mark your answer on your answer sheet.

26. Mark your answer on your answer sheet.

27. Mark your answer on your answer sheet.

28. Mark your answer on your answer sheet.

29. Mark your answer on your answer sheet.

30. Mark your answer on your answer sheet.

31. Mark your answer on your answer sheet.

PART 3

Directions: You will hear some conversations between two or more people. You will be asked to answer three questions about what the speakers say in each conversation. Select the best response to each question and mark the letter (A), (B), (C), or (D) on your answer sheet. The conversations will not be printed in your test book and will be spoken only one time.

32. What are the speakers discussing?

(A) Looking for a job
(B) Designing a website
(C) Finding a place to live
(D) Maintaining a personal relationship

33. What problem does the woman mention?

(A) Unfriendly landlord
(B) Small space
(C) Long commute
(D) High prices

34. What will the woman most likely do next?

(A) Talk to a leasing agent
(B) Call the man's friends
(C) Hire some professional help
(D) Consult some websites

35. What does Marianne want to discuss with Mr. Ford?

(A) The details of an order
(B) The designs of a catalog
(C) A schedule change
(D) Upcoming business meetings

36. Why is Mr. Ford unavailable at this time?

(A) He's out of town.
(B) He has a doctor's appointment.
(C) He's helping other customers.
(D) He has left work for the day.

37. What does the man ask Marianne to do?

(A) Provide information on her preferences
(B) Look at the product brochures
(C) Modify the design to show the company logo
(D) Pay for the business cards she ordered

38. What are the speakers discussing?

(A) Reservation for a hotel
(B) Donation to a charity
(C) A famous performer
(D) Plan for the weekend

39. Who is the woman scheduled to meet?

(A) A band member
(B) A relative
(C) An overseas sales associate
(D) A travel agent

40. What does the man offer to find out?

(A) Arrival time of a plane
(B) Location of the concert
(C) Price for a trip
(D) Ticket availability

41. What is the purpose of the call?

(A) To check the status of his order
(B) To order more products
(C) To find out prices of new glasses
(D) To get an accurate estimate of a job

42. What is the problem with the product?

(A) Its price has increased.
(B) It has been shipped to a wrong place.
(C) It's unavailable at the moment.
(D) They offer special prices online.

43. What will the woman do next?

(A) Order glasses for him
(B) Cancel the previous order
(C) Send out the shipment
(D) Log on to a computer

Go on to the next page

TEST 08

44. Where does this conversation take place?

    (A) At an office
    (B) At the airport
    (C) At a taxi stand
    (D) At a bus terminal

45. Why does the man want to leave early?

    (A) He likes to get on the plane early.
    (B) He doesn't like to hurry at the last minute.
    (C) He's afraid the traffic will be bad.
    (D) He wants to try a new way to the airport.

46. What will the woman do next?

    (A) Check the airline information
    (B) Log on to the Internet
    (C) Contact a travel agency
    (D) Change the flight schedule

47. Why does the woman say, "I'm back today with my receipt to clear things up"?

    (A) She wants to obtain a refund.
    (B) She's here to purchase new books.
    (C) She's already talked with the manager.
    (D) She is complaining about the product quality.

48. What does the woman notice while she is in the store?

    (A) Merchandize has been rearranged.
    (B) Only a few cashiers are on duty.
    (C) The store is unusually crowded.
    (D) A new section of the store has opened.

49. What is being offered today?

    (A) A signed copy of a best-selling book
    (B) A free beverage for all customers
    (C) A discount coupon for a future purchase
    (D) A complimentary piece of cake

50. Where most likely do the speakers work?

    (A) At a community park
    (B) At a gift shop
    (C) At a bicycle store
    (D) At a travel agency

51. Why did the woman change a plan?

    (A) A tour guide is unavailable.
    (B) A location is too far.
    (C) The facility is closed.
    (D) The admission fee is too expensive.

52. What does the woman suggest?

    (A) Talking to some customers
    (B) Finding a new employee
    (C) Providing a handout
    (D) Changing the bikes

53. What message does the woman give the man?

    (A) A document is needed.
    (B) A supervisor is not available.
    (C) The construction is behind schedule.
    (D) A meeting has to be held.

54. What was recently updated?

    (A) A contact list
    (B) Budget figures
    (C) A building plan
    (D) Construction equipment

55. What does the woman offer?

    (A) She would call the supervisor.
    (B) She would write the report.
    (C) She would postpone the construction.
    (D) She would make a delivery.

56. What does woman imply when she says, "We will have so much more customers"?

(A) Customers will like the new book.
(B) The discount sale will take place soon.
(C) The relocation will help the business.
(D) The woman likes to shop at his store.

57. What is the man concerned about?

(A) Reducing operating costs
(B) Completing the work in time
(C) Ordering new books for business
(D) Hiring maintenance staff

58. What will happen next week?

(A) A new manager will come.
(B) Customers can order products.
(C) New furniture will be delivered.
(D) A new store will open.

59. What is the purpose of the call?

(A) To attract more customers
(B) To promote an upcoming event
(C) To offer an cost estimate
(D) To raise money for a project

60. What would the library like to do?

(A) Survey its members
(B) Hold special workshops
(C) Buy more books
(D) Expand its facility

61. What does the man mean when he says, "it's important to support the community projects"?

(A) He will donate some money for a cause.
(B) He used to work at the library.
(C) He has children of his own.
(D) He will write a book about the story.

62. What is the conversation mainly about?

(A) Launching a new product
(B) A training schedule
(C) A possible business deal
(D) An employee evaluation

63. What will happen later this week?

(A) A procedure will be reviewed.
(B) A public announcement will be made.
(C) They will be moving into a new building.
(D) New employees will be hired.

64. What new task might the speakers be responsible for?

(A) Negotiating contract terms
(B) Making production manuals
(C) Arranging press conferences
(D) Holding training sessions

Go on to the next page

TEST 08

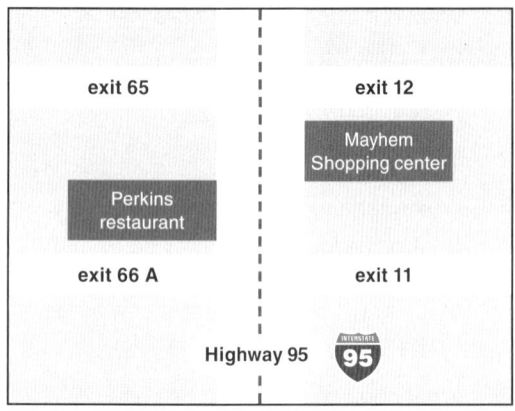

Article	Deadline
"The Presidential Candidates"	Feb 15th
"Smart Money"	March 2nd
"Nature walk in New Zealand"	March 2nd
"TECH Gizmo "	May 1st

65. What does the man want to purchase?

(A) A television set
(B) A cellular phone
(C) A briefcase
(D) A phone card

66. Why does the woman recommend Ericsson Store?

(A) It carries on the products from major manufacturers.
(B) It is close to the office.
(C) The prices are reasonable.
(D) The staff members are dependable.

67. Look at the graphic. Which exit should the man take to get to Ericsson Store?

(A) Exit 11
(B) Exit 12
(C) Exit 13
(D) Exit 14

68. What does the man ask the woman to do?

(A) Purchase the newspaper subscription
(B) Make arrangements for a meeting
(C) Increase the length of an article
(D) Correct a mistake in a document

69. Look at the graphic. Which article's deadline will be changed?

(A) The Presidential Candidates
(B) Smart Money
(C) Nature Walk in New Zealand
(D) TECH Gizmo

70. What does the woman say she will give to the man?

(A) An itinerary
(B) Customer survey results
(C) Notes from a meeting
(D) Ideas for future articles

PART 4

Directions: You will hear some talks given by a single speaker. You will be asked to answer three questions about what the speaker says in each talk. Select the best response to each question and mark the letter (A), (B), (C), or (D) on your answer sheet. The talks will not be printed in your test book and will be spoken only one time.

71. What is being advertised?

   (A) A cleaning device
   (B) Magazine subscription
   (C) Office supplies
   (D) A ticket outlet

72. Where was the product recently featured?

   (A) In a newspaper
   (B) In a promotional flyer
   (C) In a professional magazine
   (D) In a company newsletter

73. What is offered today?

   (A) Extra dust bags
   (B) Free deliver service
   (C) Personal consultation
   (D) A discounted price

74. Why is this announcement being made?

   (A) Passengers cannot find right trains.
   (B) Special promotion is being announced.
   (C) Some transportation will be delayed for a while.
   (D) A maintenance job will be conducted.

75. What should listeners do at East river Street Station?

   (A) Change trains
   (B) Receive special vouchers
   (C) Exit the station
   (D) Find the conductor

76. Why are the listeners asked to go to the customer service desk?

   (A) To get a map of train lines
   (B) To pick up their luggage
   (C) To buy tickets to the next destination
   (D) To receive a transfer coupon

77. Where is this speech probably being given?

   (A) At a product demonstration
   (B) At a shareholders' meeting
   (C) At a retirement dinner
   (D) At a customer appreciation banquet

78. What has Doug done for the last 5 years?

   (A) He increased the company sales.
   (B) He reduced the expenses.
   (C) He consulted many clients.
   (D) He developed a new program.

79. What will Doug Hanson do next month?

   (A) Travel around the world
   (B) Come back and visit his colleagues
   (C) Run his own business
   (D) Start a part-time job

80. What does the speaker indicate about the software?

   (A) It's been introduced to the market before.
   (B) It does not have any difficult functions.
   (C) It was developed by an overseas office.
   (D) Customers would be interested in buying it.

81. What will the listeners learn to do first today?

   (A) Communicate with each other
   (B) Enter the data into the system
   (C) Mail the letters to customers
   (D) Sort the information into different groups

82. According to the speaker, what should listeners do if they have problems?

   (A) Call the man
   (B) Refer to the manual
   (C) Check the website
   (D) Contact the help center

Go on to the next page

83. What is the purpose of this telephone message?

(A) To inquire about the food order
(B) To suggest a new book for the meeting
(C) To notify a member of a change
(D) To introduce a new member to the club

84. What does the woman mean when she says, "sorry for the confusion"?

(A) She's sorry to change the book of the discussion.
(B) She was confused about the direction she got before.
(C) She had to change the venue because of her personal reason.
(D) She's late for the meeting and wants to make up for it.

85. What can be inferred about John Faulkner?

(A) He is a new member.
(B) He will be at the meeting.
(C) He has a house in the area.
(D) He writes stories.

---

86. What type of company does the speaker work for?

(A) A news station
(B) An advertising company
(C) An automobile manufacturer
(D) A certified dealership

87. Why is the speaker contacting Mr. Norris?

(A) To encourage him to buy a new product
(B) To offer him a special deal
(C) To ask him to participate in a discussion
(D) To provide him with more information about the meeting

88. What is Mr. Norris asked to do by Friday?

(A) Submit a payment
(B) Visit a website
(C) Mail a registration form
(D) Return a phone call

---

89. Where does the speaker say Bestville Complex is located?

(A) In a downtown neighborhood
(B) Close to a shopping mall
(C) Next to a public transportation
(D) Near a famous mountain

90. What does the man imply when he says, "These new updated units are available"?

(A) They have just built a new apartment complex.
(B) Some units have been remodeled.
(C) They are selling appliances at the lowest prices.
(D) Some information was printed incorrectly.

91. According to the speaker, what is free for all residents of Bestville Complex?

(A) A storage space
(B) Free Internet access
(C) A swimming facility
(D) Parking spaces

#	Task Name	Duration
\multicolumn{3}{c}{**Schedules for *Grill W* Project**}

#	Task Name	Duration
1	Lay out walls	3 days
2	Rough-in plumbing	7 days
3	Sound insulation	4 days
4	Carpets & Vinyl floor	5 days
5	Clean-up	3 days

92. Where does the speaker work?

(A) An architectural firm
(B) A restaurant
(C) A tourist center
(D) A convention center

93. What is the speaker mainly discussing?

(A) Hosting a big scale banquet
(B) Organizing an international convention
(C) Renovating a property
(D) Relocating to a new facility

94. Look at the graphic. How long will the duration for Carpets & Vinyl floor?

(A) Two days
(B) Three days
(C) Four days
(D) Five days

Price List	
M-Pro Basic	$60.00
M-Pro Intensive	$100.00
Unlimited Packet	$200.00

95. Where would you hear this message?

(A) At a new employees' workshop
(B) In a language classroom
(C) At a press conference
(D) At a local job fair

96. What is the purpose of the talk?

(A) To inform participants of a closing
(B) To sort people into different groups
(C) To warn employees about a possible danger
(D) To show the features of a product

97. Look at the graphic. How much would a participant with a flyer pay for M-Pro Intensive?

(A) $ 60.00
(B) $ 80.00
(C) $ 90.00
(D) $ 100.00

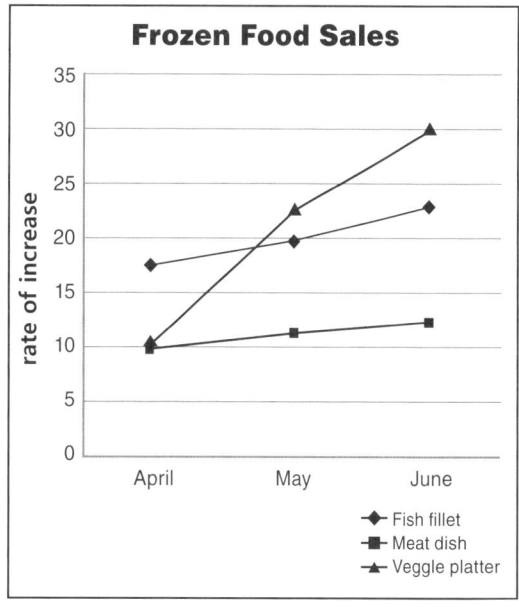

Frozen Food Sales

◆ Fish fillet
■ Meat dish
▲ Veggie platter

98. What did the speaker review yesterday?

(A) Product samples
(B) An advertising proposal
(C) Some sales data
(D) A new website

99. Look at the graphic. Which item was most loved by health conscious customers?

(A) Yogurt and Sherbet
(B) Fish fillet
(C) Meat dish
(D) Veggie platter

100. What is the purpose of the survey?

(A) To determine customer interest in new products
(B) To identify the market for frozen food
(C) To find the best way to attract new customers
(D) To ask about the recent sales experience

Go on to the next page

원쌤의 "Reality Check"

언제! 어디서! 얼마나 틀렸는지 눈 뜨고 확인하자!! ◉◉

시험 날짜: _____월 _____일

시험 장소: _____ (이어폰 ☐ 스피커 ☐)

시험 시작 시간: _____시 _____분

시험 종료 시간: _____시 _____분

파트별 점수 분석(맞은 숫자)

Part 1	
Part 2	
Part 3	
Part 4	
총 맞은 개수	

239페이지에 있는 점수 환산표를 확인해 주세요.

TEST

09

LISTENING TEST

In the Listening test, you will be asked to demonstrate how well you understand spoken English. The entire Listening test will last approximately 45 minutes. There are four parts, and directions are given for each part. You must mark your answers on the separate answer sheet.
Do not write your answers in your test book.

PART 1

Directions: For each question in this part, you will hear four statements about a picture in your test book. When you hear the statements, you must select the one statement that best describes what you see in the picture. Then find the number of the question on your answer sheet and mark your answer. The statements will not be printed in your test book and will be spoken only one time.

Sample Answer

Statement (B), "They're shaking hands," is the best description of the picture, so you should select answer (B) and mark it on your answer sheet.

1.

2.

Go on to the next page

TEST 09

3.

4.

5.

6.

Go on to the next page

TEST 09

PART 2

Directions: You will hear a question or statement and three responses spoken in English. They will not be printed in your test book and will be spoken only one time. Select the best response to the question or statement and mark the letter (A), (B), or (C) on your answer sheet.

7. Mark your answer on your answer sheet.

8. Mark your answer on your answer sheet.

9. Mark your answer on your answer sheet.

10. Mark your answer on your answer sheet.

11. Mark your answer on your answer sheet.

12. Mark your answer on your answer sheet.

13. Mark your answer on your answer sheet.

14. Mark your answer on your answer sheet.

15. Mark your answer on your answer sheet.

16. Mark your answer on your answer sheet.

17. Mark your answer on your answer sheet.

18. Mark your answer on your answer sheet.

19. Mark your answer on your answer sheet.

20. Mark your answer on your answer sheet.

21. Mark your answer on your answer sheet.

22. Mark your answer on your answer sheet.

23. Mark your answer on your answer sheet.

24. Mark your answer on your answer sheet.

25. Mark your answer on your answer sheet.

26. Mark your answer on your answer sheet.

27. Mark your answer on your answer sheet.

28. Mark your answer on your answer sheet.

29. Mark your answer on your answer sheet.

30. Mark your answer on your answer sheet.

31. Mark your answer on your answer sheet.

PART 3

Directions: You will hear some conversations between two or more people. You will be asked to answer three questions about what the speakers say in each conversation. Select the best response to each question and mark the letter (A), (B), (C), or (D) on your answer sheet. The conversations will not be printed in your test book and will be spoken only one time.

32. What does the man ask the woman to do?

    (A) Check the flight schedule
    (B) Reserve a seat at a restaurant
    (C) Go to see a doctor at the hospital
    (D) Change the appointment time

33. What will the man do tomorrow morning at 10 a.m.?

    (A) Visit a hospital
    (B) Meet a client
    (C) Wait in the lobby
    (D) Go over some file

34. When will the man be back to the office?

    (A) At 12:00 p.m.
    (B) At 1:00 p.m.
    (C) At 2:00 p.m.
    (D) At 3:00 p.m.

35. Where do the speakers most likely work?

    (A) At a post office
    (B) At a restaurant
    (C) At an employment agency
    (D) At a marketing firm

36. What does the woman suggest?

    (A) Find a reliable supplier
    (B) Improve food quality
    (C) Change serving staff
    (D) Hire more people

37. What are they going to do this afternoon?

    (A) Talk to more customers
    (B) Change dinner schedules
    (C) Write some documents
    (D) Meet with the general manager

38. Why is the woman calling?

    (A) To ask for a discount
    (B) To change the interior of her house
    (C) To subscribe a newspaper
    (D) To inquire about a class

39. What is the woman concerned about?

    (A) The cost of tuition
    (B) Class hours
    (C) Housing options
    (D) Professional experience

40. What does the man offer to do?

    (A) Find a job for her
    (B) Give her a scholarship
    (C) Send the woman some information
    (D) Accept the woman's application

41. What will the man do in Milan next month?

    (A) Attend a conference
    (B) Visit corporate headquarters
    (C) Meet with some clients
    (D) Purchase some products

42. What does the woman ask the man about?

    (A) The length of his stay
    (B) The topic of his presentation
    (C) The cost of his tickets
    (D) The name of his clients

43. What does the woman recommend?

    (A) Getting a group discount
    (B) Visiting a museum
    (C) Meeting with local residents
    (D) Taking a bus tour

Go on to the next page

44. What does the man apologize for?

(A) Not passing the test
(B) Forgetting the delivery
(C) Not participating in the training
(D) Missing a meeting

45. What will happen at the factory on Monday?

(A) Some employees will be evaluated.
(B) The policies will be changed.
(C) An inspection will be conducted.
(D) A demonstration will be given.

46. What is the man asked to provide in Grover City?

(A) Move some machinery
(B) Give some opinion
(C) Lay off some staff
(D) Train some employees

47. Why is the man calling?

(A) He wants to reserve a room.
(B) He wants to stay in a different room.
(C) He wants to change the date of arrival.
(D) He wants to confirm a reservation.

48. What does the woman ask the man to do?

(A) To give his home address
(B) To tell his name in full
(C) To provide her with some number
(D) To explain the reason for his visit

49. What can be inferred about the man?

(A) He stayed at this hotel before.
(B) He lost his reservation number.
(C) He will arrive on a different date.
(D) He likes to stay in a room with a view.

50. What are the speakers discussing?

(A) Training classes
(B) Hiring procedure
(C) Performance evaluation
(D) Efficient communication

51. What does the woman imply when she says, "you can take them during your work hours"?

(A) The company will pay for the registration.
(B) The man has changed his work hours.
(C) Classes are work-related topics.
(D) The work schedules are too tight these days.

52. What does the woman suggest the man do?

(A) Speak with the supervisor
(B) Visit the personnel office
(C) Update the software
(D) Refer to the online site

53. What kind of products are the speakers discussing?

(A) Office equipment
(B) Healthy food
(C) Cleaning supplies
(D) Kitchen supplies

54. Why has the Aquaria products never been used before?

(A) They're rather expensive.
(B) They are complicated to use.
(C) They're not environmentally friendly.
(D) Their products relatively new in the industry.

55. What is the man asked to do?

(A) Clean up the alley of the hotel
(B) Cancel the previous orders
(C) Move some furniture to the side
(D) Give a product demonstration

56. What does the woman want the man to do?

(A) Provide flower arrangements
(B) Change the display in the store
(C) Plan a dinner party for her
(D) Cancel her order for tomorrow

57. When is the event taking place?

(A) Tonight
(B) Tomorrow morning
(C) Tomorrow afternoon
(D) Tomorrow evening

58. What does the man mean when he says, "we have to treat them as a special order"?

(A) Special decorations will be made.
(B) There will be a delivery charge.
(C) They have to make them in a rush.
(D) The sales price has gone up.

---

59. Why is Mr. Thomson leaving his position?

(A) To teach at a university
(B) To pursue other interests
(C) To start his own business
(D) To transfer to an overseas division

60. Where does Mr. Thomson most likely work?

(A) At an employment agency
(B) At a travel agency
(C) At a law firm
(D) At a publishing firm

61. What will take place on Friday?

(A) An office party
(B) A job interview
(C) A press conference
(D) An awards ceremony

Construction Schedule

#	Task Name	Dates
1	Approval	March 28th
2	Design	April 15th
3	Demolition	May 1st
4	Construction	August 20th
5	Final Completion	September 1st

62. What is under construction?

(A) A tunnel
(B) A highway
(C) A parking garage
(D) An office building

63. Why has the construction schedule been changed?

(A) There are not enough workers.
(B) They didn't have enough money.
(C) The weather has been bad.
(D) They couldn't get permission from the authorities.

64. Look at the graphic. Which task has to be extended?

(A) Approval
(B) Design
(C) Demolition
(D) Final completion

Go on to the next page

Lunch Specials

Gourmet Cheese Sampler	$12
Healthy Mediterranean Soup	$ 8
Spicy Carpaccio Salad	$10
Giant Combo Sandwich	$12

All specials come with a drink of your choice.

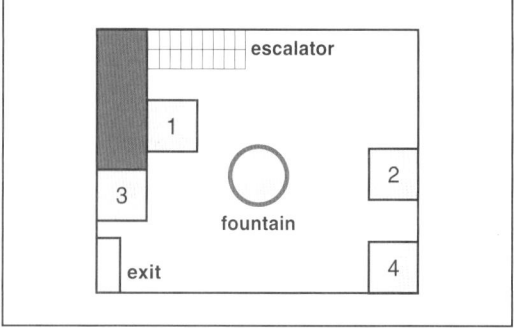

65. What type of event is the man organizing?

(A) A dealers' meeting
(B) A client lunch
(C) A retirement party
(D) A department luncheon

66. What does the woman mention about the café?

(A) Cancellations require 24 hours' notice.
(B) The menu changes seasonally.
(C) It received recognition from local diners.
(D) It has many rooms to accommodate different sizes of groups.

67. Look at the graphic. What menu item does not contain meat?

(A) The sampler
(B) The soup
(C) The salad
(D) The sandwich

68. Why is the woman calling?

(A) To finalize a renovation project
(B) To inquire about the property
(C) To confirm a delivery address
(D) To attend a professional conference

69. What type of business does the woman want to open?

(A) A family restaurant
(B) A skin-care shop
(C) A hair salon
(D) An art supply store

70. Look at the graphic. Which location will the woman probably see?

(A) 1
(B) 2
(C) 3
(D) 4

PART 4

Directions: You will hear some talks given by a single speaker. You will be asked to answer three questions about what the speaker says in each talk. Select the best response to each question and mark the letter (A), (B), (C), or (D) on your answer sheet. The talks will not be printed in your test book and will be spoken only one time.

71. Who is this message intended for?

(A) People who have technical problems
(B) The weather forecasters
(C) The morning commuters
(D) The company's employees

72. What caused the office closure?

(A) Updates on equipment
(B) Inspection on the facility
(C) Weather conditions
(D) Maintenance job

73. What are the listeners asked to do?

(A) Work using online system
(B) Come to work after lunch
(C) Enter another password
(D) Record the automated message

---

74. Who probably is making the announcement?

(A) A building resident
(B) A traffic officer
(C) A property manager
(D) An auto technician

75. What is said about the sedan?

(A) Its headlights are on.
(B) It has parked on level 1.
(C) The driver does not have handicapped permit.
(D) It is blocking the entrance.

76. Where should a visitor to the building park?

(A) In any of the spaces on level 2
(B) In front of the exit
(C) In vacant spaces
(D) In the color marked area

---

77. Where most likely is the announcement being made?

(A) In a factory
(B) In an electronics store
(C) In an employment agency
(D) In a park

78. What will happen at three o'clock?

(A) The work will begin at the factory.
(B) The factory will be closed for the day.
(C) Some machines will be turned off.
(D) Some videos will be shown.

79. Who is Douglas Xing?

(A) A factory supervisor
(B) A personnel officer
(C) A line worker
(D) A training manager

---

80. According to the message, what happened today?

(A) A delivery was attempted.
(B) An order was received.
(C) Someone from the flower shop called.
(D) A party has been arranged.

81. What does woman mean when she says, "do not have a long shelf time"?

(A) They have to wait for a long time to buy the flowers.
(B) The address was incorrectly recorded.
(C) The flowers are perishable products.
(D) The flowers are not selling well these days.

82. What will happen at 9 a.m. tomorrow?

(A) A deliver person will visit again.
(B) The flowers will be discarded.
(C) New order should be made.
(D) A store will open.

Go on to the next page

137

83. Where is this talk probably taking place?

(A) In a power plant
(B) In a government agency
(C) In an auditorium
(D) In a radio station

84. What is the topic of Ms. Lorain's talk?

(A) Fuel prices
(B) Alternative energy
(C) Financial planning
(D) Developing countries

85. What has Ms. Lorain recently been invited to do?

(A) To design a new generation automobile
(B) To call for a professional meeting
(C) To ask questions to a panel of scientists
(D) To conduct research with other members

---

86. What is being advertised?

(A) A stationery store
(B) A suburban property
(C) An office space
(D) An equipment rental

87. What is said about Bingham Creative?

(A) It only designs office buildings.
(B) It provides free utilities for tenants.
(C) It is hiring new employees.
(D) It has won awards before.

88. What does the woman imply when she says, "act fast and grab this unique opportunity"?

(A) The building is famous for its unique design.
(B) The units could sell out quickly.
(C) The deadline is getting closer.
(D) The discount amount is much bigger than ever.

---

89. What is the main purpose of this talk?

(A) To reserve a seat in the training class
(B) To describe the process of getting a raise
(C) To clarify a change in work hours
(D) To announce a new payroll system

90. Why does the man say, "to calculate and track our work records more accurately and efficiently"?

(A) To pay for the price of new software
(B) To encourage employees to work harder
(C) To introduce a new online tutorial link
(D) To emphasize the merits of new software

91. How can the listeners get more information?

(A) By reading a memo
(B) By visiting the website
(C) By stopping by at the payroll office
(D) By looking over the program manual

---

92. What type of business does the speaker probably work for?

(A) A travel agency
(B) An environmentalists' group
(C) An apparel company
(D) A financial institute

93. What's the main purpose of the meeting?

(A) To train new employees
(B) To expand into an overseas market
(C) To review next year's budget
(D) To discuss new products

94. What are the employees asked to do?

(A) Taste different food samples
(B) Meet employees from overseas branches
(C) Contact possible designers for the next season
(D) Provide opinions on some designs

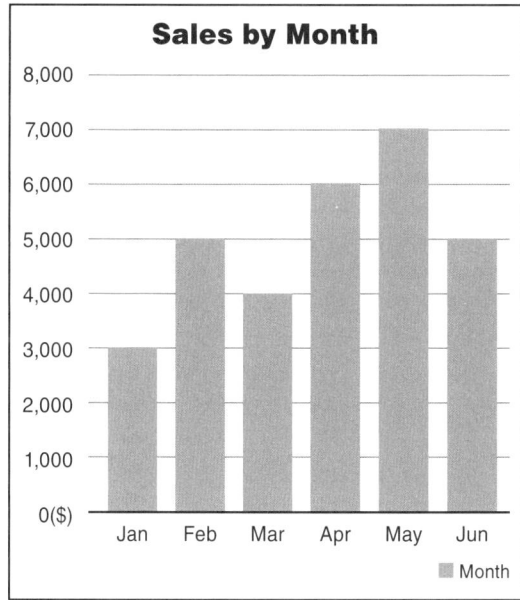

Sales by Month

Ridgeway Street

Parkway Street   Maple Avenue

95. What is the purpose of this speech?

(A) To welcome new staff
(B) To present awards to employees
(C) To expand into overseas markets
(D) To report successful sales results

96. Look at the graphic. Which month did the new pastel line of products make a huge increase in sales?

(A) March
(B) April
(C) May
(D) June

97. What will happen next month?

(A) The company will open another branch.
(B) Some employees will get promotions.
(C) They will meet foreign visitors.
(D) Employees will receive bonuses.

98. What is the purpose of the announcement?

(A) To welcome new employees
(B) To inform new security policies
(C) To address some employee concerns
(D) To solicit new clients

99. What will become available to employees in May?

(A) Flexible working hours
(B) Transportation to the bus stations
(C) New business offices
(D) Additional parking spaces

100. Look at the graphic. Which number shows where shuttle buses are supposed to stop?

(A) 1
(B) 2
(C) 3
(D) 4

Go on to the next page

TEST 09

원쌤의 "Reality Check"

언제! 어디서! 얼마나 틀렸는지 눈 뜨고 확인하자!! ◉◉

시험 날짜: _____월 _____일

시험 장소: _____ (이어폰 ☐ 스피커 ☐)

시험 시작 시간: _____시 _____분

시험 종료 시간: _____시 _____분

파트별 점수 분석(맞은 숫자)

Part 1	
Part 2	
Part 3	
Part 4	
총 맞은 개수	

239페이지에 있는 점수 환산표를 확인해 주세요.

TEST
10

LISTENING TEST

In the Listening test, you will be asked to demonstrate how well you understand spoken English. The entire Listening test will last approximately 45 minutes. There are four parts, and directions are given for each part. You must mark your answers on the separate answer sheet.
Do not write your answers in your test book.

PART 1

Directions: For each question in this part, you will hear four statements about a picture in your test book. When you hear the statements, you must select the one statement that best describes what you see in the picture. Then find the number of the question on your answer sheet and mark your answer. The statements will not be printed in your test book and will be spoken only one time.

Sample Answer

Statement (B), "They're shaking hands," is the best description of the picture, so you should select answer (B) and mark it on your answer sheet.

1.

2.

Go on to the next page

TEST 10

3.

4.

5.

6.

PART 2

Directions: You will hear a question or statement and three responses spoken in English. They will not be printed in your test book and will be spoken only one time. Select the best response to the question or statement and mark the letter (A), (B), or (C) on your answer sheet.

7. Mark your answer on your answer sheet.

8. Mark your answer on your answer sheet.

9. Mark your answer on your answer sheet.

10. Mark your answer on your answer sheet.

11. Mark your answer on your answer sheet.

12. Mark your answer on your answer sheet.

13. Mark your answer on your answer sheet.

14. Mark your answer on your answer sheet.

15. Mark your answer on your answer sheet.

16. Mark your answer on your answer sheet.

17. Mark your answer on your answer sheet.

18. Mark your answer on your answer sheet.

19. Mark your answer on your answer sheet.

20. Mark your answer on your answer sheet.

21. Mark your answer on your answer sheet.

22. Mark your answer on your answer sheet.

23. Mark your answer on your answer sheet.

24. Mark your answer on your answer sheet.

25. Mark your answer on your answer sheet.

26. Mark your answer on your answer sheet.

27. Mark your answer on your answer sheet.

28. Mark your answer on your answer sheet.

29. Mark your answer on your answer sheet.

30. Mark your answer on your answer sheet.

31. Mark your answer on your answer sheet.

PART 3

Directions: You will hear some conversations between two or more people. You will be asked to answer three questions about what the speakers say in each conversation. Select the best response to each question and mark the letter (A), (B), (C), or (D) on your answer sheet. The conversations will not be printed in your test book and will be spoken only one time.

32. Why did the man call?
    (A) To find out when the doctor is available
    (B) To cancel an appointment
    (C) To report an emergency
    (D) To take a special exam

33. What does the woman offer to do for the caller?
    (A) Contact the doctor for him
    (B) Review some medical record
    (C) Assign him to a different project
    (D) Reschedule his appointment

34. Why does the man decide to call her back later?
    (A) He needs to wait for a call from his company.
    (B) He needs directions to the doctor's office.
    (C) He wants to stay in Asia longer.
    (D) He does not know when he will be free.

35. What is stated about Ms. Long?
    (A) She is looking for a job overseas.
    (B) She has been recently promoted.
    (C) She has traveled overseas a lot.
    (D) She is moving into a new house.

36. What will Ms. Long need to do?
    (A) Make a presentation to the board
    (B) Train new staff
    (C) Work for public relations
    (D) Hire new employees

37. What does the woman say about her friend Elliot?
    (A) He is a marketing expert.
    (B) He has a lot of experience.
    (C) He will be interested in the job.
    (D) He is from France.

38. According to the speakers, what is the problem with the television?
    (A) The product is broken.
    (B) The shipment is incomplete.
    (C) The order was sent to a wrong place.
    (D) The wrong computer model was sent.

39. What does the man recommend doing?
    (A) Buying another remote control
    (B) Complaining to the manager
    (C) Finding a receipt
    (D) Checking the list

40. What time does the store close?
    (A) At 1 o'clock
    (B) At 5 o'clock
    (C) At 6 o'clock
    (D) At 7 o'clock

41. What problem are they talking about?
    (A) Their business received customer complaints.
    (B) Their business is out of supplies.
    (C) A shipment of merchandise has been delayed.
    (D) Some employees are not available for consultation.

42. What does the man say he will do this afternoon?
    (A) Place an order
    (B) Meet with a supervisor
    (C) Update a database
    (D) Call up a technician

43. What is the man asked to do immediately?
    (A) Create an inventory list
    (B) Update the work schedule
    (C) Unpack some boxes
    (D) Go to a store

Go on to the next page

44. Why does the woman want to talk to Mr. Gonzales?

(A) To inquire about his former colleague
(B) To confirm the time of an interview
(C) To introduce him to new employees
(D) To invite him to a sales conference

45. What will the woman do tomorrow morning?

(A) Accept a job offer
(B) Meet with Mr. Gonzales
(C) Arrange a travel plan
(D) Interview an applicant

46. What does the man offer to do?

(A) Give Mr. Gonzales' number
(B) Stop by at the woman's office
(C) Email the information
(D) Have someone call her

47. What are the speakers discussing?

(A) Attending a seminar
(B) Trying food from other countries
(C) Scheduling a flight
(D) Entertaining a visitor

48. What does the Raymond Adams plan to do Friday afternoon?

(A) Attend a lecture
(B) Visit his relatives
(C) Meet with his partner
(D) Plan for the next trip

49. What will the speakers probably do on Friday evening?

(A) Visit an art museum
(B) Attend a theatric performance
(C) Have a business meeting
(D) Eat at a restaurant

50. What does the man imply when he says, "Do you have any problems using our service"?

(A) He wants to change his mobile phone service.
(B) His company recently moved into a new place.
(C) He thinks she might not be satisfied with his company.
(D) He has the same problem before.

51. What has recently happened to the woman?

(A) She relocated to a new place.
(B) She got promoted at her company.
(C) She found a better company to do business with.
(D) She misplaced her phone and lost track of it.

52. What does the man offer to do?

(A) Meet the woman in person
(B) Send another bill to the address
(C) Provide a special coupon for her
(D) Waive some fees

53. What are the speakers mainly discussing?

(A) Ways to reduce a travel budget
(B) Possible locations for a conference
(C) Whom they should take to the event
(D) Plans for an upcoming business trip

54. What problem do the speakers have?

(A) Their business cards didn't arrive.
(B) The reservation was made on the wrong date.
(C) The transportation arrangements are not complete.
(D) Some of the conference materials are not ready.

55. What does the woman suggest they do?

(A) Contact a hotel
(B) Cancel the order
(C) Postpone a decision
(D) Reserve an extra space

56. What are the speakers discussing?

(A) Starting new employment
(B) Relocating to a new place
(C) Interviewing potential employees
(D) Scheduling a lunch appointment

57. What does the man mean when he says, "I don't mind working late as long as the pay is competitive"?

(A) He used to work at the competitor's company.
(B) He wants to receive a high salary.
(C) He doesn't like to work overtime.
(D) His work hours are pretty flexible.

58. When was the man's interview?

(A) Yesterday
(B) Last week
(C) Two weeks ago
(D) Two months ago

---

59. What does the man ask the woman to do?

(A) Wear safety gears
(B) Check a procedure
(C) Find some data
(D) Hire some temporary workers

60. Why is the woman unable to help?

(A) She is conducting an experiment.
(B) She is delivering a speech at the meeting.
(C) She is packing some materials.
(D) She needs to complete a data entry.

61. What does the woman say she will do tomorrow?

(A) Meet with a researcher
(B) Give presentation in front of the board
(C) Help the man with the test
(D) Begin writing a new report

	Beginner	Professional	Business'
Model #	PX 40	PX 50	PX 70
Set up fee	$20	waived	waived
Speed	8 pages/min	10 pages/min	12 pages/min
Colors	Black/White	Black/Silver	Black/White

62. What are the speakers talking about?

(A) Latest news from a magazine
(B) Price estimate for a job
(C) Features of two products
(D) Standards of quality control

63. Look at the graphic. Which model will the man be likely to purchase?

(A) PX 40
(B) PX 50
(C) PX 70
(D) Wait for a new model

64. What will the woman probably do next?

(A) She will talk with the manager.
(B) She will demonstrate the printer.
(C) She will find a box of product from a stockroom.
(D) She will receive the payment from the man.

Go on to the next page

TEST 10

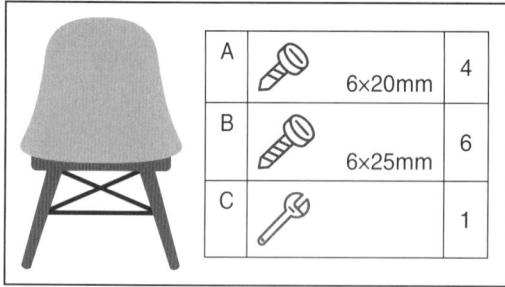

A	6×20mm	4
B	6×25mm	6
C		1

65. Where does the man most likely work?

(A) At a local restaurant
(B) At a shipping company
(C) At a furniture store
(D) At an assembly factory

66. Look at the graphic. What is the woman missing?

(A) Part A
(B) Part B
(C) Part C
(D) Assembly instructions

67. What does the man offer to do?

(A) Cancel the original order
(B) Arrange a delivery
(C) Provide some assembly instructions
(D) Take the woman to the store

Launching Schedule

#	Task Name	Dates
1	Concept meeting	Jan 15th
2	Proto type	Feb 15th
3	Marketing Research	April 1st
4	Production	May 1st
5	Launching show	May 15th

68. What business does the woman work for?

(A) A magazine publisher
(B) A vehicle manufacturer
(C) An advertising firm
(D) A professional research center

69. Why has there been some delay?

(A) They had to modify the initial prototypes.
(B) The research costed more than expected.
(C) Communicating in global environment was difficult.
(D) Some machinery in the factory malfunctioned.

70. Look at the graphic. Which date is no longer accurate?

(A) Feb 15th
(B) April 1st
(C) May 1st
(D) May 15th

PART 4

Directions: You will hear some talks given by a single speaker. You will be asked to answer three questions about what the speaker says in each talk. Select the best response to each question and mark the letter (A), (B), (C), or (D) on your answer sheet. The talks will not be printed in your test book and will be spoken only one time.

71. What is the main purpose of this announcement?
(A) To encourage people to visit an exhibit
(B) To introduce a gift idea
(C) To inform extended hours
(D) To announce a closing time

72. When will the gift shop in the museum close?
(A) At 4:00
(B) At 4:10
(C) At 5:00
(D) At 5:10

73. What will happen next month?
(A) A new exhibit will be held.
(B) A coat room will be added.
(C) Online registration service will begin.
(D) A section will be closed for renovation.

74. What is this announcement about?
(A) A change in security practice
(B) An ordering procedure for new equipment
(C) A plan to evaluate factory's employees
(D) A schedule for the regular inspection

75. According to the announcement, why should some employees go to the security office?
(A) To pick up an instruction booklet
(B) To register the new program
(C) To get an identification badge
(D) To receive orientation materials

76. What does the man imply when he says, "call your department to clear your ID"?
(A) Call an emergency hot line for information.
(B) The department store is out of inventory.
(C) You cannot access the building without an ID.
(D) Employees should keep their IDs at their offices.

77. What is the purpose of this talk?
(A) To introduce an instruction video
(B) To promote a new product
(C) To change the order she had placed
(D) To welcome a group of new employees

78. What will the listeners be reviewing?
(A) Detailed terms of a contract
(B) Specific images they have gathered
(C) Many helpful online sites
(D) Various functions of a camera

79. What are the listeners asked to do?
(A) Carry the handbook all the time
(B) Sign up at the online site
(C) Explore the functions on their own
(D) Send the images to their company

80. What is the purpose of the speech?
(A) To welcome new employees
(B) To inform a schedule change
(C) To present an employee award
(D) To report company's successful year

81. What kind of company does the speaker probably work for?
(A) An advertising agency
(B) An airline company
(C) A soft drinks company
(D) An accounting firm

82. What does the woman imply when she says, "helped a lot to increase our clients' sales"?
(A) They used to work at the clients' companies.
(B) The commercials for the clients were effective.
(C) Creativity is the most important factor in the advertisement.
(D) Ms. Wilson will become an executive of this company soon.

Go on to the next page

83. What type of event does Stewards Food specialize in?

(A) Outdoor events
(B) Corporate functions
(C) International business
(D) Family celebrations

84. What is available on the Stewards Food's website?

(A) Chef's contact information
(B) Pictures of the service staff
(C) Price estimates for various functions
(D) Sample menus for the event

85. According to the advertisement, how can listeners request a price estimate?

(A) By linking to a website
(B) By calling a catering specialist
(C) By sending the request form by fax
(D) By contacting the person in charge

86. Where does the caller probably work?

(A) At a print shop
(B) At an art gallery
(C) At a publishing company
(D) At a bookstore

87. What is the message concerned about?

(A) Ordering more products
(B) Handling customer complaints
(C) Setting up a new display
(D) Writing an article for the next month's issue

88. What does the caller ask Amy to do?

(A) Keep a detailed record
(B) Locate a missing item
(C) Create a work schedule
(D) Contact customers for an input

89. Where are the listeners?

(A) At a technical training
(B) At an auto maker's conference
(C) On an assembly floor
(D) At an annual sales seminar

90. What is the purpose of the talk?

(A) To explain today's schedule
(B) To inform changes in the program
(C) To get a discount coupon for an item
(D) To promote new electronic equipment

91. What does the woman mean when she says, "The outer appearance can be customized"?

(A) Customers buy products solely depend on its appearance.
(B) There will be extra charges for changing the outer designs.
(C) The products could look different from one another.
(D) The company is the only one which offers this kind of premium service.

92. Who is Mark Planko?

(A) A radio show host
(B) A news reporter
(C) A psychologist
(D) A company executive

93. What will be the main subject of the program?

(A) An advertising technique
(B) A new radio program
(C) New writing technique
(D) New product campaign

94. What did Mark Planko do recently?

(A) He launched a new product.
(B) He got an award for his advertisement.
(C) He published some research.
(D) He traveled around the world.

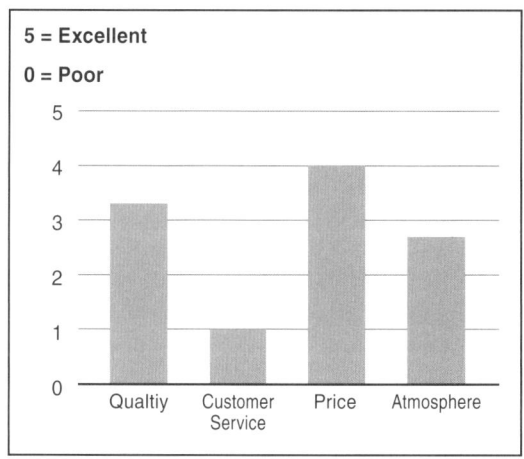

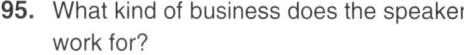

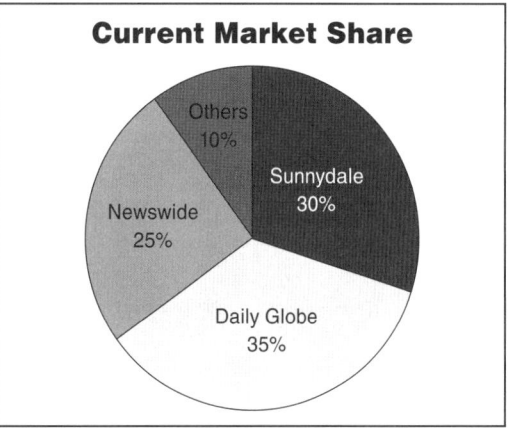

95. What kind of business does the speaker work for?

(A) A restaurant chain
(B) A marketing research firm
(C) A cleaning service
(D) An assembly factory

96. Look at the graphic. What does the speaker want to discuss with the listeners?

(A) Quality
(B) Customer service
(C) Price
(D) Atmosphere

97. What will Mr. Bones do?

(A) Survey the customers again
(B) Calculate where the money is leaking
(C) Locate an unprofitable branch
(D) Create a detailed report

98. Look at the graphic. Which company will have the biggest market share next month?

(A) Newswide
(B) Daily Globe
(C) Sunnydale
(D) Starlight Magazine

99. Who is Jack Johnson?

(A) A company executive
(B) A newspaper editor
(C) A mayor of the city
(D) A radio reporter

100. What event took place this morning?

(A) A news conference was held.
(B) A merger contract was signed.
(C) The president made a special announcement.
(D) They moved into a new headquarters building.

스파르타

TOEIC
실전 LC 1000제

정답
및
스크립트

ANSWER KEY

TEST 1

1. (A)	2. (C)	3. (B)	4. (A)	5. (C)
6. (B)	7. (C)	8. (B)	9. (A)	10. (B)
11. (B)	12. (A)	13. (C)	14. (A)	15. (A)
16. (A)	17. (B)	18. (C)	19. (B)	20. (B)
21. (B)	22. (B)	23. (B)	24. (C)	25. (A)
26. (A)	27. (C)	28. (A)	29. (A)	30. (C)
31. (A)	32. (A)	33. (C)	34. (B)	35. (C)
36. (D)	37. (D)	38. (A)	39. (C)	40. (D)
41. (B)	42. (C)	43. (D)	44. (B)	45. (C)
46. (D)	47. (C)	48. (D)	49. (B)	50. (C)
51. (B)	52. (C)	53. (B)	54. (C)	55. (D)
56. (B)	57. (D)	58. (A)	59. (D)	60. (A)
61. (B)	62. (A)	63. (D)	64. (A)	65. (D)
66. (A)	67. (D)	68. (A)	69. (B)	70. (B)
71. (A)	72. (C)	73. (D)	74. (D)	75. (B)
76. (D)	77. (B)	78. (D)	79. (B)	80. (B)
81. (D)	82. (A)	83. (C)	84. (D)	85. (D)
86. (A)	87. (D)	88. (B)	89. (D)	90. (C)
91. (B)	92. (B)	93. (D)	94. (B)	95. (C)
96. (B)	97. (C)	98. (D)	99. (B)	100. (D)

TEST 3

1. (D)	2. (B)	3. (C)	4. (B)	5. (C)
6. (A)	7. (B)	8. (A)	9. (C)	10. (A)
11. (B)	12. (B)	13. (A)	14. (A)	15. (C)
16. (A)	17. (C)	18. (A)	19. (B)	20. (A)
21. (C)	22. (C)	23. (A)	24. (A)	25. (A)
26. (A)	27. (A)	28. (A)	29. (A)	30. (C)
31. (C)	32. (D)	33. (D)	34. (C)	35. (A)
36. (C)	37. (D)	38. (A)	39. (C)	40. (D)
41. (A)	42. (D)	43. (C)	44. (A)	45. (D)
46. (D)	47. (B)	48. (B)	49. (D)	50. (C)
51. (B)	52. (A)	53. (D)	54. (D)	55. (B)
56. (C)	57. (A)	58. (D)	59. (D)	60. (B)
61. (D)	62. (D)	63. (C)	64. (B)	65. (A)
66. (C)	67. (C)	68. (C)	69. (C)	70. (B)
71. (B)	72. (D)	73. (C)	74. (B)	75. (A)
76. (C)	77. (A)	78. (B)	79. (C)	80. (C)
81. (C)	82. (B)	83. (C)	84. (D)	85. (A)
86. (C)	87. (C)	88. (D)	89. (C)	90. (B)
91. (D)	92. (A)	93. (C)	94. (D)	95. (C)
96. (A)	97. (D)	98. (D)	99. (B)	100. (C)

TEST 2

1. (B)	2. (D)	3. (D)	4. (C)	5. (B)
6. (A)	7. (B)	8. (B)	9. (A)	10. (C)
11. (A)	12. (B)	13. (A)	14. (C)	15. (C)
16. (B)	17. (C)	18. (B)	19. (B)	20. (A)
21. (C)	22. (B)	23. (C)	24. (A)	25. (A)
26. (A)	27. (B)	28. (A)	29. (B)	30. (A)
31. (B)	32. (C)	33. (B)	34. (C)	35. (B)
36. (D)	37. (C)	38. (D)	39. (A)	40. (C)
41. (B)	42. (A)	43. (D)	44. (A)	45. (D)
46. (C)	47. (C)	48. (D)	49. (A)	50. (A)
51. (B)	52. (D)	53. (C)	54. (D)	55. (A)
56. (B)	57. (D)	58. (C)	59. (D)	60. (B)
61. (A)	62. (D)	63. (B)	64. (B)	65. (C)
66. (B)	67. (A)	68. (D)	69. (A)	70. (B)
71. (B)	72. (C)	73. (D)	74. (D)	75. (B)
76. (C)	77. (A)	78. (D)	79. (B)	80. (B)
81. (D)	82. (C)	83. (D)	84. (C)	85. (B)
86. (D)	87. (D)	88. (B)	89. (C)	90. (D)
91. (C)	92. (D)	93. (B)	94. (D)	95. (C)
96. (A)	97. (D)	98. (A)	99. (B)	100. (A)

TEST 4

1. (D)	2. (C)	3. (A)	4. (C)	5. (D)
6. (C)	7. (C)	8. (B)	9. (A)	10. (A)
11. (B)	12. (C)	13. (B)	14. (C)	15. (C)
16. (A)	17. (A)	18. (C)	19. (B)	20. (B)
21. (C)	22. (C)	23. (A)	24. (A)	25. (A)
26. (C)	27. (A)	28. (A)	29. (B)	30. (C)
31. (A)	32. (D)	33. (D)	34. (A)	35. (B)
36. (C)	37. (D)	38. (C)	39. (D)	40. (C)
41. (C)	42. (D)	43. (B)	44. (A)	45. (D)
46. (A)	47. (C)	48. (A)	49. (D)	50. (C)
51. (B)	52. (D)	53. (C)	54. (B)	55. (D)
56. (C)	57. (B)	58. (C)	59. (A)	60. (D)
61. (C)	62. (B)	63. (D)	64. (D)	65. (A)
66. (D)	67. (B)	68. (A)	69. (B)	70. (A)
71. (D)	72. (C)	73. (C)	74. (A)	75. (D)
76. (C)	77. (A)	78. (D)	79. (C)	80. (C)
81. (B)	82. (B)	83. (C)	84. (A)	85. (B)
86. (A)	87. (B)	88. (B)	89. (C)	90. (A)
91. (C)	92. (D)	93. (C)	94. (A)	95. (B)
96. (A)	97. (C)	98. (D)	99. (C)	100. (D)

TEST 5

1. (D)	2. (B)	3. (A)	4. (C)	5. (B)
6. (B)	7. (B)	8. (C)	9. (A)	10. (A)
11. (A)	12. (C)	13. (B)	14. (A)	15. (B)
16. (B)	17. (C)	18. (A)	19. (C)	20. (A)
21. (B)	22. (C)	23. (A)	24. (B)	25. (C)
26. (C)	27. (C)	28. (B)	29. (C)	30. (C)
31. (B)	32. (C)	33. (B)	34. (A)	35. (B)
36. (D)	37. (C)	38. (A)	39. (C)	40. (A)
41. (B)	42. (A)	43. (D)	44. (A)	45. (C)
46. (D)	47. (B)	48. (C)	49. (A)	50. (D)
51. (A)	52. (C)	53. (A)	54. (C)	55. (B)
56. (B)	57. (C)	58. (C)	59. (D)	60. (A)
61. (C)	62. (D)	63. (A)	64. (C)	65. (B)
66. (C)	67. (B)	68. (D)	69. (C)	70. (C)
71. (A)	72. (B)	73. (C)	74. (C)	75. (C)
76. (D)	77. (B)	78. (C)	79. (D)	80. (A)
81. (D)	82. (C)	83. (B)	84. (D)	85. (C)
86. (D)	87. (A)	88. (C)	89. (D)	90. (C)
91. (B)	92. (B)	93. (D)	94. (D)	95. (C)
96. (A)	97. (C)	98. (D)	99. (D)	100. (B)

TEST 7

1. (B)	2. (D)	3. (B)	4. (D)	5. (A)
6. (C)	7. (A)	8. (B)	9. (B)	10. (A)
11. (C)	12. (A)	13. (A)	14. (A)	15. (A)
16. (B)	17. (C)	18. (C)	19. (A)	20. (C)
21. (A)	22. (B)	23. (C)	24. (B)	25. (A)
26. (C)	27. (A)	28. (A)	29. (C)	30. (A)
31. (B)	32. (C)	33. (C)	34. (D)	35. (D)
36. (C)	37. (D)	38. (B)	39. (D)	40. (A)
41. (B)	42. (B)	43. (C)	44. (B)	45. (D)
46. (D)	47. (B)	48. (B)	49. (D)	50. (D)
51. (C)	52. (C)	53. (A)	54. (B)	55. (B)
56. (C)	57. (D)	58. (D)	59. (A)	60. (A)
61. (D)	62. (A)	63. (B)	64. (C)	65. (C)
66. (D)	67. (B)	68. (B)	69. (A)	70. (C)
71. (A)	72. (A)	73. (C)	74. (D)	75. (C)
76. (C)	77. (C)	78. (C)	79. (B)	80. (B)
81. (D)	82. (D)	83. (C)	84. (D)	85. (D)
86. (D)	87. (A)	88. (B)	89. (A)	90. (B)
91. (D)	92. (B)	93. (A)	94. (B)	95. (A)
96. (C)	97. (D)	98. (B)	99. (B)	100. (D)

TEST 6

1. (D)	2. (A)	3. (D)	4. (C)	5. (B)
6. (B)	7. (C)	8. (A)	9. (C)	10. (B)
11. (A)	12. (C)	13. (C)	14. (A)	15. (C)
16. (A)	17. (C)	18. (B)	19. (A)	20. (C)
21. (A)	22. (A)	23. (B)	24. (A)	25. (C)
26. (A)	27. (B)	28. (C)	29. (B)	30. (A)
31. (A)	32. (D)	33. (C)	34. (B)	35. (C)
36. (A)	37. (D)	38. (B)	39. (D)	40. (D)
41. (C)	42. (B)	43. (A)	44. (A)	45. (D)
46. (C)	47. (A)	48. (B)	49. (D)	50. (B)
51. (A)	52. (C)	53. (B)	54. (B)	55. (D)
56. (D)	57. (B)	58. (A)	59. (D)	60. (C)
61. (B)	62. (C)	63. (D)	64. (C)	65. (C)
66. (B)	67. (D)	68. (D)	69. (B)	70. (B)
71. (A)	72. (D)	73. (C)	74. (B)	75. (A)
76. (D)	77. (C)	78. (C)	79. (D)	80. (D)
81. (B)	82. (A)	83. (D)	84. (B)	85. (A)
86. (A)	87. (C)	88. (C)	89. (B)	90. (C)
91. (A)	92. (D)	93. (B)	94. (D)	95. (C)
96. (B)	97. (A)	98. (C)	99. (C)	100. (C)

TEST 8

1. (D)	2. (B)	3. (D)	4. (B)	5. (C)
6. (C)	7. (A)	8. (B)	9. (A)	10. (C)
11. (B)	12. (A)	13. (A)	14. (C)	15. (A)
16. (C)	17. (B)	18. (B)	19. (A)	20. (B)
21. (A)	22. (C)	23. (B)	24. (C)	25. (A)
26. (A)	27. (B)	28. (C)	29. (B)	30. (A)
31. (C)	32. (C)	33. (D)	34. (D)	35. (A)
36. (D)	37. (A)	38. (D)	39. (B)	40. (D)
41. (A)	42. (C)	43. (D)	44. (A)	45. (C)
46. (B)	47. (A)	48. (D)	49. (B)	50. (C)
51. (B)	52. (C)	53. (A)	54. (C)	55. (D)
56. (C)	57. (B)	58. (D)	59. (D)	60. (D)
61. (A)	62. (C)	63. (B)	64. (D)	65. (B)
66. (C)	67. (B)	68. (C)	69. (C)	70. (D)
71. (A)	72. (C)	73. (D)	74. (C)	75. (A)
76. (D)	77. (C)	78. (B)	79. (D)	80. (C)
81. (B)	82. (D)	83. (C)	84. (C)	85. (D)
86. (B)	87. (C)	88. (D)	89. (D)	90. (B)
91. (C)	92. (A)	93. (C)	94. (C)	95. (D)
96. (D)	97. (C)	98. (C)	99. (D)	100. (A)

TEST 9

1. (B)	2. (D)	3. (D)	4. (C)	5. (A)
6. (D)	7. (B)	8. (A)	9. (A)	10. (B)
11. (B)	12. (A)	13. (B)	14. (A)	15. (C)
16. (A)	17. (C)	18. (A)	19. (B)	20. (A)
21. (C)	22. (A)	23. (A)	24. (B)	25. (C)
26. (A)	27. (B)	28. (C)	29. (A)	30. (C)
31. (C)	32. (D)	33. (A)	34. (C)	35. (B)
36. (D)	37. (C)	38. (D)	39. (B)	40. (C)
41. (C)	42. (A)	43. (D)	44. (D)	45. (C)
46. (B)	47. (D)	48. (C)	49. (D)	50. (A)
51. (C)	52. (D)	53. (C)	54. (A)	55. (D)
56. (A)	57. (D)	58. (C)	59. (B)	60. (C)
61. (A)	62. (B)	63. (C)	64. (C)	65. (D)
66. (C)	67. (B)	68. (B)	69. (C)	70. (A)
71. (D)	72. (C)	73. (A)	74. (C)	75. (D)
76. (D)	77. (A)	78. (C)	79. (D)	80. (A)
81. (C)	82. (D)	83. (C)	84. (B)	85. (D)
86. (C)	87. (D)	88. (B)	89. (D)	90. (D)
91. (A)	92. (C)	93. (D)	94. (D)	95. (D)
96. (B)	97. (D)	98. (C)	99. (D)	100. (A)

TEST 10

1. (B)	2. (B)	3. (C)	4. (D)	5. (B)
6. (D)	7. (C)	8. (B)	9. (A)	10. (A)
11. (C)	12. (B)	13. (C)	14. (A)	15. (A)
16. (C)	17. (A)	18. (C)	19. (B)	20. (B)
21. (B)	22. (C)	23. (B)	24. (A)	25. (C)
26. (C)	27. (C)	28. (B)	29. (C)	30. (A)
31. (C)	32. (B)	33. (D)	34. (D)	35. (B)
36. (D)	37. (C)	38. (B)	39. (D)	40. (C)
41. (B)	42. (A)	43. (D)	44. (A)	45. (D)
46. (D)	47. (D)	48. (C)	49. (D)	50. (C)
51. (A)	52. (D)	53. (D)	54. (C)	55. (A)
56. (A)	57. (B)	58. (D)	59. (B)	60. (D)
61. (A)	62. (C)	63. (A)	64. (C)	65. (C)
66. (C)	67. (B)	68. (B)	69. (C)	70. (B)
71. (D)	72. (C)	73. (A)	74. (A)	75. (C)
76. (C)	77. (A)	78. (D)	79. (B)	80. (C)
81. (A)	82. (B)	83. (B)	84. (D)	85. (A)
86. (D)	87. (C)	88. (A)	89. (B)	90. (D)
91. (C)	92. (C)	93. (A)	94. (C)	95. (A)
96. (B)	97. (D)	98. (C)	99. (D)	100. (A)

1회

1.	(A)	2.	(C)	3.	(B)	4.	(A)	5.	(C)
6.	(B)	7.	(C)	8.	(B)	9.	(A)	10.	(B)
11.	(B)	12.	(A)	13.	(C)	14.	(A)	15.	(A)
16.	(A)	17.	(B)	18.	(C)	19.	(B)	20.	(B)
21.	(B)	22.	(B)	23.	(B)	24.	(C)	25.	(A)
26.	(A)	27.	(C)	28.	(A)	29.	(A)	30.	(C)
31.	(A)	32.	(A)	33.	(C)	34.	(B)	35.	(C)
36.	(D)	37.	(D)	38.	(A)	39.	(C)	40.	(D)
41.	(B)	42.	(C)	43.	(D)	44.	(B)	45.	(C)
46.	(D)	47.	(C)	48.	(D)	49.	(B)	50.	(C)
51.	(B)	52.	(C)	53.	(B)	54.	(C)	55.	(D)
56.	(B)	57.	(D)	58.	(A)	59.	(D)	60.	(A)
61.	(B)	62.	(A)	63.	(D)	64.	(A)	65.	(D)
66.	(A)	67.	(D)	68.	(A)	69.	(B)	70.	(B)
71.	(A)	72.	(C)	73.	(D)	74.	(D)	75.	(B)
76.	(D)	77.	(B)	78.	(D)	79.	(B)	80.	(B)
81.	(D)	82.	(A)	83.	(C)	84.	(D)	85.	(D)
86.	(A)	87.	(D)	88.	(B)	89.	(D)	90.	(C)
91.	(B)	92.	(B)	93.	(D)	94.	(B)	95.	(C)
96.	(B)	97.	(C)	98.	(D)	99.	(B)	100.	(D)

Part 1

1. (A) The man is standing on a ladder.
   (B) The man is climbing up the stairs.
   (C) The man is carrying some lumber.
   (D) The man is painting on the wall.

2. (A) The desk is full of books.
   (B) The curtains have been pulled shut.
   (C) The monitor is sitting on a desk.
   (D) The clock is hanging on the wall.

3. (A) The woman is selling some jewelry.
   (B) The woman is leaning toward the display.
   (C) The woman is wrapping up a present.
   (D) The woman is negotiating the price.

4. (A) The man is protecting his face with a mask.
   (B) The man is lighting the candles.
   (C) The man is working at his desk.
   (D) The man is fixing the pipe at a factory.

5. (A) The students are standing around the table.
   (B) The woman is handing out some documents.
   (C) The woman is explaining something.
   (D) The students are writing something on the board.

6. (A) Customers are paying for their purchases.
   (B) Various items have been arranged on the table.
   (C) Customers are shopping at a supermarket.
   (D) Books are being placed on the shelf.

Part 2

7. When can we reschedule the interview?
   (A) Not in my backyard.
   (B) It might be possible.
   (C) Are you free on Thursday?

8. Who helps the registration at the Information Technology seminar?
   (A) Down the hallway.
   (B) The receptionist.
   (C) You have to sign up first.

9. That's the car we want, isn't it?
   (A) Yes, it's that red one.
   (B) No, send it later.
   (C) I saw several of them.

10. Where can I find more office supplies?
    (A) It was surprising to know.
    (B) In the cabinet by the door.
    (C) Yes, I'll bring some over.

11. Do you have a used copy of this book?
    (A) On the front page.
    (B) Sorry, we don't.
    (C) The copier is broken.

12. Why was the printing paper moved out of the supply closet?
    (A) To be closer to the copiers.
    (B) From the office supplier.
    (C) I'll get it later today.

13. Did you hire someone to replace Jeffrey?
    (A) Sometime next week.
    (B) No, we have to order new parts.
    (C) Yes, she will start next Monday.

14. Why are we getting new keys for the conference room?
    (A) They are changing the locks.
    (B) The new secretary starts next week.
    (C) Next to the locksmith's.

15. The clock in the employees' lounge needs new batteries.
    (A) I'll go get some right away.
    (B) No, thank you. I'm fine.
    (C) We need to change the location.

16. Our deadline has been extended to next Wednesday.
    (A) That's good news.
    (B) Extension 135, I think.
    (C) Yes, we need more money.

17. Wasn't there a coffee shop at Elga Street?
    (A) No, no coffee for me please.
    (B) Yes, but it moved to another place.
    (C) Turn left at the next corner, please.

18. Has the mail for our department arrived yet?
    (A) We haven't received any phone calls.
    (B) Yes, we should put extra postage.
    (C) I'll go check right away.

19. Where should I send the updated sales report?
    (A) By seven o'clock.
    (B) To the Milwaukee office.
    (C) The sales are up to 10 percent.

20. Would you like to sit inside, or out on the patio?
    (A) Put the files inside the envelope.
    (B) I think it's too windy outside.
    (C) Sure, two more tables, please.

21. Which building will the new employees work at tomorrow?
    (A) No, he's not that new.
    (B) At the Emerson Building.
    (C) We don't work on the weekend.

22. What did Mr. Peterson say about my proposal?
    (A) The office was moved last week.
    (B) He said it was quite reasonable.
    (C) I don't think he will be here soon.

23. Do you want me to type this letter for you?
    (A) No, it should be sent by express.
    (B) Thanks, I really appreciate it.
    (C) I haven't met her yet.

24. Haven't you signed the contract with Fair Trading?
    (A) The contact number has been changed.
    (B) Yes, it was excellent design.
    (C) No, I need to review it first.

25. We would like you to work with us in the product development team.
(A) That sounds interesting.
(B) The due date has been postponed.
(C) Yes, I'll have one more please.

26. Does Mr. Kenneth know the accounting meeting date has been changed?
(A) Yes, I informed him yesterday.
(B) No, the reservation was cancelled.
(C) Nobody knows what's going on.

27. Don't you think the price for our new printer was too expensive?
(A) I didn't think he was coming.
(B) Yes, I would love to buy one.
(C) I thought it was acceptable.

28. Who changed the layout of the blueprints?
(A) The project architect.
(B) The president won't like it.
(C) Yes, we can accommodate it.

29. Do you know why the bank is closed?
(A) I think it's a national holiday.
(B) I'd like to open an account.
(C) No, I don't know anybody here.

30. There is no way we could finish this project in time.
(A) We definitely need a new projector.
(B) Don't worry. The plane should get here on time.
(C) I'll go talk to Mr. Anderson about the extension.

31. You can sign the lease agreement by the end of this week.
(A) Okay, I'll do it by tomorrow.
(B) It's been assigned to someone else.
(C) It was sent a few weeks ago.

Part 3

Questions 32 through 34 refer to the following conversation.

M Did you hear that there will be a street parade today in celebration of the holiday in front of our building?

W I saw the news this morning too. We'd better hurry to the airport since heavy traffic is expected all over the city. Should we leave right after the meeting?

M Good idea. Since the flight departure time is 9 in the evening, we should arrive there two hours before at the latest.

W We're finishing a little over 5 so we can leave at 6. That should give us enough time.

W Alright, just remind me when we should get ready.

32. Where are the speakers?
(A) In an office
(B) At a restaurant
(C) At the airport
(D) In the parade

33. Why is the traffic jam expected?
(A) Many people are going on a picnic.
(B) Construction is ongoing.
(C) There will be a street parade.
(D) There was an accident on the street.

34. What time will the speakers leave?
(A) At 5 p.m.
(B) At 6 p.m.
(C) At 7 p.m.
(D) At 9 p.m.

Questions 35 through 37 refer to the following conversation.

M Hi, Ms. Casey. This is Brandon Alexander from Pablo Water Company. We've found out that you haven't paid your bill for the last 3 months.

W I know, but there was a problem. I haven't been receiving my bills since I moved into my new apartment. Didn't I give you my new address before?

M Let me check. According to our data base, your address is 809 Orchard Avenue. Is that correct?

W No, that's my old apartment. I thought I had informed every company of the new address, but I must have forgotten your company. Let me tell you the new one.

35. What is the purpose of the call?
(A) To promote a new service
(B) To make a complaint
(C) To inform a customer of unpaid bills
(D) To confirm a schedule

36. According to the woman, what was the problem?
(A) She was not aware of the new services.
(B) She could not meet the deadline.
(C) She was unfairly treated by a staff member.
(D) She may have forgotten to notify some change.

37. What will the man probably do next?
(A) Call a colleague
(B) Provide her with a discount
(C) Explain the procedure
(D) Update some information

新 Questions 38 through 40 refer to the following conversation with three speakers.

M Hi Angela, Hi Daniela. How are the trainees in your departments going? I know you've had to train several new bank cashiers this year.

W1 They're doing really well. In fact, as of this month, I no longer have any trainees. Mine became all full-time cashiers.

W2 5 out of six trainees in our department became full time, too.

M That's perfect. Now that you have enough cashiers, do you think some of the more experienced ones might be interested in training to become a loan officer?

W2 I heard the loan department is a bit short-handed.

M That is true. And since we might have a couple of loan officers who are transferring to another location next month, we definitely need more people in the loan department.

W1 I can certainly ask them. I'll send you the names of anyone who's interested.

W2 If it's that urgent, we'll put that in our top priority. We can let you know by the end of the day tomorrow. Right, Angela?

38. Where do the speakers most likely work?
(A) At a bank
(B) At a supermarket
(C) At an employment firm
(D) At a business school

39. What does the man say he wants to do?
(A) Register for a management class
(B) Work as a cashier
(C) Hire a new loan officer
(D) Open a new account

40. What do the women say they will send the man tomorrow?
(A) Handouts from a presentation
(B) Brochures for financial services
(C) An application for the new position
(D) A list of some names

Questions 41 through 43 refer to the following conversation.

W It's almost our lunch break. Let's try something different for lunch today! How about some Indian food at the restaurant down the street from our office? They've recently opened and have become quite famous for tasty food.

M Oh, I already took my family there last weekend, but it was not as impressive as people say. There were too many people and the service wasn't good at all because it was too busy.

W Really? I had no idea. Where should we go then?

M Actually, why don't we just have some delivery food and eat here? There is still much to be done before the afternoon's meeting.

41. Where is the conversation probably taking place?
(A) In a restaurant
(B) In the office
(C) On the street
(D) At the park

42. What does the man say about the restaurant?
(A) It was too expensive.
(B) It was as good as its reputation.
(C) It was below his expectations.
(D) It was far away from the office.

43. What will the speakers probably do?
(A) Go out to eat
(B) Leave for the day
(C) Take a walk
(D) Order some food

Questions 44 through 46 refer to the following conversation.

W Good morning. You have reached Dr. Henry's office. This is Laura. How may I help you?

M Hi, this is Joel Phillips. I'd like to reschedule my appointment today at three o'clock to another time tomorrow. Is that possible?

W I'm afraid the appointments are already fully booked for this week. Mr. Phillips, you've already waited two weeks to make this reservation and you really should have your teeth examined. Is there any way you can come today as arranged?

M I know, but I am at an urgent meeting with my client right now and I might not make it to the three o'clock appointment. Well, I'll try to conclude everything quickly in the meeting so that I can arrive at your clinic on time. Thank you.

44. Where does the woman work?
(A) At a theater
(B) At a dental clinic
(C) At a travel agency
(D) At a restaurant

45. How long did it take for the man to make a reservation?
(A) Three hours
(B) One week
(C) Two weeks
(D) Three weeks

46. What does the man say he will do?
(A) Cancel his appointment with his client
(B) Look for some reviews
(C) Book another time
(D) Finish the work early

Questions 47 through 49 refer to the following conversation.

M Did you hear that Mr. Russell has been promoted to the general manager of our headquarters in New York office?

W I wasn't told, but I knew that he would be promoted soon. He deserves the position for his dedication and effort. Anyway what's going to happen to his vacancy then?

M As far as I know, the company will be hiring his replacement in our office and another secretary to work with him in the head office. Since he will relocate to New York in May, the recruitment should be expedited in this month. Do you have anyone in mind?

W Well, I have a friend whom I used to work with. She is a hard worker and she's in between jobs at the moment. I'll just call her and ask if she's interested.

47. What is the conversation mainly about?
(A) A vacation trip
(B) Office supply purchase
(C) Changes in personnel
(D) Software installation

48. What does the woman mean when she says, "I knew that he would be promoted soon"?
(A) She was notified about the news before.
(B) She is very close to Mr. Russell.
(C) She wants to get promoted, too.
(D) She thinks Mr. Russell has worked hard.

49. What will the woman do next?
(A) Call Mr. Russell
(B) Talk to a former colleague
(C) Interview an applicant
(D) Make a reservation

Questions 50 through 52 refer to the following conversation.

W Thank you for coming. Mr. Langston. I asked you to come in today because our current shipping company is not quite satisfactory. We've heard that your company provides good services at reasonable prices. So, tell me about your company.

M Yes, Ms. Wilson. I'm pleased to introduce to you what we do. Before doing so, however, could you please tell me about your company's needs first, so that I can suggest our services to meet your requirements?

W Well, we manufacture heavy machinery such as tractors and cranes. We cover deliveries on our own except for international orders. That's why we're outsourcing these overseas orders to businesses like yours.

M We specialize in international deliveries. I'd also like to know your priorities regarding product shipments and reasons why you found your current contractor unsatisfactory.

50. Why did the woman invite the man?
(A) To request a refund
(B) To sign a business contract
(C) To obtain more information
(D) To rent some equipment

51. What kind of company does the woman work for?
(A) A shipping company
(B) A heavy equipment company
(C) A real estate agency
(D) A law firm

52. What is the woman most likely to do next?
(A) Give a lecture
(B) Prepare for shipment
(C) Answer the questions
(D) Sign a contract

Questions 53 through 55 refer to the following conversation.

W Here is my car key. By what time do you think I should get back to pick up my car?

M After rotating the tires and changing the oil, we still need to perform a safety inspection at the end. Because we are currently pretty busy working on other customers' cars, yours should be done by 5, I think.

W Can I come by 6:30, then? I leave work at 6 and it takes about 30 minutes to come here.

M Sure, you can come by any time before 8 and that's when we close.

W Can you tell me where the nearest bus station is? I have to go back to the office soon.

M The bus stop is about 200 meters down the street. There are buses going into the city every 10 minutes or so.

W Thanks. Can you give me a call if the work finishes early? I need my car back as soon as possible.

53. Where most likely are the speakers?
(A) At a bus stop
(B) In an auto repair shop
(C) In an office
(D) On the road

54. According to the woman, when does she expect to be back?
(A) By 5 p.m.
(B) By 6 p.m.
(C) By 6:30 p.m.
(D) By 8 p.m.

55. What does the woman ask the man to do?
(A) Order more parts
(B) Drop her keys off
(C) Close the shop later than usual
(D) Notify any change

Questions 56 through 58 refer to the following conversation.

M Hello, Ms. Lena. This is Peter Lewis from CPM Industries. I'm calling regarding your interview last week. We've made a decision to offer you a job as a graphic designer.

W Thank you, Mr. Lewis. It's a relief to hear the news. I've been waiting for your call. I believe working for CPM Industries is a perfect opportunity to use my skills and abilities for my future career. I accept the offer.

M Oh great! When do you think you can start working?

W I'll need at least two weeks to notify the company and find a suitable replacement.

M Okay, I'll make a note of it. You also need to come down to our office to fill out some papers. Let me know when it will be more convenient for you.

56. Who is the man calling?
(A) A business owner
(B) A job applicant
(C) A photographer
(D) A journalist

57. What does the woman mean when she says, "It's a relief to hear the news"?
(A) She's been sick for the last few days.
(B) She had applied for this company before.
(C) She is working for a newspaper company.
(D) She was worried she might not get the job.

58. According to the man, why does the woman have to see him?
(A) To complete some documents
(B) To submit a certification
(C) To celebrate an anniversary
(D) To start working

Questions 59 through 61 refer to the following conversation .

M Carol, I tried to book the rooms for the whole team for the conference in Arlington, but all the hotels in town are full. We should have made the reservation sooner.

W Well, I know a hotel about 20 miles outside the city. Let me check online first. I'm sure they'll have enough rooms available for the team.

M Hmm. 20 miles? We'll have to rent a van to commute each day so we may end up going over our travel budget.

W Actually, I think we'll be fine. Hotels located outside the city tend to be less expensive. The money we'll be saving on rooms can be used to rent a van.

M Okay. That makes sense. Let's check with the hotel.

59. What problem are the speakers mainly discussing?
(A) A flight has been canceled.
(B) Tickets are all sold out.
(C) The registration has not been completed.
(D) Hotel rooms are unavailable.

60. What solution does the woman suggest?
(A) Reserving rooms in another area
(B) Postponing a business trip
(C) Calling a travel agent
(D) Taking public transportation

61. What does the man imply when he says, "That makes sense"?
(A) They may be late for the conference.
(B) They may not exceed the budget.
(C) They may have missed the deadline.
(D) The rooms may be too small for the group.

Questions 62 through 64 refer to the following conversation.

W Richard, did you get any messages from the technical support team about my desktop? All my data about the presentation for our new clients were stored in that computer and I cannot open any of it.

M Well, I called them this morning again but they said that they won't be able to send someone until tomorrow around 3.

W Oh, no. That's going to be too late. I'm meeting with one of the new clients to propose ways to boost the sales in her company. It is my first time to meet her in person and I need to make a good impression to win the contract. Could you please call them again and ask them to take a look at my computer?

M Sure. I understand how important the presentation is to execute the contract. I'll let you know after making the call.

62. What problem does the woman have?
(A) Her presentation materials are inaccessible.
(B) There are a number of mistakes in her report.
(C) The technical support team is out of the office all day.
(D) The meeting is canceled due to the inclement weather.

63. When was the technician supposed to arrive?
(A) This morning
(B) This afternoon
(C) Tomorrow morning
(D) Tomorrow afternoon

64. What will the man do next?
(A) Make a call
(B) Help her presentation
(C) Contact her client
(D) Repair her computer

新 Questions 65 through 67 refer to the following conversation and map.

W What will we do to thank the major sponsors of our museum this year? It's almost November and we should do something to remind them of us.

M Well, let's do more than just send out thank-you cards like we did last year. How about making picture frames with our museum's name and logo on them?

W Hey, that's actually a good idea. In that way, they could always remember us every time they look at the frame. However, we have to make sure the frame looks elegant and stylish and not like a free giveaway.

M I have an idea. I know a premium gift shop on Main Street which handles personalized gifts such as cups and trophies. They're only a block away from us. I'll stop by their store after lunch.

W Actually, they just moved to a new location at the corner of Beacon Street and Carton Avenue across from Boise Cafe. Let me call them first to find out whether they take large orders.

65. What do the speakers want to do?
(A) Plan a party for customers
(B) Conduct a training session for employees
(C) Mail out some information to participants
(D) Show their appreciation to sponsors

66. What did the organization send out last year?
(A) Thank you cards
(B) Money orders
(C) Picture frames
(D) Monogrammed cups

67. Look at the graphic. What number shows where the gift 新 shop is located?
(A) 1
(B) 2
(C) 3
(D) 4

新 Questions 68 through 70 refer to the following conversation and schedule.

M Welcome back, Helena. Did you have fun during the holiday?

W More than I can say. I had a wonderful time.

M Where have you been? I spent most of my vacation time repainting and repairing my house.

W I went to Thailand with one of my friends. There was a beautiful beach in front of the hotel where we stayed. We loved the beach so much that we stayed there 5 days instead of 3 days we originally had planned.

M Really? Actually, I went there last year, too. I also liked the beach a lot. Did you do a lot of sightseeing?

W We actually didn't do any sightseeing. We were more interested in swimming and relaxing on the beach. It was the most enjoyable vacation I've ever had except that I got a little sunburn and it still hurts.

M I'm glad you enjoyed your vacation.

68. What is the conversation mainly about?
(A) Taking a vacation
(B) Winning a prize
(C) Testing a program
(D) Booking a flight

69. Look at the graphic. In which location has the woman 新 decided to stay longer?
(A) At Bangkok
(B) At Phuket
(C) At Chiangmai
(D) At home

70. What does the woman say was the problem with her vacation?
(A) Her flight was delayed.
(B) She got too much sun.
(C) Her schedule was too tight.
(D) One of her friends got sick.

Part 4

Questions 71 through 73 refer to the following news report.

Good morning listeners, this is 102.7 FM, your favorite station for local news, weather and traffic. Because of a sudden snowstorm last night, the morning commute is worse than usual. City officials are still working hard to clean up the road but there are delays on major highways and bridges. Please use extra caution because the roads are slippery and as the temperature goes down this afternoon, the conditions will get worse. Here is a reminder that on Friday, Lincoln Bridge will reopen after two weeks of construction to reinforce the foundation of this historic bridge. We'll be right back with more news on the presidential election next month. But, first let's listen to some messages from those who sponsor this program. We'll be right back.

71. When is the report being broadcasted?
(A) In the morning
(B) At noon
(C) In the afternoon
(D) At midnight

72. What is causing the traffic delay?
(A) Road construction
(B) Electric repairs
(C) Bad weather
(D) An accident in a highway

73. What will people hear next?
(A) An interview with the guest
(B) An emergency weather report
(C) A presidential election
(D) An advertisement

Questions 74 through 76 refer to the following telephone message.

Hello, this is Jennifer Johnson from Ashley Furniture. This message is for Marilyn Lowe about the order you have placed last week. Ms, Lowe, I'm afraid the sofa you ordered isn't available in the chocolate brown leather you wanted. This particular shade of leather has been discontinued by the manufacturer because it wasn't selling well. I did find other similar colors of leather such as dark brown and espresso color. If you order in these colors, your sofa will be ready in one month as we had promised. Why don't you stop by at the shop and I'll show you the samples of these leathers. Thank you.

74. What is the purpose of the message?
(A) To explain a change in the invoice
(B) To ask for the mailing address
(C) To respond to a customer complaint
(D) To report a problem with the order

75. Why has the product been discontinued?
(A) The style was out of date.
(B) The color was not popular.
(C) The quality was below expectation.
(D) The manufacturer has been changed.

76. What does the speaker suggest the customers do?
(A) Speak with a manager
(B) Cancel the order
(C) Wait for the new model
(D) Visit the store

Questions 77 through 79 refer to the following broadcast.

Good evening and thank you for listening to Radio 101.5. I'm sorry to inform our listeners that due to an unexpected problem with transmission equipment, we won't be broadcasting our normally scheduled live news from the election site. Instead, I'll host a special discussion with our guest, Barbara Fisher, a political commentator for the National Party. She used to work at numerous government agencies and recently published a book on our nation's political history and major players in it. Tonight, she will explain what changes we can expect after the election. Welcome to our show, Barbara.

77. Who most likely is the speaker?
(A) A well-known reporter
(B) A radio host
(C) A technical staff
(D) A political commentator

78. Why has the schedule changed?
(A) The election was delayed.
(B) The live performance was cancelled.
(C) A studio is not available at the moment.
(D) Some equipment is not working.

79. What has Barbara Fisher recently done?
(A) She joined a political party.
(B) She wrote a book.
(C) She moved to a suburb.
(D) She received a prestigious award.

Questions 80 through 82 refer to the following telephone message.

Hi, Peter, this is Steven from the shipping department. I just got your fax message concerning tomorrow's deliveries to corporate clients. The problem is that the coversheet says there will be a five-page fax but I only received three of them. We need to assign trucks and personnel who will be in charge of shipping to our clients. So, the sooner we get detailed information, the better. I might be leaving the office to check on the warehouse, but I'll tell my assistant to double check the status of the fax when she receives it. You may call Ms. Elaine Thompson at extension 5362 after you send the whole fax and confirm with her. Thank you.

80. What is the problem with the fax message?
(A) It is blurring.
(B) It is incomplete.
(C) It has been damaged.
(D) It's been sent to a wrong place.

81. What has the speaker requested?
(A) Give him a call
(B) Fix the fax machine
(C) Confirm the appointment time
(D) Send the information again

82. What is Peter asked to do?
(A) Contact Ms. Thompson for help
(B) Deliver the item soon
(C) Check the order form again
(D) Place the coversheet on top of the document

Questions 83 through 85 refer to the following announcement.

Everyone, please direct your attention to this side. The beautiful flowers you see here are tulips. Tulips are perennial flowers that people can enjoy for many years once you plant the bulbs in the cold ground. Unlike what most people think, tulips are the most popular garden flowers rather than roses. As you can see, there is a wide variety of colors and patterns in this class. That is why they are loved by so many people around the world. If you are interested in knowing which could be your favorite, don't worry about it. I'm going to walk you through all the details of these fascinating flowers with you. After that, we will move on to the next room where we look at exotic flowers from tropical regions of the world. But, first, let's get acquainted with these mosaic colored tulips on your right.

83. Who probably is making this announcement?
(A) A local farmer
(B) A museum administrator
(C) A tour leader
(D) A store manager

84. What can be said about tulips?
(A) They are annual plants.
(B) They are from tropical regions.
(C) They have strange names.
(D) They are the most popular flowers.

85. What does the speaker mean when she says, "I'm going to walk you through"?
(A) The tour will begin soon.
(B) They'll move to another location.
(C) She'll distribute some materials.
(D) She'll give more information about the flowers.

Questions 86 through 88 refer to the following advertisement.

Thank you for your interest in buying your first house or apartment through Riverview Property. We specialize in buying, selling, and maintaining top quality properties near the famous Ontario lakes. Our company has an excellent reputation because our staff members are knowledgeable and experienced real estate agents. They have served hundreds of people to find their ideal houses. So, how can we do this? First this morning, I'll show you a short video explaining the steps of buying your house through Riverview Property. After this, you'll have the basic ideas of how you can proceed with this major decision in your life. Then, I'll hand out a questionnaire to determine your preferences, so that we can focus on individual customer's needs and interests.

86. Who most likely are the listeners?
(A) Potential customers
(B) New employees
(C) Maintenance staff
(D) Job applicants

87. According to the speaker, what contributes to the company's good reputation?
(A) Affordable prices
(B) Scenic neighborhood
(C) Convenient location
(D) Capable staff

88. What will the speaker give the listeners after the video?
(A) Individual presentations
(B) A questionnaire
(C) Viewing of the property
(D) Sample products

Questions 89 through 91 refer to the following news report.

Now, let's check the local news here. The city council of Maple Creek has approved the plan to build a new public swimming pool near the city park. Plans for the swimming pool will include indoor and outdoor swimming pools connected together. It will also have a separate pool for children under the age of 12 so that they can use the facility safely. A small picnic area and family site will be added to the poolside. Sitting mayor, Elizabeth Greenfield spoke about the new swimming pool at a press conference yesterday. She expressed enthusiasm, saying that the new recreation area will provide the much needed place for area residents to exercise and have fun together. Construction will begin in January and will take approximately 3~4 months to finish. We expect to see the opening ceremony in May just in time for summer.

89. What is the report mainly about?
(A) A city park
(B) A new city hall
(C) Exercising equipment
(D) A public swimming pool

90. Who is Elizabeth Greenfield?
(A) A news reporter
(B) A building architect
(C) A city official
(D) An event coordinator

91. 新 What does the man imply when he says, "She expressed enthusiasm"?
(A) She was eager to go to the park.
(B) She is excited about the new project.
(C) She wants to have a bigger family.
(D) She is happy to be reelected as a mayor.

新 Questions 92 through 94 refer to the following announcement and receipt.

Thank you for coming to Cinemark Theater. At our Orlando Cinemark Theater, we do our best to ensure your pleasant viewing of the film. Please refrain from talking loud, using mobile phones, and making unnecessary noise for other audience members. Also, you may not bring in outside food or drinks. When you go out after the show, please put all your trash in the trash bins located next to the exit doors. We would like to remind you that you can now buy tickets through our convenient Cinemark online system. If you reserve your tickets online, we'll give out special coupons for complimentary snacks for you and your family to enjoy. Just show your receipt to an agent at the ticket booth to exchange for your special coupons. Thank you and enjoy the movie.

92. What is the speaker doing?
(A) Introducing an actress of a movie
(B) Explaining precautions before viewing
(C) Selling tickets for an event
(D) Cleaning up the area for the audience

93. What are the listeners asked to do?
(A) Use a mobile phone
(B) Take some notes
(C) Put the receipt in the bag
(D) Discard the trash in the can

94. 新 Look at the graphic. What special gift will be available to a customer with this receipt?
(A) Price discount
(B) Popcorns
(C) Free programs
(D) Autographs by celebrities

新 Questions 95 through 97 refer to the following announcement and list.

Good morning employees. I want to remind everyone that our factory is scheduled for a safety inspection this Friday. The inspectors will arrive at the plant floor at 10 in the morning and they will start by looking through the maintenance records, so be sure to submit any updated paperwork to the supervisor today. It is important to have current records for machinery maintenance and repair. After that, the inspectors will move on to the production floor to see that line workers are following standard procedures. They'll send us the inspection report and we'll set up a meeting for next week so we can talk about the results. I will be posting the check list for you to focus on before the actual inspection occurs. If any of you find a problem you cannot handle on your own, such as the one with concerning new employees, you should let your managers know about it as soon as possible. Let us do our best to get the best results.

95. What will the inspectors do first?
(A) Meet with the supervisors
(B) File a complaint to the authority
(C) Check the updated records
(D) Set up a follow-up meeting

96. Why will the listeners meet next week?
(A) To meet with inspectors
(B) To discuss some results
(C) To learn about the procedures
(D) To train new employees

97. 新 Look at the graphic. Which area should the managers be notified about?
(A) Record keeping procedures
(B) Regular machine maintenance
(C) Safety training for new employees
(D) Aisle cleaning and maintenance

Questions 98 through 100 refer to the following telephone message and map.

Hello. Mr. Peters, this is Howard Rays from Fire and Hazard Prevention Bureau. I've been inspecting fire exits of the whole baseball stadium for the last two days. Most of the exit doors and fire extinguishers are working fine. But, I'm afraid some of the signs for emergency exits are broken in the hallway near the entrances to K, L, X section of the stadium right behind the score board. This could be potentially dangerous when a number of spectators try to find the exit paths in the event of an emergency. I will send you an e-mail with the exact locations of the broken signs this afternoon. Give me a call if you have any questions. Thank you.

98. What has the speaker finished inspecting?
(A) Street lamps
(B) First aid kits
(C) Electricity lines
(D) Building's exits

99. 新 Look at the graphic. Where does the man suggest signs to be checked?
(A) Area 1
(B) Area 2
(C) Area 3
(D) Area 4

100. What will the speaker send in his e-mail?
(A) An estimate for the repair job
(B) Suggestions for better conditions
(C) A manual for emergency evacuation
(D) Locations of problematic areas

2회

1.	(B)	2.	(D)	3.	(D)	4.	(C)	5.	(B)
6.	(A)	7.	(B)	8.	(B)	9.	(A)	10.	(C)
11.	(A)	12.	(B)	13.	(A)	14.	(C)	15.	(C)
16.	(B)	17.	(C)	18.	(B)	19.	(B)	20.	(A)
21.	(C)	22.	(B)	23.	(C)	24.	(A)	25.	(A)
26.	(A)	27.	(B)	28.	(A)	29.	(B)	30.	(A)
31.	(B)	32.	(C)	33.	(B)	34.	(C)	35.	(B)
36.	(D)	37.	(C)	38.	(D)	39.	(A)	40.	(C)
41.	(B)	42.	(A)	43.	(D)	44.	(A)	45.	(D)
46.	(C)	47.	(C)	48.	(D)	49.	(A)	50.	(A)
51.	(B)	52.	(D)	53.	(C)	54.	(D)	55.	(A)
56.	(B)	57.	(D)	58.	(C)	59.	(D)	60.	(B)
61.	(A)	62.	(D)	63.	(B)	64.	(B)	65.	(C)
66.	(B)	67.	(A)	68.	(D)	69.	(A)	70.	(B)
71.	(B)	72.	(C)	73.	(D)	74.	(D)	75.	(B)
76.	(C)	77.	(A)	78.	(D)	79.	(B)	80.	(B)
81.	(D)	82.	(C)	83.	(D)	84.	(C)	85.	(B)
86.	(D)	87.	(D)	88.	(B)	89.	(C)	90.	(D)
91.	(C)	92.	(D)	93.	(B)	94.	(D)	95.	(C)
96.	(A)	97.	(D)	98.	(A)	99.	(B)	100.	(A)

Part 1

1.
(A) The woman is cutting out some patterns.
(B) The woman is chopping some wood.
(C) The lumber is being loaded.
(D) The woman is putting on safety goggles.

2.
(A) The men are shaking hands.
(B) The men are exchanging business cards.
(C) Both men are wearing suits and ties.
(D) The men are standing across from each other.

3.
(A) Pedestrians are walking around the park.
(B) Cars are being parked near the building.
(C) Trees are being planted in a garden.
(D) The bench is unoccupied at the moment.

4.
(A) The frames are being hung on the wall.
(B) The men are talking to each other on the phone.
(C) Documents have been spread out on the desk.
(D) One man is pointing something on the board.

5.
(A) A woman is shopping for some food.
(B) Some clothes have been hung on racks.
(C) A sales clerk is reaching into a box.
(D) Some bags have been placed on the floor.

6.
(A) Some people are having their hair cut.
(B) Some people are trimming branches.
(C) Some people are sitting around the table.
(D) Some people are putting on aprons.

Part 2

7. Where will the guest speakers stay during the convention?
(A) The last day of the event.
(B) At a nearby hotel.
(C) I'll be leaving tomorrow.

8. How many handouts should we prepare for the meeting?
(A) Not until tomorrow.
(B) At least two dozen.
(C) I'll do it right away.

9. Did you go to the market yesterday?
(A) Yes, I bought some vegetables.
(B) The price has been marked down.
(C) Yes, I'm going there soon.

10. Why weren't you at the company picnic on Saturday?
(A) Actually, Sunday is better for me.
(B) It will take place in a park.
(C) Something came up.

11. What forms of identification should I need?
(A) A passport or a driver's license will do.
(B) I don't need anything, thank you.
(C) Please fill out this form first.

12. Which printer would be better for the home usage?
(A) The machine needs to be repaired.
(B) I would recommend the one in this corner.
(C) We can give you a 10 percent discount.

13. Haven't you taken this course before?
(A) Yes, but it was a long time ago.
(B) The classes will be held in the auditorium.
(C) No, one will be enough for me.

14. Who's sponsoring this charity event to benefit the city library?
(A) It will be held next Saturday.
(B) At the convention center downtown.
(C) The Benson Corporation is.

15. Why don't you get a loan from the bank?
(A) Seventy five dollars per day.
(B) I'll get it for you right away.
(C) You're right. I should do that.

16. Do you carry the latest model of this cassette player?
(A) It's too heavy to hold.
(B) Sorry, we don't.
(C) The appliance store.

17. What's the extension for the personnel department?
(A) Find the extension cord from the top drawer.
(B) It contains personal information.
(C) I believe it's 327.

18. It's a beautiful day today, isn't it?
(A) I arranged it myself.
(B) Yes, It truly is.
(C) Yes, we should be back soon.

19. Haven't you met Cindy Conrad before?
(A) I believe Cindy will arrive soon.
(B) Yes, at the company banquet last winter.
(C) No, it's too far away from here.

20. Should I get tickets for 10 o'clock, or 12 o'clock?
(A) Either one will be fine with me.
(B) Yes, let's get the express service.
(C) It will last at least two hours.

21. You ordered the new printer for the accounting team, didn't you?
(A) Yes, the copy machine is not broken.
(B) Sure, let me take a look at it.
(C) Yes, it should be here soon.

22. It's too cold in here.
(A) Let's open the window.
(B) Why don't you put your sweater on?
(C) No, I don't have his number.

23. Do you want me to give you a ride to the convention?
(A) Give me a call when you get home.
(B) Keep the change, please.
(C) Thank you. That would be great.

24. How do you like your new job so far?
(A) The work is quite interesting.
(B) I don't like him at all.
(C) You can send it by e-mail or fax.

25. Would you like to leave now, or stay a little longer?
(A) I'd rather go if it's okay with you.
(B) I'm not sure why.
(C) A little over to the right, please.

26. Can you tell me where the nearest gas station is?
(A) It's just one block up this road.
(B) I think the store is open today.
(C) No, it leaves every 30 minutes.

27. Why don't we hire some more staff for the holiday season?
(A) Sure, the new product demonstration.
(B) That would be a wise thing to do.
(C) The sale starts from Monday, the 25th.

28. When did you learn about Mr. Stalk's transfer?
(A) Just today.
(B) By transporting goods by ship.
(C) It should be finished soon.

29. Don't you want to join our company baseball team?
(A) It might rain tomorrow.
(B) Sorry, I'm too busy these days.
(C) I'd like to see a different one, please.

30. The director's flight will arrive at LaGuardia Airport at 7 tomorrow evening.
(A) I can pick him up if you want.
(B) Some of the directories list the wrong numbers.
(C) We should delay our flights then.

31. We have to discuss the budget figures before we present them to the board.
(A) OK, I can figure it out myself.
(B) Oh, is there something wrong with them?
(C) In the last year's budget report.

Part 3

Questions 32 through 34 refer to the following conversation.

W Hi, I'm in room 805. I checked in two days ago. This is already the third time I'm having problems with the shower. You need to do something about it.
M I'm sorry, ma'am. If you can give us more detailed information about your problem, we could fix it far more quickly.
W Well, the water is so weak and it suddenly turns into cold water in the middle of shower. I suggest you find out what the problem is.
M I feel so bad about your inconvenience. Why don't I move you to one of our suite rooms to make up for your trouble?

32. What is the woman's problem?
(A) She was overcharged.
(B) Her room is too small.
(C) Facility is not working properly.
(D) She checked in too late.

33. How long has the woman stayed in her room?
(A) One day
(B) Two days
(C) Three days
(D) Five days

34. What does the man offer?
(A) Move to another hotel
(B) Give her a refund
(C) Change the room
(D) Investigate the problem himself

Questions 35 through 37 refer to the following conversation.

M Hi, I'm looking for a guitar to learn with. Do you have one for beginners?
W Sure we do. Is there anything particular you're looking for?
M I was hoping to get the one that is reasonably priced.
W I understand. But the problem with guitars in the lower price range is that they can be hard to tune. A lot of beginners end up quitting because the notes don't sound right.
M Well, the guitar is actually for me, and I have a little of experience of playing other instruments, so I don't think that will be a problem.
W In that case, the guitars you should look at are on this wall.
M They look fine to me. Is there anything else I should know about before starting playing?
W Well, I suggest buying some music books, too. We have a large selection of beginner's books to get you started with your new guitar.

35. Who is the woman?
(A) A school teacher
(B) A sales clerk
(C) A librarian
(D) A songwriter

36. What problem does the woman mention?
(A) All classes have been filled up.
(B) A musical instrument cannot be returned.
(C) Only advanced level books are available.
(D) Inexpensive guitars are difficult to tune.

37. What does the woman suggest the man do?
(A) Sign up for lessons
(B) Attend a guitar concert
(C) Purchase some books
(D) Visit the store again later

Questions 38 through 40 refer to the following conversation.

W Good afternoon. Do you need any help finding something? I'm the manager of the store.
M I'm fine. I just came here to look for a birthday present for my brother and I found a jacket that he would like.
W That's great. Before you pay for it, however, let me give you a great offer. If you sign up for our Frequent Shoppers Card, you'll get 15% off all your charges that you will pay today. Would you like an application form?
M Yes, please. That sounds like a good deal. I guess I have to get the membership first to get a discount.

38. Why is the man at the store?
(A) To see the manager
(B) To meet with his brother
(C) To apply for the card
(D) To purchase a present

39. What special offer is currently available?
(A) A discount card
(B) Extended warranty
(C) Personalized gift wrapping
(D) Free delivery

40. What will the man most likely do next?
(A) Speak to the manager
(B) Join the fitness club
(C) Sign up for the card
(D) Apply for the position

Questions 41 through 43 refer to the following conversation.

W   Adam, one of the overseas sales managers will be visiting us next week. He's never been to New York before and I'd like to show him around. Have you ever taken the city tour bus?

M   Well, if he has some time, it would be a good idea. Or, you could take him out on musical shows on Broadway. Everybody loves the show.

W   He should be leaving next Monday to meet with the managers in the west coast.

M   Why don't you call the ticket office now and find out what shows still have seats left? They sell out pretty quickly, you know.

41. According to the woman, what will happen next week?
(A) She will be transferred.
(B) A colleague will visit.
(C) A sale will begin.
(D) A new show will be introduced.

42. What does the woman ask about?
(A) City tours
(B) Broadway shows
(C) Flight schedules
(D) Contact information

43. What does the man suggest the woman do?
(A) Find out where the hotel is
(B) Call the manager right away
(C) Reserve the city tours
(D) Check the ticket availability

新 Questions 44 through 46 refer to the following conversation with three speakers.

W1   Excuse me. We just saw a sign by the store entrance about your interior design service.

M   My wife and I are interested in doing some remodeling in our kitchen. Can you help us with that?

W2   Certainly. We can help you choose everything from appliances and cabinets to paint colors.

M   That sounds great. How do we get started?

W2   Before we begin, I just want to let you know that we're offering a special promotion this month, 15% off any home-improvement purchase you make in our store.

W1   That is wonderful news. It is a good thing we decided to stop by at the store.

W2   First, I can set up an appointment for one of our designers to come out to your home. That way, the designer can see your kitchen and give you some ideas.

44. What is the couple planning to do?
(A) Remodel a kitchen
(B) Open a restaurant
(C) Build a new house
(D) Hire a real estate agent

45. What is available only until the end of the month?
(A) A free gift with a purchase
(B) An extended warranty
(C) Free installation service
(D) A fifteen percent discount

46. What does the store manager offer to do?
(A) Place an order
(B) Give a promotional catalog
(C) Set up a home visit
(D) Contact customer service

Questions 47 through 49 refer to the following conversation.

M   Since you've been feeling well lately, I think we can reduce the dose of your medication. Do you want us to send a new prescription to your pharmacist?

W   Thank you, Dr. Young. But, I recently changed my pharmacy, so could you send the prescription to them? Last month, I moved to a small apartment in Pine-view Complex and I found out it has a small pharmacy inside the building.

M   Sure, just don't forget to give the number of the new pharmacy to the receptionist when you leave.

47. What are the speakers discussing?
(A) Getting a surgery
(B) Moving into a new place
(C) Filling a prescription
(D) Renovating an apartment

48. What happened to the woman last month?
(A) She changed the doctor.
(B) Her condition got worse.
(C) She found a new roommate.
(D) She moved to a new apartment.

49. What information will the woman give the receptionist?
(A) A telephone number
(B) Discount coupons
(C) The name of an employee
(D) The location of the pharmacy

Questions 50 through 52 refer to the following conversation.

W   Is there any way I can get to Los Angeles as soon as possible? My flight from New York didn't arrive on time, so I missed my connecting flight.

M   Well, let me check. We don't have any direct flights, but if you're willing to stop over in San Francisco, there's a flight leaving in 20 minutes. That will be your best choice for now.

W   As long as it gets me to Los Angeles in one piece, I'll take it. Would there be any extra charge?

M   No, ma'am. You're fine. Here is your ticket and please hurry to gate number 20. The ground crew will be waiting for you.

50. What is the woman's problem?
(A) She missed her flight.
(B) She lost her ticket.
(C) She wants a direct flight.
(D) She couldn't find her luggage.

51. What is the woman's final destination?
(A) New York
(B) Los Angeles
(C) San Francisco
(D) Miami

52. What does the man mean when he says, "You're fine"?
新 (A) He likes the woman's appearance.
(B) She is going to miss the flight.
(C) He will take the woman to the gate.
(D) She doesn't have to pay for the charge.

Questions 53 through 55 refer to the following conversation.

M Thank you for coming, Ms. Wilson. As the last stage of our interview process, we're interviewing the top three candidates for the position of our online sales manager. Could you tell us more about your previous job experience?

W Well, I've been working at Sanwa Electronics for the last 5 years and I was awarded as the employee of the year in 2007 by making record-breaking sales.

M That is pretty impressive. Do you mind telling us why you would want to leave your current job?

W Well, I'm going back to school to get my master's degree in business administration, but I still want to work full-time. This position has the flexibility that will allow me to work and study at the same time.

53. What position is the woman interviewing for?
(A) An electrician
(B) A service representative
(C) A sales manager
(D) A school administrator

54. What is said about Sanwa Electronics?
(A) It makes quality electronic appliances.
(B) The products are sold in many countries.
(C) It was established in the year 2007.
(D) It gives out awards to employees.

55. Why does the woman say she wants to change jobs?
(A) She will be attending classes.
(B) She wants to make more money.
(C) She wants to work closer to home.
(D) She would like to have more responsibilities.

Questions 56 through 58 refer to the following conversation.

M Becky, how was your sales presentation? I was afraid you might be feeling nervous about meeting all the board members.

W It didn't go well at all. I spent so much time preparing the slides, but unfortunately, the projector just stopped in the middle of the presentation. It was a complete disaster.

M That's awful. How did you manage?

W Luckily, the copy center was close, so I ran over and made enough copies for everyone to look at. I did my best and tried to sound strong and confident.

M You did the best you could do. I'm sure everyone understood that it wasn't your fault.

W I'm feeling exhausted now that it's over.

56. What problem did the woman have?
(A) She was too nervous to talk aloud.
(B) Some equipment malfunctioned.
(C) Some of her slides weren't ready.
(D) Some of the board members didn't show up.

57. What did the woman do to solve the problem?
(A) She postponed the presentation.
(B) She asked for a new projector.
(C) She took a break in the middle.
(D) She made some extra copies.

58. Why does the woman say, "I'm feeling exhausted"?
(A) Because she didn't sleep well last night.
(B) Because there was a natural disaster.
(C) Because she worked hard for the presentation.
(D) Because the copy machine was broken.

Questions 59 through 61 refer to the following conversation.

M Rebecca, I wanted to remind you that we'll be having our office painted this weekend. The painters will move the furniture and paint the whole office, and make sure you clear everything off your desk before you leave today.

W Sure, Mr. Roy. But, we will have to start working on Monday and I'm concerned about ventilation. Do you think the air in the office would be clean enough to work on Monday?

M Don't worry, I specifically requested the workers use a special kind of paint that gives off less fume. They claim that the room will be cleared of all smells just after a few hours. We'll see on Monday I guess.

59. According to the speakers, what will happen this weekend?
(A) Workers will be relocated.
(B) New furniture will be delivered.
(C) A painting will be purchased.
(D) An office will be painted.

60. What is the woman asked to do?
(A) Choose a paint color
(B) Remove items from the desk
(C) Open the windows
(D) Contact the delivery person

61. What has the man requested that the workers do?
(A) Use a specific type of product
(B) Place all the furniture back in its places
(C) Finish the work in time
(D) Use some fans to dry off the paint

新 Questions 62 through 64 refer to the following conversation and ticket.

W I can't believe the train hasn't come in yet. I wonder what could possibly be wrong. Do you think there has been an accident?

M Well, the ticket agent said that the tracks are being worked on and it's causing delays up to 30 minutes. I'm afraid I might be late for work. I have to be at the company by 8:30 to get ready for a 9:00 opening.

W I've been taking the train for a long time, and this is the first time this has happened. The train is supposed to be so reliable, you know.

M You're right. This is strange. I take the train because it stops just a few streets from the bank where I work. In 5 years as a teller, I've never been late for work.

62. Why is the woman concerned?
(A) She is late for her appointment.
(B) She couldn't get a loan from a bank.
(C) The weather has not been nice.
(D) The train got delayed.

63. Look at the graphic. When is likely the new departure time
新 for the man's train?
(A) 7:30 a.m.
(B) 8:00 a.m.
(C) 8:30 a.m.
(D) 9:00 a.m.

64. Where does the man work?
(A) At a weather agency
(B) At a bank
(C) At a training center
(D) At a repair shop

169

新 Questions 65 through 67 refer to the following conversation and guide.

W Hi, Tony. This is Angela. I'm just checking in. How's everything going up here? Are you checking the lights of the Olsen Energy offices yet? They've been asking to fix them for days.

M Actually, it is taking longer than I thought it would. I changed the light bulbs of the rooms, but they won't turn on. So I decided to check the electric wires in the back room. I'm just going to get the keys from the maintenance room.

W Well, before you start working on the wiring, could you come downstairs? I need some help moving the big table in one of the conference rooms on the fourth floor. We need to repaint the wall.

M Sure, I'll be right up. This is a good time for me to take a break anyway.

65. Who most likely are the speakers?
(A) Interior designers
(B) Appliance store clerks
(C) Maintenance crew
(D) Office receptionists

66. Look at the graphic. Where is the man currently working?
新 (A) On the first floor
(B) On the second floor
(C) On the third floor
(D) On the fourth floor

67. What are the speakers probably going to do next?
(A) Move a table
(B) Install a new lighting fixture
(C) Fix the machine
(D) Make a conference call

新 Questions 68 through 70 refer to the following conversation and list.

M Hi, our employees are participating in a trade convention in two weeks and we'd like to order T-shirts with our company's logo on them. What options would you recommend?

W Well, we have a wide variety of colors and styles. After you choose the T-shirts you want, we can either print or sew the design on them.

M I would prefer sewing. It looks more professional. How long would it take to have 100 T-shirts sewed with our logo on them? We don't have that much time.

W First, we need to know how complicated your logo is to give you a detailed estimate. However, if you visit our website, we have posted the standard price list for different options. You can check the price there for the basic sewing for 100 people plus the price of the T-shirts you choose as well.

M OK, I'll do that right away.

W Meanwhile, if you want to expedite the process, please update your company's logo on your online order form and click for estimate request.

68. What information does the woman provide?
(A) Discount on larger orders
(B) Designing tips for company logos
(C) Sales strategy to treat customers
(D) Availability of different styles and options

69. What is the man concerned about?
(A) When the order will be complete
(B) Where the order will be delivered to
(C) Who he should contact for more information
(D) What kind of payment options he has

70. Look at the graphic. How much will the man's order cost?
新 (A) $300.00
(B) $500.00
(C) $700.00
(D) $1000.00

Part 4

Questions 71 through 73 refer to the following telephone message.

Hello, my name is Charles Xing. I'm calling because I'm interested in holiday packages to France that your company offers. My wife and I have been looking for an affordable trip and one of my colleagues recommended your tours. I heard you have a variety of tours for people with different interests. We want to spend more time in Paris and learn about different architecture and history of the area. I'll be on a business trip this weekend and I'd like to meet with you before I leave on Saturday. Could you call me at 555-2859 and let me know when you are available this week? Thank you.

71. Why is the speaker calling?
(A) To inquire about employment opportunity
(B) To find more about packaged tours
(C) To book a business trip
(D) To request a price discount

72. How did the speaker learn about the agency?
(A) From a newspaper
(B) From a website
(C) From an acquaintance
(D) From a family member

73. What will the speaker do on Saturday?
(A) Visiting his family
(B) Take a history class
(C) Return from work
(D) Leave for a trip

Questions 74 through 76 refer to the following advertisement.

Are you tired of wondering who to call whenever you have problems with your appliances? Now, one call does it all. You can get a service contract for all your appliances — refrigerator, television, washer and dryer and even your water heater — covered in one easy contract. With the monthly fee of as low as 10 dollars, Care-For-You offers high quality maintenance and repair service on all your appliances. Should you have any troubles, just call us day or night, 7 days a week. We will be there for you. And if you call us now, we will take 15% off from your first bill. But hurry, this offer is good for next ten days only. So, call today and wash away your worries.

74. What is offered in this advertisement?
(A) A sale on office equipment
(B) An extended warranty on mattress
(C) Reduced prices on a refrigerator
(D) A service contract for appliances

75. Why does the man say, "call us day or night, 7 days a week"?
新 (A) To sell new appliances to customers
(B) To emphasize the company's service
(C) To encourage to log in their website
(D) To explain the refund policy

76. How long is the special offer good for?
(A) For one day
(B) For seven days
(C) For ten days
(D) For fifteen days

Questions 77 through 79 refer to the following announcement.

Everyone, I have an announcement before you start your shift. We're going to upgrade some of the machinery in the ceramics factory. The new machines will do the same function of mixing and taking the air out of the soil mixture, but they'll do it more quickly. This upgrade will help us speed up our production of new line of ceramic dinnerware and tea wares almost 30 to 40 percent faster than before. Everyone must be trained on using the new equipment before they start using it. The training will be conducted department by department during your regular working hours so that the whole operation won't be affected by it. You'll get an e-mail today explaining your team's exact training date and time.

77. What type of merchandise does the factory produce?
(A) Ceramic ware
(B) Electronics
(C) Packaged food
(D) Office supplies

78. Why is the factory getting new equipment?
(A) To manufacture different products
(B) To replace broken machinery
(C) To cut down the production cost
(D) To increase production

79. According to the speaker, how will the employees receive training?
(A) The will take online courses.
(B) They will take turns.
(C) They will receive certificates afterwards.
(D) Someone from the main office will teach them.

Questions 80 through 82 refer to the following telephone message.

Hello, this is Vanessa Adams from the accounting department. I'm calling about the problem with your expense report you've submitted for your trip to New York last month. You have submitted the report and receipts on the payment you made on your one week trip. I'm afraid some of the restaurant receipts don't match the amounts you've entered in your expense report. Also, a couple of dates don't match the dates on your itinerary. I'm sure you would like to be reimbursed for these expenses as soon as possible, but I can't approve the payment until these discrepancies are corrected. I would like you to stop by at the accounting office today or tomorrow to discuss this matter. Thank you.

80. What department does the speaker work for?
(A) Human resources
(B) Accounting
(C) Banking
(D) Purchasing

81. 新 What does the woman imply when she says, "receipts don't match the amounts"?
(A) There has been a scheduling conflict.
(B) The restaurant complained about the process.
(C) The discount amount has not been applied.
(D) Information on receipts is inaccurate.

82. What does the speaker ask the listener to do?
(A) Make their payment
(B) Talk to his supervisor
(C) Visit her office soon
(D) Contact her through the phone

Questions 83 through 85 refer to the following talk.

Thank you all for coming to Lakeville Complex Residents' Association meeting. My name is Lisa Arnold and I'm the new building manager. It is a great pleasure to see all of you. As the manager, my first job should be preparing for the annual safety inspection next month. As you know, passing this inspection is very important in managing this size of property. So, please feel free to let me know any repairs that should be done before the inspection. I would set up a special bulletin board in front of the manager's office, so that you can put any comments or suggestions on the board concerning the problems with our complex. I'll check the board every day and make sure that the problems are fixed as soon as possible.

83. Who is the speaker?
(A) A real estate agent
(B) A local resident
(C) A service representative
(D) A building manager

84. What does the speaker say her first task will be?
(A) Communicating well with tenants
(B) Getting in touch with the city council
(C) Passing the annual inspection
(D) Installing new safety equipment

85. What are the listeners asked to do?
(A) Introduce themselves to each other
(B) Give their feedbacks to her
(C) Call her if there is an emergency
(D) Make a decision on a certain issue

Questions 86 through 88 refer to the following announcement.

As you know, each year our company supports a local improvement project. And this year, we have decided to support a local charity called Green Peace. Green Peace is a nonprofit organization focusing on planting more trees and educating people on the importance of greener planet. We've decided to purchase about 100 trees and each one of you will plant them together with local residents. Now, I will be distributing copies of an article we got from Green Peace. This article explains in terms of what we should do to protect our environment, especially by saving trees first. You should read it before the volunteering project scheduled for next Friday.

86. What are the listeners asked to do?
(A) Join a nonprofit organization
(B) Take care of your garden better
(C) Donate some money
(D) Plant trees for a cause

87. Who provided the article that the speaker is distributing?
(A) A company officer
(B) A newspaper reporter
(C) A government official
(D) A charity organization

88. What type of information about trees does the article contain?
(A) Where they should send the donation
(B) How to protect trees for better environment
(C) How to volunteer for the on-going projects
(D) Which environmental agency to contact

Questions 89 through 91 refer to the following news report.

This is WXG, your evening business report. Today, Dudley Motor Corporation's Chairman Michael Santos announced that they will increase the production of the company's most popular model, the DW-3000. The sales of this production have steadily increased in almost all global markets since its introduction in last March. Mr. Santos thinks that the compact size and affordable price are the key factors in this model's success. As of next month, DW-3000 will be the only car model produced at the company's factory in Spring Valley, Australia. Mr. Santos will expect this will ease the strain on meeting the increased global supplies.

89. Who is Michael Santos?
(A) A marketing expert
(B) A design staff
(C) A corporate executive
(D) A newspaper reporter

90. What did Michal Santos announce?
(A) Introduction of a new line of products
(B) The construction of a new factory
(C) A change in product features
(D) Increased production of a popular product

91. What does the man imply when he mentions, "DW-3000 will be the only car model produced in Australia"?
(A) Additional safety precautions will be taken in the factory.
(B) They're going to expand to Australian auto market.
(C) They will focus on meeting the demand of one product model.
(D) They're going to close down some manufacturing facilities.

Questions 92 through 94 refer to the following advertisement.

If you are looking for a job or considering a career change, come to Ocean City's 10th Annual Job Fair. The fair will take place in the city's convention center from August 10 through August 12. Over 100 small and medium sized companies will look for their new and experienced employees in the fair. Again, this year, Radio WXN is one of the sponsors of the fair and you can listen to WXN for live updates every hour throughout the convention period. Admission is free but the participants should register beforehand to receive official name cards and other information. Candidates must bring their resumes and up-to-date employment history and current contact information. Please visit the job fair website at www.oceanjobfair.govt. for the complete list of companies and organizations participating in the event.

92. What is the purpose of the event?
(A) To solicit more sponsors
(B) To inform schedule changes
(C) To advertisement a particular company
(D) To publicize job openings

93. Who is one of the sponsors of the event?
(A) A employment agency
(B) A radio station
(C) A web-designing firm
(D) A non-profit organization

94. According to the speaker, what can be found on the website?
(A) Steps to register in a fair
(B) Recommendations from the hiring manger
(C) History of the city's events being held
(D) A list of participating organizations

新 Questions 95 through 97 refer to the following news report and map.

Good morning and thank you for listening to MZ morning traffic with Julie Park. The last night's storm did quite some damage on the road and the morning commute is not easy today. Lincoln Tunnel is backed up almost 10 miles because broken trees are blocking the entrance of one of the lanes to downtown. The police are already at the scene directing the clean-up but it will take at least another hour, so, if you're on Highway 95, I would recommend the Route 65 instead of the tunnel. Most of the major roads are moving smoothly but please take caution of the slippery road conditions because of the storm. Stay tuned. I'll be right back with more detailed road conditions after the short message from our sponsors.

95. What is the problem with the tunnel?
(A) The repair work is being conducted.
(B) There has been an accident.
(C) The entrance has been blocked.
(D) The road is being repaved.

96. 新 Look at the graphic. Which exit are the motorists advised to take?
(A) Exit 6
(B) Exit 7
(C) Exit 8
(D) Stay on Highway 95

97. What will the listeners most likely hear next?
(A) News on road conditions
(B) Weather updates
(C) An interview with the police
(D) An advertisement

新 Questions 98 through 100 refer to the following announcement and coupon.

Before we start, I'd like to remind everyone about our new discount coupon promotions. As you know, discount coupons for our product have been printed in local newspapers. But, starting next month, customers will also receive coupons electronically by e-mail. We'd like the cashiers to mention this to customers as they're checking out of the store. Ask them if they would be interested in receiving discount coupons through e-mail. These special e-coupons offer premium discounts and special deals to be used on different weekdays. For example, on Mondays and Tuesdays all vegetable are 50% off after 4 o'clock and on Wednesdays and Thursdays, all dairy products are 50% off and so on. This change will attract more customers to the store on weekdays as well as the weekends. We can also obtain more information about our customers to serve them better in the future.

98. What is the announcement about?
(A) A new store promotion
(B) A going-out-of-business sale
(C) A change in payment method
(D) Recent customer complaints

99. Who most likely are the listeners?
(A) Marketing researchers
(B) Store employees
(C) Supermarket customers
(D) Website designers

100. Look at the graphic. What day is the coupon valid on?
(A) Monday
(B) Wednesday
(C) Weekends
(D) Any of the weekdays

3회

1. (D)	2. (B)	3. (C)	4. (B)	5. (C)
6. (A)	7. (B)	8. (A)	9. (C)	10. (A)
11. (B)	12. (B)	13. (A)	14. (A)	15. (C)
16. (A)	17. (C)	18. (A)	19. (B)	20. (A)
21. (C)	22. (C)	23. (A)	24. (A)	25. (A)
26. (A)	27. (A)	28. (A)	29. (A)	30. (C)
31. (C)	32. (D)	33. (D)	34. (C)	35. (A)
36. (C)	37. (D)	38. (A)	39. (C)	40. (D)
41. (A)	42. (D)	43. (C)	44. (A)	45. (D)
46. (D)	47. (B)	48. (B)	49. (D)	50. (C)
51. (B)	52. (A)	53. (D)	54. (D)	55. (B)
56. (C)	57. (A)	58. (D)	59. (D)	60. (B)
61. (D)	62. (D)	63. (C)	64. (B)	65. (A)
66. (C)	67. (C)	68. (C)	69. (C)	70. (B)
71. (B)	72. (D)	73. (C)	74. (B)	75. (A)
76. (C)	77. (A)	78. (B)	79. (C)	80. (C)
81. (C)	82. (B)	83. (C)	84. (D)	85. (A)
86. (C)	87. (C)	88. (D)	89. (C)	90. (B)
91. (D)	92. (A)	93. (C)	94. (D)	95. (C)
96. (A)	97. (D)	98. (D)	99. (B)	100. (C)

Part 1

1.
(A) The woman is putting on some gloves.
(B) The lens of an equipment are being cleaned.
(C) The scientific instrument has been placed in a case.
(D) The woman is inspecting something on a table.

2.
(A) Books are being arranged on the shelf.
(B) They are working at the table.
(C) The woman is writing on the board.
(D) They're studying English at the library.

3.
(A) The car is being parked in front of the house.
(B) Trees are being planted near the road.
(C) The vehicles are standing by the road.
(D) Pedestrians are crossing the road together.

4.
(A) People are boarding an aircraft.
(B) Some people are gathered near the bus.
(C) The bus has stopped at a traffic sign.
(D) Some people are waiting to check in to a hotel.

5.
(A) Farmers are cutting grass in a pasture.
(B) Animals are being fed at a barn.
(C) A fence runs along the edge of the road.
(D) Some workers are fixing the fence in a garden.

6.
(A) Some items have been arranged on the shelf.
(B) The man is standing on a ladder against the wall.
(C) Some bottles are being labeled by the woman.
(D) They are stacking some boxes in a warehouse.

Part 2

7. Where did Mr. Yang go?
(A) About a week ago.
(B) To the warehouse.
(C) With his family.

8. Why did you miss your flight?
(A) I woke up late this morning.
(B) There were too many applicants.
(C) I miss them very much.

9. Did you bring your business cards?
(A) I don't think it will.
(B) He brought something new.
(C) Yes, they're in my briefcase.

10. You'll be coming to London for the International publishers' conference, won't you?
(A) I hope so.
(B) No, I don't want one.
(C) Yes, international flight.

11. Which restaurant should we invite the guests at?
(A) It starts at seven o'clock tonight.
(B) How about the one Tom recommended?
(C) Around 200 people including guest speakers.

12. Would you like to try the new Indian restaurant?
(A) I'll take the check, please.
(B) Sure, I heard its food is excellent.
(C) We should visit the country one more time.

13. When will the marketing proposal be completed?
(A) By the end of Wednesday.
(B) I think Ms. Wilson is the one.
(C) I can't complain.

14. I heard it's going to rain this afternoon.
(A) Do you have an umbrella with you?
(B) I'd rather take the train instead.
(C) Sometime tomorrow will be better for me.

15. Should we send the invitation card today or next week?
(A) Let's invite everyone to the party.
(B) They're predicting rain for tomorrow.
(C) Next Monday might be better.

16. The mail has just arrived, right?
(A) Actually, it came early this morning.
(B) We should put them in the outgoing box.
(C) Yes, it's just the right size.

17. How many applications did we receive today?
(A) Three years of experience in sales.
(B) We should mail it by three o'clock.
(C) I haven't counted them yet.

18. Isn't Mr. Elliot attending the seminar in Singapore?
(A) That's what I heard.
(B) Sorry, I'm too busy today.
(C) Yes, at the international terminal.

19. We need to ask for more time to finish this article.
(A) No, I don't need anything, thank you.
(B) Are there any problems?
(C) The performance was finished earlier.

20. What should we call our new line of clothes?
(A) Something fun and easy to remember.
(B) I don't go shopping that often.
(C) Let's find out the dress code of the party.

21. Who was the man standing next to you?
(A) It's right next to the door.
(B) I'll be waiting for you here when you come back.
(C) Someone I met at the new employees' orientation.

22. Haven't you read over our benefits policy?
(A) It was so interesting that I want to watch it again.
(B) Yes, I have a pen right here.
(C) No. I haven't had time yet.

23. What do you think will happen when the merger deal is signed?
(A) We might have to find a new job.
(B) The sign needs to be replaced right away.
(C) Sure, we need to be there as soon as possible.

TEST 03

173

24. Has the dishwasher been fixed yet?
(A) No, but someone is coming this afternoon.
(B) Yes, the interest rate has been fixed.
(C) They'll fax everything today.

25. How may I help you?
(A) I'm looking for some winter coats.
(B) Sure, I'd love to assist you in any ways.
(C) By express or regular delivery.

26. Why haven't the reimbursement of the travel expenses been processed yet?
(A) Some receipts were missing.
(B) The shipping procedure has to be changed.
(C) There were some delays at the airport.

27. When can we expect to receive shipment of auto parts?
(A) By later this week.
(B) The expected costs went up.
(C) Put them in the delivery area.

28. I need twenty copies of this report by tomorrow.
(A) Do you want them to be color-copied?
(B) I don't need anything, thank you.
(C) Tomorrow is better for me.

29. Do you have some time to review the agenda or are you busy?
(A) I can look at it now.
(B) I'm not late for the meeting.
(C) It should be ready in no time.

30. Do we have to pack the boxes by tomorrow?
(A) Yes, let's use different materials.
(B) They usually use the air-mail.
(C) We still have a few more days.

31. Why don't we work on the competitor analysis this afternoon?
(A) No, the competition is getting fierce.
(B) I don't usually work on the weekend.
(C) Actually, tomorrow is better for me.

Part 3

新 Questions 32 through 34 refer to the following conversation with three speakers.

M Cindy, can you help the building design for CamTech today? It's supposed to be finished by the end of the week and there's still a lot to do.

W1 I'd be happy to help, but I can't do it today. I have a meeting with a potential client this afternoon.

M Well, that could easily be handled by any employee. CamTech is one of the biggest accounts and you've worked with them before.

W1 Okay, then. I'll check if someone can cover this meeting for me. Maria, can you come over here?

W2 Yes, what is it Ms. Novak? Mr. Yang?

M Cindy has an important project to deal with this afternoon and we're wondering if you could meet one of the new clients this afternoon.

W1 All you have to do is just to interview them about what they want and how much they're willing to spend.

W2 Okay, just give me any materials related to them before the meeting.

M Well, if everything is all set, I'll let Greg, the project manager, know about it right away. He is going to be so relieved.

32. What does the man ask Cindy to do?
(A) Reschedule a client meeting
(B) Arrange the company banquet
(C) Train her assistants
(D) Work on a building design

33. Why does the man want Cindy to do the work?
(A) Because she can save more money than other employees.
(B) Because the deadline is approaching quickly.
(C) Because she had won the award for the excellent design.
(D) Because she has worked for the client before.

34. What will the man likely do next?
(A) Sign the contract
(B) Hire Maria instead of Cindy
(C) Notify another employee about the change
(D) Meet with a new client

Questions 35 through 37 refer to the following conversation.

W Hi, I just received 24 conference chairs I ordered from your company's website, but two of the chair legs are broken. I think there must have been a problem with the delivery.

M Oh, I'm really sorry about that. Would you like me to send you the replacements?

W No, that's not necessary. Now that I've seen them, I think 22 chairs will be enough for our needs. So, I think I want a refund for the two chairs.

M We can do that. I'll refund your money to your account. Meanwhile, I email you a prepaid shipping label so you can send the broken chairs back to us.

35. What is the woman calling about?
(A) A damaged product
(B) A late shipment
(C) Travel arrangements
(D) Computer problems

36. What does the woman want the man to do?
(A) Confirm a reservation
(B) Send some replacement parts
(C) Refund a purchase
(D) Return a phone call

37. According to the man, what will the woman receive by e-mail?
(A) A cost estimate
(B) A product brochure
(C) A revised invoice
(D) A shipping label

Questions 38 through 40 refer to the following conversation.

W Charlie, can you take me home after work today? My car is still in the shop.

M Sorry, I have to leave work early today. I have to go to the airport to pick up Mr. Yamamoto from the Tokyo office. His plane should arrive around three.

W Oh, well. I guess I can take the bus, then. The bus station is not that far from here, right?

M No, it's only a couple of blocks down Maple Street. Do you want me to give you more detailed directions?

38. What does the woman ask for?
(A) A ride to a place
(B) Help with a report
(C) Directions to the office
(D) Mr. Yamamoto's itinerary

39. Where does the man need to go in the afternoon?
(A) To the woman's house
(B) To Tokyo branch
(C) To the airport
(D) To the bus station

40. What does the man offer to do?
(A) Meet her at the airport
(B) Work overtime tonight
(C) Change the schedule
(D) Give some information

Questions 41 through 43 refer to the following conversation.

W Hey, Matt. You like Ben Taylor, right? Have you seen the new movie where he plays a role of a secret agent? The review in the newspaper said it is really exciting and moving. It broke the record of box-office sales.
M No. My friends and I tried to buy tickets last Saturday but they were sold out. So, I was disappointed.
W Well, the article said more theaters will be showing the movie from next week. Why don't you check its official website for more locations?

41. How did the woman learn about the movie?
(A) By reading a review
(B) By talking to a friend
(C) By listening to the radio
(D) By checking the internet

42. What does the man mean when he says, "So, I was 新 disappointed"?
(A) She didn't like the movie.
(B) The actors didn't do a good job.
(C) The theater was too crowded.
(D) Tickets were unavailable.

43. What does the woman suggest the man do?
(A) Wait until the DVD version comes out
(B) Arrive early to avoid the crowd
(C) Find another place to watch the movie
(D) Change his seat to another one

Questions 44 through 46 refer to the following conversation.

M Have you reviewed the resume of Steven Johnson? His experiences are pretty impressive.
W I have noticed he won pretty big contracts from a big international trader last year, too. Do you think he would be a good fit for our company?
M Well, we have to see him in person before making any decision. Should I arrange a formal interview with him?
W Actually, I'll be out of town next week, so why don't we set up a schedule in the following week?

44. What are the speakers discussing?
(A) A job candidate
(B) A newly won contract
(C) Company expansion
(D) A travel arrangement

45. What has Steven Johnson done before?
(A) He had applied for this company before.
(B) He's been exercising a lot.
(C) He made a reservation at a restaurant.
(D) He won a big contract with a foreign company.

46. When will the speakers meet Mr. Johnson?
(A) Today
(B) Tomorrow
(C) Next week
(D) In two weeks

Questions 47 through 49 refer to the following conversation.

W Edward, I was wondering if you can help me. I've been trying to access my e-mail account and I keep getting an error message that I'm using the incorrect password.
M Well, I don't think I can help you with that. Why don't you call Technical Support? They should be able to reset your password.
W I've been trying to talk with them already. They must have left for the day.
M There might be a special number we could use after hours for tech problems. Let me look it up in our online directory.

47. What is the woman's problem?
(A) She forgot her password.
(B) She cannot use the e-mail system.
(C) She forgot to meet an accountant.
(D) She lost her Identification card.

48. Who has the woman been trying to contact?
(A) A computer manufacturer
(B) A technical support staff
(C) A customer service representative
(D) A building security

49. What does the man offer to do?
(A) Visit the security office
(B) Change the password
(C) Give her a direction to an office
(D) Find a telephone number

Questions 50 through 52 refer to the following conversation.

M Hello, Ms. Diaz. I'm returning your call about the wedding invitations you ordered. You said that the event no longer being held at Hilton Plaza. Is that correct?
W Yes, We've decided to use a different hotel which is more conveniently located for our guests.
M We don't usually allow last-minute change without any penalty, but you're in luck. We haven't started printing them yet.
W That's good news. The new place is the Ball Room of the Mountain Lodge Hotel.
M Well, it's not accurate to receive the information through the phone. Could you please log onto our online account and update your order?
W I'll do that. The only problem is I won't have access to a computer by the end of the day today.
M That's okay. We won't start working on yours until tomorrow morning. Just make sure you get everything spelled right on your order.

50. Where most likely does the man work?
(A) At a post office
(B) At an Internet company
(C) At a print shop
(D) At a travel agency

51. What has changed about the event?
(A) Its starting time
(B) Its location
(C) The number of guests
(D) The room size

52. What does the man ask the woman to do?
(A) Revise her order online
(B) Confirm her telephone number
(C) Call another vendor
(D) Rent an equipment for the event

Questions 53 through 55 refer to the following conversation.

W I just read an annual report for Mandy's division and their sales have almost doubled since she became the manager of her sales team.

M I agree. I think she is really talented in terms of motivating her staff. I heard she encourages everyone to share their sales strategies at a weekly meeting.

W Yes, I think that helps new sales representatives to improve their skills a lot. Maybe we should <u>ask other managers to follow Mandy's example.</u>

53. What does the woman say she just read?
(A) A training manual
(B) A book review
(C) A company newsletter
(D) An annual report

54. According to the man, what happens at the weekly meetings?
(A) Individual projections are given.
(B) A manager reviews sales figures.
(C) Products are demonstrated.
(D) Employees discuss the strategies.

55. 新 What does the woman imply when she says, "ask other managers to follow Mandy's example"?
(A) Mandy broke the record of highest sales.
(B) Mandy did a great job of leading her team.
(C) Other managers don't like Mandy very much.
(D) Mandy was just promoted to a manager.

Questions 56 through 58 refer to the following conversation.

W Hello, This is Angela from Summerville Health Clinic. Your sales person dropped some information on one of your new products, the Easy Thermo?

M Yes, we started supplying these to many pediatric hospitals and they all loved it. Easy Thermo looks friendly and is easy to operate. So, children are less scared of medical procedures, not to mention its accuracy.

W Well, our staff would like to see the product and try them on ourselves. Could you send us samples?

M Sorry, ma'am. We don't give out sample equipment, but I would be glad to visit and show you the product in person. I think the short demonstration will answer any questions you might have.

56. Why is the woman calling?
(A) To place an order
(B) To return a product
(C) To inquire about a product
(D) To confirm an appointment

57. Who most likely is the man?
(A) A sales representative
(B) A medical personnel
(C) A physician
(D) A machine operator

58. What does the man offer to do?
(A) Send some samples through mail
(B) Give some discounts on a new product
(C) Process an urgent order
(D) Give a product demonstration

Questions 59 through 61 refer to the following conversation.

M Hi, Stella. I'm having trouble getting the sales figures for the international market. I need those numbers for my presentation tomorrow.

W Those records should be in the company online database. Don't you have the password to use it?

M I do, but for some reasons, it's not working this morning. I already talked with someone in the technical support. But, it's not fixed yet and I'm in a hurry.

W Well, I should have that data in my computer. I can email them to you. Let me know if you haven't received them in a few minutes.

59. What is the man having difficulty doing?
(A) Contacting the technical support
(B) Getting permission from a supervisor
(C) Winning a contract from a client
(D) Accessing some information

60. Who does the man say he has requested help from?
(A) A software programmer
(B) The technology department
(C) An overseas manager
(D) The accounting department

61. What does the woman say she will do?
(A) Revise some document
(B) Prepare a sales presentation
(C) Post a memo on the board
(D) Send an e-mail

Questions 62 through 64 refer to the following conversation.

W Hey, Kendrick. Have you heard the news that we finally purchased digital microscopes in our laboratory?

M Really? That is good news. I'm a little surprised though since those microscopes are rather expensive and I thought we already spent our budget for this year.

W I guess the administration has finally realized the importance of having high-quality equipment at a teaching hospital like ours.

M True. With these advanced and improved images, <u>it would be much easier</u> to train our medical students from this semester.

62. What are the speakers mainly discussing?
(A) Updating software
(B) Lack of staff
(C) Medical surgeries
(D) Laboratory equipment

63. What is the man surprised at?
(A) A deadline has been extended.
(B) More teachers were hired.
(C) A purchase has been approved.
(D) Tuition has been increased.

64. 新 What does the man mean when he says, "it would be much easier"?
(A) Students these days are much smarter than before.
(B) New equipment will be very helpful in teaching students.
(C) Medical advances in the industry have been amazing.
(D) Hospital staff has to be trained to provide better services.

新 Questions 65 through 67 refer to the following conversation with three speakers and list.

W	Hey, George, Hi Scott. We're thinking about selling some of the new natural tiles that have been introduced to the market. Do you think our customers will like the ceramic ones?
M1	Well, I heard they've been sold in other locations and customers actually favor them over other types of tiles.
M2	They are supposed to be environmentally friendly and good for your health, too.
M1	But aren't the ceramic ones are much more expensive than the regular tiles?
M2	True, but they are usually cheaper than the natural marble ones.
W	Some of our customers would like to have affordable construction materials. There is no point in bringing them in if our customers won't like them.
M1	I'm sure the manufacturer has a wide selection of new tiles. Why don't we take a look at its website?
W	Good idea. There should be some new ceramic tiles with a reasonable price range.

65. What is the store planning to do?
(A) Introduce a new product
(B) Manufacture new tiles
(C) Survey customers
(D) Lower the product prices

66. What is the woman concerned about?
(A) The packaging might be weak.
(B) The environmentalist might complain.
(C) A product will not sell well.
(D) Customers will call the authority.

67. 新 Look at the graphic. Which model will the speakers likely order?
(A) MT215
(B) MT320
(C) CA101
(D) CA201

新 Questions 68 through 70 refer to the following conversation and invitation.

W	Hi, the radio announcer at your station just mentioned the details of a play that is about to open next week. I'm calling because he gave the wrong information about it.
M	Oh, thanks for calling. We used the information from an official invitation that the production sent us. Something must have changed after that.
W	Well, there was a last-minute change and we had to move the performance to Marcus Theater. The time is still at seven though.
M	I'll make sure that the announcer will give an update right away with the information about the new venue. Thanks and good luck on the opening night.

68. Why is the woman calling?
(A) To ask about the admission fee
(B) To book a performance space
(C) To correct an error
(D) To ask for directions

69. 新 Look at the graphic. What information on the invitation is no longer accurate?
(A) The name of the play
(B) The starring actress
(C) The name of the theater
(D) The time of the performance

70. What does the man say will happen next?
(A) Play tickets will be given away.
(B) An announcement will be made.
(C) A traffic report will be given.
(D) An official apology will be made.

Part 4

Questions 71 through 73 refer to the following broadcast.

Good morning, this is Jeffrey Morgan in the weather room with your hourly weather update. We will have more unseasonably warm weather today. We can expect sunny skies with temperatures approaching almost 17 degrees Celsius in some parts. The national weather bureau said the high pressure system flowing from the Pacific Ocean is keeping us from winter rains and winds. Things are likely to change from next week, though. The high pressure system will begin to break down from Monday afternoon and the high temperature should drop down to below ten degrees, which is the average at this time of the year. It is 5 o'clock now, and we will have the next weather report in exactly one hour along with hourly traffic updates.

71. What does the speaker suggest about today's weather?
(A) It will rain all day.
(B) It will be unusually warm.
(C) It will change later today.
(D) It will be similar to last year's.

72. What will likely happen next week?
(A) The weather report will be at a different time.
(B) The summer will begin sooner.
(C) There will be sunnier days.
(D) The temperature will decrease.

73. When will the next weather report take place?
(A) In twenty minutes
(B) In half an hour
(C) In an hour
(D) In a day

Questions 74 through 76 refer to the following advertisement.

The Oasis Art Supplies is pleased to announce the opening of its newest store in Grover City. Like all of our other stores, we guarantee that our new location will sell quality art materials at the lowest prices. To celebrate the grand opening, we are hosting a special contest this Saturday. You can submit any kind of art you made and visitors to the store will vote on their three favorites. The lucky winners will receive 500 dollars of art supplies from our store. For complete schedules for the contest and other activities that we have planned for the day, please visit our website at www.artoasis.com. We hope to see you all there.

74. What type of business is being advertised?
(A) Museum
(B) Art supplies
(C) Online education
(D) Office equipment

75. What will the contest winners receive?
(A) Free products
(B) Back-state passes
(C) Tickets to a concert
(D) Cash prizes

76. According to the advertisement, what is found on the website?
(A) Procedure for registration
(B) Directions to different locations
(C) Schedules for an event
(D) Lists of products on sale

Questions 77 through 79 refer to the following introduction.

I know you guys have a lot of work to do, so let's get started. First, I'm happy to announce that two new graphic designers will be joining our department and if any of you can help with their training next week, I'd really appreciate it. Please let me know after the meeting if you're available for them next week. Next, I'd like to mention that everything is right on schedule for next month's release of new stationery. We've worked for the last 6 months to create new logos and characters for this line, and the advertising team has been working hard to make the next month's launching successful. So, I'd like to introduce David from the advertising department to show how it's going to be done. David, I'll let you take it from here.

77. What department does the speaker work for?
(A) Graphic designing team
(B) Sales team
(C) Advertisement department
(D) Human resources division

78. What does the speaker need help with?
(A) Promoting new products
(B) Training new employees
(C) Scheduling works for the next 6 months
(D) Meeting the supervisor for consultation

79. What is scheduled to happen next month?
(A) They will move to a new location.
(B) The new employees will start working.
(C) A new product will be available.
(D) An advertising campaign will be changed.

Questions 80 through 82 refer to the following talk.

Thank you all for volunteering to be on the interview committee. My name is Ben Wiley, personnel manager for new recruits, and I'll be in charge of conducting this year's peer interview process. We have over 50 candidates competing for 3 positions we're offering this year. From tomorrow, you'll start the first round of interviews where you talk to the applicants and have lunch with them. After that, you'll be given a score sheet to mark their impression and communications skills. Sometime next week, personnel director will conduct second interviews. Your scores will play an important role when the president makes a final decision early next month. Now, let me hand out the envelopes that contain the résumés of your assigned interviewees and their profiles.

80. What is the purpose of the talk?
(A) To create jobs for new employees
(B) To determine the number of positions
(C) To explain the interview process
(D) To make a lunch appointment

81. Who will conduct the first round of interviews?
(A) A personnel manager
(B) A personnel director
(C) A committee of volunteers
(D) A company president

82. What will happen next?
(A) They will apply for the job.
(B) The will receive some information.
(C) They will meet the president.
(D) They will meet the new employees.

Questions 83 through 85 refer to the following announcement.

Hello everyone. Let me start off by making a short announcement. I'd like to remind you that we'll be doing some maintenance work on our electrical system this weekend. We've found a potential hazard in workplace from last week's regular system check-up and have decided to work on it. Electronic power throughout the building will be shut off at 8 p.m. on Friday and will be back on Sunday afternoon. The work should take about 48 hours, so everything should be done by the end of the day on Sunday. All systems will be up and running on Monday when you come back to work. To prevent any damage to your equipment, please turn off your computers and other electronic devices before you leave work on Friday afternoon. We're sorry to cause you any trouble, but the regular safety inspection and maintenance job are a necessary part of our company procedures for us to work safely and efficiently. Thank you for your cooperation.

83. What type of work is scheduled?
(A) Software upgrade
(B) Weekend getaway trips
(C) Electronic maintenance
(D) Telephone system installation

84. What are the employees asked to do?
(A) Contact the security office
(B) Upgrade your software
(C) Email the necessary information
(D) Shut down some equipment

85. What does the man imply when he says, "We're sorry to cause you trouble"?
新
(A) He's justifying the company procedure.
(B) He made a mistake when doing some electrical job.
(C) He's complimenting employees for their good work.
(D) He is angry because something bad had happened during the construction.

Questions 86 through 88 refer to the following talk.

Good morning everyone, before we begin the weekly meeting, I'd like to introduce our new senior vice president for overseas sales, Rachel Park. As you know, we have interviewed a number of qualified applicants and Rachel was our top choice. She has extensive experience in overseas sales. She used to work in Paris, Milan, Tokyo, and Seoul. At her last job, she was in charge of managing Asian branches at AD-Pro, our major competitor. We are thrilled that she has accepted our offer. Please welcome Ms. Park and I hope everyone stays after the meeting to say hello to Rachel and have some refreshments.

86. What is the main purpose of the talk?
(A) To announce a job opening
(B) To discuss the opening of an overseas branch
(C) To welcome a new employee
(D) To introduce a new company procedure

87. What is said about Rachel Park?
(A) She accepted an award from the company.
(B) She speaks several different languages.
(C) She used to work at a competitor.
(D) She plans to move to an Asian country.

88. What will happen after the meeting?
(A) New products will be released.
(B) Job description will be posted.
(C) They will take a break for a while.
(D) Food and beverages will be served.

Questions 89 through 91 refer to the following telephone message.

Hello, Mr. Mitchell, this is Amy Watson at General Laboratory in San Paolo. We have received your resume for the position of mechanical engineer and we are very impressed with it. Especially, our senior managers would meet with you to discuss your career at the General Laboratory. Are you available to visit our lab sometime next week? Ideally, if you could visit us before Thursday, you could meet most of our senior engineers since most of our engineers are really busy on Fridays. We're so excited to finally meet you in person. Please give me a call back at 11-55-575-2145 with your preferences and I'll take care of your flight and hotel arrangements.

89. What is the purpose of the call?
(A) To request an application
(B) To confirm a delivery
(C) To schedule an interview
(D) To place an order

90. What does the woman imply when she said, "to finally meet you in person"?
(A) He had applied for this company before.
(B) She hasn't seen him face to face.
(C) She wants to meet him and his family.
(D) She is happy that he accepted the position.

91. What does the speaker ask Mr. Mitchell to do?
(A) Reserve a hotel room
(B) Provide reference information
(C) Take personal belongings with him
(D) Return a telephone call

Questions 92 through 94 refer to the following telephone message and schedule.

Hello, this is Dennis Wales from Brooks Industries. I'm calling about a mistake on the bill we received early today. We're being charged for four deliveries of materials made in August for one ton of steel pipes and two spools of copper wires. As you know, we usually get four deliveries each month, but in August our production was down for a while because of some equipment problems. So, we received only three deliveries on the August 5th, August 12th, and August 27th. Other information on payment method and order quantity on these dates are correct but the incorrect charge for another delivery must be erased from our account. We've been doing business with your company for over a year and this has never happened before. Can you please send us a corrected statement as soon as possible and I hope this kind of mistake won't happen again.

92. What is the speaker calling about?
(A) To report a mistake
(B) To schedule a delivery
(C) To place an order
(D) To receive a refund

93. Look at the graphic. Which date of the charge should be corrected?
(A) August 5th
(B) August 12th
(C) August 21st
(D) August 27th

94. What does the speaker request?
(A) A formal letter of apology
(B) A written confirmation
(C) A price list of each item
(D) A corrected bill

Questions 95 through 97 refer to the following announcement and ticket.

Can I have your attention, please? We have an urgent announcement for all passengers for Singapore Airlines flight SL902 leaving for Chicago in one hour. Due to the congested condition of the runway, the departure gate for flight 902 to Chicago has been changed from 15B to 12A. The departure time for this flight is 9:45 a.m. as is printed on your boarding pass. We're truly sorry for the inconvenience. Once again, all passengers with tickets for the flight SL902 are advised to proceed to Gate 12A for 9:45 departure.
The agents at the boarding gate will help you with the process. If you have any questions or concerns, please consult with a gate agent or use one of our information hot-line telephones available at each terminal. Thank you.

95. What is the reason for the announcement?
(A) A ticket has been recovered from the airport.
(B) The flight has been cancelled.
(C) Some important information has to be updated.
(D) The gate agent is not available at the moment.

96. Look at the graphic. What information is incorrectly printed?
(A) 15B
(B) 9:45 P. M.
(C) 56C
(D) SL902

97. What should listeners have to do if they have a question?
(A) Wait until the boarding is completed
(B) Proceed to the main terminal
(C) Visit the information booth
(D) Use a designated telephone

Questions 98 through 100 refer to the following announcement and schedule.

Good morning everyone and welcome to your first day at Kingsville Electronics. My name is May and I am the sales manager of the South New York region. Let me start off by saying how happy I'm to have you as a part of the Kingsville Electronics sales team. I'm thrilled to have such a talented group of new employees in our sales force. Since you've already received your company manuals, we will start up today by reviewing some of the most important department procedures and policies. We will have a short break at noon and then in the afternoon, you will meet some of the senior sales representatives and other colleagues you'll work with. Oh, there is an error in your printed schedule. There will be a change, a switch, in times for the last two sessions. Some of the senior sales agents won't be here until 3 so we'll postpone it a little bit. Our team has continuously topped the sales record of the national average and we hope you could do the same excellent job in the future.

98. Who most likely are the listeners?
(A) Electronic engineers
(B) Laboratory technicians
(C) Department store employees
(D) Sales representatives

99. What have the listeners already been given?
(A) Employee ID badges
(B) Company manuals
(C) Social security codes
(D) Personal pin numbers

100. Look at the graphic. What will be the last program on the schedule?
(A) Program introduction
(B) Company policy & procedure
(C) Meet the colleagues
(D) Group activities

4회

1.	(D)	2.	(C)	3.	(A)	4.	(C)	5.	(D)
6.	(C)	7.	(C)	8.	(B)	9.	(A)	10.	(A)
11.	(B)	12.	(C)	13.	(B)	14.	(C)	15.	(C)
16.	(A)	17.	(A)	18.	(C)	19.	(B)	20.	(B)
21.	(C)	22.	(C)	23.	(A)	24.	(A)	25.	(A)
26.	(C)	27.	(A)	28.	(A)	29.	(B)	30.	(C)
31.	(A)	32.	(D)	33.	(D)	34.	(A)	35.	(B)
36.	(C)	37.	(D)	38.	(C)	39.	(D)	40.	(C)
41.	(C)	42.	(D)	43.	(B)	44.	(A)	45.	(D)
46.	(A)	47.	(C)	48.	(A)	49.	(D)	50.	(C)
51.	(B)	52.	(D)	53.	(C)	54.	(B)	55.	(D)
56.	(C)	57.	(B)	58.	(C)	59.	(A)	60.	(D)
61.	(C)	62.	(B)	63.	(D)	64.	(D)	65.	(A)
66.	(D)	67.	(B)	68.	(A)	69.	(B)	70.	(A)
71.	(D)	72.	(C)	73.	(C)	74.	(A)	75.	(D)
76.	(C)	77.	(A)	78.	(D)	79.	(C)	80.	(C)
81.	(B)	82.	(B)	83.	(C)	84.	(A)	85.	(B)
86.	(A)	87.	(B)	88.	(B)	89.	(C)	90.	(A)
91.	(C)	92.	(D)	93.	(C)	94.	(A)	95.	(B)
96.	(A)	97.	(C)	98.	(D)	99.	(C)	100.	(D)

Part 1

1. (A) He's planting some flowers in a green house.
(B) He's picking some fruits in an orchard.
(C) He's holding a box of files with both hands.
(D) He's taking care of some plants.

2. (A) The woman is setting up a projector.
(B) Most of the people in the room are standing.
(C) The presentation is being given at a lecture hall.
(D) The woman is handing out some papers.

3. (A) They're rowing a boat in the water.
(B) They're racing with one another.
(C) Some boats are docked at a pier.
(D) Some boats are being pulled up to the shore.

4. (A) They are cooking meals together.
(B) They are setting the table for a dinner.
(C) Some people are spending some time together.
(D) Some people are having a family picnic outdoors.

5. (A) Cars are being towed for repairs.
(B) A car is being parked on the driveway.
(C) Some vehicles are chasing each other.
(D) Some smoke is rising into the air.

6. (A) The woman is standing next to the man.
(B) Both of them are wearing short-sleeved shirts.
(C) Both of them are having their hands together.
(D) The man is sitting higher than the woman.

Part 2

7. What time would be better for you?
(A) He should be here any time now.
(B) It's been three times this month.
(C) Let me see if I'm available.

8. How long has it been since your last trip to Tokyo office?
(A) Three day ago.
(B) About 6 months.
(C) It was a very long flight.

9. Who wants to take charge of the new project?
(A) I can do it.
(B) The old one works fine.
(C) The headquarters will be relocated.

10. We should be able to open up a store as scheduled.
(A) We will need some extra help to do that.
(B) Will you close the door for me?
(C) I'd like to buy some new cosmetics.

11. Where are the designs for the renovation to the Acne Building?
(A) Sorry, the sign was wrong.
(B) In Ms. Chavez's office.
(C) With an additional fee.

12. That is the restaurant we went together last week, right?
(A) Let's order some pizza instead.
(B) No, he is not coming today.
(C) Yes, their service was great.

13. How do you clean this computer screen?
(A) The programmers will help.
(B) With a dry cloth.
(C) From a TV studio.

14. Can you pass me that yellow folder?
(A) I already passed the test.
(B) Where should we meet?
(C) Here you go.

15. This coat will have to be dry-cleaned.
(A) The synthetic fabrics.
(B) No, I didn't have to.
(C) How much would that cost?

16. Which assignment should I work on first?
(A) Start with Craig contract.
(B) He was assigned to a different team.
(C) It should be done by this afternoon.

17. Have you already looked at the menu?
(A) I ordered a salad and some bread.
(B) They already arrived at the station.
(C) I looked everywhere for him.

18. What's the procedure for turning off the heating system?
(A) Let's turn to the right.
(B) It's a part of the process.
(C) I'll show you in a minute.

19. Turn left at Cremont Road.
(A) Sure, I'll turn it down.
(B) Is that the next street?
(C) Let's stop by at the store.

20. When does Sally usually leave the office?
(A) She doesn't live around here.
(B) Around half past five on the weekdays.
(C) She didn't leave me any message.

21. Will Mr. Becker be arriving by train tomorrow?
(A) The training was postponed.
(B) Yes, I'm leaving for my vacation.
(C) We should ask Ms. Norris about it.

22. Would you like to join the selection committee I belong to?
(A) Sorry, but I'm already full.
(B) Take care of the personal belongings.
(C) I'd like that, thank you.

23. I'm available if you need any help completing the company newsletter.
(A) Thanks but I'm almost done.
(B) We should ask for more money.
(C) Yes, she was really helpful.

24. Isn't Mr. Brawley visiting us today?
(A) He'll be here around two.
(B) The visitors must wear name tags.
(C) Tomorrow is the company anniversary.

25. The Jazz concert starts at 8 o'clock.
(A) We'd better hurry then.
(B) No, the plane leaves at seven.
(C) It was the best performance.

26. Won't Ms. Lopez be available on Tuesday?
(A) Early next month.
(B) Yes, it started at five.
(C) She'll still be out of town.

27. Let's call Amy to ask about the new commercial.
(A) I have her number here.
(B) I'd rather buy a different one.
(C) The advertisement will be on air tomorrow.

28. Why did they reject the proposal?
(A) There was an important section missing.
(B) Please press the eject button.
(C) I'm sure he will pass the test.

29. If we can afford it, we should hire some temporary workers for the holiday.
(A) The permanent jobs have more benefits.
(B) I'll take a look at the budget.
(C) That was a long time ago.

30. Are you done putting together the marketing proposal for the meeting?
(A) Let me take a look around.
(B) The market won't be closed until 5.
(C) Do you need it already?

31. Can you tell me where the customer service desk is?
(A) Take the elevator to the top floor.
(B) Yes, the service contract includes all repairs.
(C) Sorry, but that is our store policy.

Part 3

Questions 32 through 34 refer to the following conversation.

W Hi, I'd like to go to Woodberry Shopping Center. Would this bus take me there?
M No, it won't. The route I'm driving goes up to Jersey Hospital. You'll have to take number 98 bus which will go east to the shopping mall.
W Thanks, does the bus stop here?
M No, you'll have to take it from the opposite side of the road. Go across the street and the bus stop for east bound is right next to the florist's shop.

32. Who is the woman talking to?
(A) A receptionist
(B) A traffic officer
(C) A doctor
(D) A bus driver

33. Where does the woman want to go?
(A) To a bus terminal
(B) To a doctor's office
(C) To a florist's shop
(D) To a shopping center

34. What does the man tell the woman to do?
(A) Take a different bus
(B) Get off the bus right away
(C) Look at the map
(D) Come back again

Questions 35 through 37 refer to the following conversation.

M Thanks for telling me about the painting courses at the community center. I signed up for it earlier today and now I need to get some supplies. Can you recommend a good art supplies store near here?
W I like the one on Washington Street next to the history museum.
M I think I've seen the commercial about the store before.
W Actually, I just got an e-mail about a sale the store's having this week. You'll get extra savings this week.
M Hmm. Washington Street is kind of far from me but I think I can get there this weekend.
W I'll send you the e-mail I got from them. With the special discount, it's definitely worth the trip to the store.
M I hope so. My class starts from next week. I need to buy the supplies this week.

35. What did the man do today?
(A) He started a new job.
(B) He registered for a class.
(C) He met an instructor.
(D) He made some purchase online.

36. What does the man want to purchase?
(A) A textbook
(B) A painting
(C) Some art supplies
(D) Some postage stamps

37. What does the woman say she will do?
(A) Teach a class
(B) Drive the man to the museum
(C) Postpone the event until next week
(D) Forward an e-mail

Questions 38 through 40 refer to the following conversation.

M Hi, could you tell me where I can find some strawberries?
W Strawberries are in the fruit section at the end of aisle number two. We also have various kinds of fruit salads and cakes including strawberry ones.
M Oh, I didn't know that. Where can I find the cakes, then?
W In the bakery section at the back of the store. I recommend the strawberry cake with some whipping cream.

38. Where are the speakers?
(A) At a farm
(B) At a restaurant
(C) At a supermarket
(D) At a product fair

39. What does the man ask about?
(A) The price of a dessert
(B) Whereabout of a person
(C) Availability of seats left
(D) The location of a product

40. What does the woman recommend?
(A) Speak with the manager
(B) Check the directions to the farm
(C) Buy a kind of food
(D) Look at the menu again

Questions 41 through 43 refer to the following conversation.

W   Brad, if you have time this afternoon, I would like to meet with you to discuss your job performance report. I know we are originally scheduled to meet on Thursday, but I have to visit the Sydney office because of some urgent matter.

M   Let me check my schedule. Hmm. I have a conference call around two in the afternoon. I could meet you before 2 o'clock or after 4.

W   Let's meet right after lunch. This won't take long. We just have to go through the points I made and make sure you understand them.

M   Okay, I'll stop by your office just after 1 o'clock, then.

41. Why does the woman want to meet with the man?
(A) To schedule an interview
(B) To offer a job in Sydney
(C) To discuss a performance review
(D) To meet the new supervisor

42. Why does the woman reschedule the meeting?
(A) She needs to visit her family.
(B) She needs to see her doctor.
(C) She has to work overtime.
(D) She has to visit another branch.

43. What time will the meeting take place?
(A) At lunch time
(B) At one o'clock
(C) At two o'clock
(D) At four o'clock

Questions 44 through 46 refer to the following conversation.

W   Excuse me, I'm calling from room 2207. I was heading out for the shopping district in downtown and I just noticed that it's raining outside. Unfortunately, I forgot my umbrella. Is there any place near the hotel where I can buy one?

M   Oh, you don't need to buy one. We have complimentary umbrellas available here at the front desk. I can have someone bring one up to your room, if you'd like.

W   That's okay, I'll just stop by at the desk on my way out.

M   Well, if you'd prefer that way, that's okay. I'll be here all evening. But keep in mind that most of the stores in downtown shopping district close at around nine. So, you might want to hurry.

44. Who most likely is the man?
(A) A hotel receptionist
(B) A tour guide
(C) A convenience store clerk
(D) A police officer

45. What does the man offer to do?
(A) Update an itinerary
(B) Check a price
(C) Provide a local map
(D) Have an item delivered

46. What does the man notify the woman about?
(A) A closing time
(B) An additional fee
(C) A road closure
(D) A departure date

Questions 47 through 49 refer to the following conversation.

W   The finance department gave me the sales report from our new pet shop in Middletown, and this quarter's sales figures are much lower than we were expecting.

M   Yes, I read that report, too. Happy Pet, our competitor has been there for a long time and customers feel really loyal to it. We should do something about it.

W   Hmm, maybe we should advertise more in the local market.

M   That's a good idea. I can look over the sales figures again, so we can focus our ads on the products customers most want to buy.

47. What problem does the woman mention?
(A) The weather has not been good.
(B) The competitor launched a new product.
(C) Sales are below their expectation.
(D) They need to expand the market.

48. How does the woman suggest they address the problem?
(A) By increasing advertisement
(B) By hiring more staff
(C) By reducing prices
(D) By extending business hours

49. What does the man offer to do?
(A) Contact the manager
(B) Investigate the competitor
(C) Develop a new product
(D) Review some data

Questions 50 through 52 refer to the following conversation.

M   Hello, this is Jim Anderson. We talked on the phone last Friday. I have an appointment with you on Wednesday at 10:30 to talk about a small business loan. Would there be any documents I should bring that day?

W   Yes, Mr. Anderson. You should bring statements that show your annual income, your business account, and any other loan payments that you're currently making to other financial institutes. Also, you should bring the official loan application form.

M   I have all the documents ready, but I still haven't received your bank's application form.

W   That's okay. We have everything here at the bank. You can fill it out on Wednesday.

50. What are the speakers discussing?
(A) Applying for a job
(B) Missing an appointment
(C) Getting a loan
(D) Upcoming deadline

51. When does the man have the appointment?
(A) Monday
(B) Wednesday
(C) Thursday
(D) Friday

52. Why does the woman say, "We have everything here at the bank"?
(A) She will open a bank account for him.
(B) He doesn't have to worry about closing time.
(C) He wants to change his appointment
(D) He can finish the process at the bank.

新 Questions 53 through 55 refer to the following conversation with three speakers.

M1 Barbara, Peter, since the store has been doing so well, I think now we'll be able to hire a few assistants.

W Good idea. If we train them to handle things here at the store, then we will have more time to research the latest trends in the fashion industry.

M2 That is true. The clothing lines we've had in stock have sold really well, but I'd like to expand our women's clothing and start carrying athletic wear as well.

M1 Yes, and our children's wear has sold a lot better than we expected. We could really grow in this area, too.

W OK, why don't I post a help-wanted ad on a couple of employment websites?

M2 Could you do that? I can also try to contact some of the agencies.

W The sooner we get help, the sooner we can follow through with our plans.

53. Who most likely are the speakers?
(A) Fitness instructors
(B) Website designers
(C) Clothing store owners
(D) Costume designers

54. What will the speakers like to have more time to do?
(A) Review applications
(B) Investigate fashion trends
(C) Design clothing
(D) Build a new website

55. What does the woman say she plans to do?
(A) Fix a window display
(B) Contact a supplier
(C) Train new employees
(D) Post some advertisement

Questions 56 through 58 refer to the following conversation.

M Have you seen the blueprints for the new building project in downtown? They're quite impressive.

W Yes, I agree. It will be the best design that our department has ever come up with. The boss wants to meet with us and get our feedback before he presents it at the boarding meeting this Thursday.

M Maybe you and I should get together before the meeting to discuss what we can improve.

W That's a good idea. Today is already Monday. How about we see each other first thing tomorrow?

M Sure, I'll stop by at your office tomorrow morning then.

56. Who most likely are the speakers?
(A) Board members
(B) Department managers
(C) Designing staff
(D) Receptionists

57. Why do they have to see the supervisor?
(A) To discuss future projects
(B) To share their opinions
(C) To be introduced at the meeting
(D) To improve the service quality

58. What does the woman imply when she says, "How about we see each other first thing tomorrow"?
(A) The boss wants to change the building design.
(B) They're not going to be busy all day.
(C) They don't have enough time before the deadline.
(D) She's not available in the afternoon.

Questions 59 through 61 refer to the following conversation.

M Thank you for agreeing to this interview, Ms. Swift. Since your organic moisturizing cream featured in the trade fair last month, our magazine has tried to write an article about your business. Can you tell me how you got started?

W Well, I've had skin problems for a long time. So, I decided to develop a cream from ingredients that I can trust. I used only the certified organic vegetables and fruits to make the special cream. I loved it and I guess more people like it, too.

M That's an amazing story. I heard now you're selling almost 5,000 jars a month.

W Yes, and since my company took part in the trade fair, we've been working around the clock to keep up with the high demand.

59. Why is the man interviewing Ms. Swift?
(A) She started her own company.
(B) She grew vegetables in her garden.
(C) She is an event coordinator.
(D) She volunteered for the interview.

60. What product is being discussed?
(A) Organic food
(B) Trade magazine
(C) New recipe
(D) Moisturizing cream

61. According to Ms. Swift, what happened after the trade fair?
(A) She expended to overseas.
(B) She opened up a store.
(C) Sales have increased drastically.
(D) Customers have been calling her.

新 Questions 62 through 64 refer to the following conversation and list.

M Excuse me, I'd like to send this package to New York and I want it to be arrived there no later than Friday, the 15th. It's a birthday present for my sister and her party is on Saturday.

W Well, let me weigh it first. Hold on for a second, If you send it by regular mail, it will take about 3 to 5 days, but if you use the express mail, however, we guarantee the delivery in 2 business days with extra charge.

M Well, that is very expensive, but I guess I have no choice. I don't want my sister to have a party without a present. I'll take the faster option.

W Okay, why don't you fill out this form first? Did you put anything fragile inside the box?

62. What are the speakers talking about?
(A) Giving a delivery address
(B) Sending a gift to a family member
(C) Buying some stamps at the post office
(D) Traveling to New York

63. Look at the graphic. How much would the man have to pay?
新 (A) 10 dollars
(B) 12 dollars
(C) 18 dollars
(D) 22 dollars

64. What will the man probably do next?
(A) Buy some gifts
(B) Wait for two more days
(C) Put the items in the box
(D) Complete some paperwork

新 Questions 65 through 67 refer to the following conversation and schedule.

W Excuse me. My name is Andrea Peterson. It's almost 2 o'clock and I believe our accounting team has a meeting in this room in about 5 minutes. I was hoping you could wrap up soon.

M Well, I'm pretty sure I signed up for this room for another hour. Why don't we check the schedule board on the wall?

W Oh, you're right. That is strange. I was so sure that I've signed up for the room from 2 o'clock. I'd better get back and check the online calendar on my computer.

M That's okay. I know the schedules could be confusing.

W I'll try to be back in an hour. Sorry to interrupt your work.

65. What are the speakers talking about?
(A) The confusion of meeting schedule
(B) The cost of accounting software
(C) The contents for the next report
(D) The location of a sales presentation

66. How do the speakers resolve the issues?
(A) By contacting the receptionist
(B) By searching the online help link
(C) By reducing the time for the meeting
(D) By looking at some information on the board

67. Look at the graphic. What team does the man work for?
新 (A) Maintenance department
(B) New product development team
(C) Accounting department
(D) Facility Department

新 Questions 68 through 70 refer to the following conversation and map.

M Stephanie, I'm worried. We've got a new editor starting next week and I'm afraid we don't have enough room for him on this floor.

W I've been thinking about it too. I heard there are some empty offices upstairs. Why don't we move Jacky upstairs so that we can have space for the new employees? In that way, we could help the new employee get used to our editorial department first.

M Good idea. Jacky's seat is near the entrance and closest to the stairs. The new employee will be able to meet many people from other departments.

W We also need Jacky to help us with administrative work, too. We use her services on a daily basis.

M For the time being, we should handle our administrative work on our own until we find the space for Jacky. We don't have any other choice. We cannot leave the new employee alone in nowhere.

68. Why is the man concerned?
(A) There is not enough office space.
(B) They need to hire more people.
(C) They have to publish more magazines.
(D) He's being transferred to an office upstairs.

69. What does the woman recommend to do?
(A) Hire part-time staff
(B) Move some employees
(C) Work after hours
(D) Train the new employees

70. Look at the graphic. Which area will the new employee be
新 seated?
(A) Area 1
(B) Area 2
(C) Area 3
(D) Area 4

Part 4

Questions 71 through 73 refer to the following news report.

And now, for our 7 o'clock local news. At the press conference earlier this afternoon, Dr. Edgar Wolfe, a renowned physician working at the Lincoln Hospital in downtown announced that it will be opening the second facility to accommodate the city's growing population. The existing hospital has served the local residents for over 15 years and is known for its experienced physicians and kind staff. According to Dr. Wolfe, the construction for the new location will start next month and it will be ready to treat patients in about a year.

71. Who is Edgar Wolfe?
(A) A regional manager
(B) A city official
(C) A news announcer
(D) A local doctor

72. What did the Lincoln Hospital announce?
(A) It will hire more medical personnel.
(B) It will be updating its official website.
(C) It will be adding another location.
(D) It will be installing state-of-the-art equipment.

73. How long has the Lincoln Hospital been operating?
(A) For seven years
(B) For ten years
(C) For fifteen years
(D) For twenty years

Questions 74 through 76 refer to the following advertisement.

Are you looking to change or enhance your career? Do you want to work and enjoy your life, too? Then, call the Middleton Business Center today. The center offers professional development programs such as public speaking skills, resume-writing techniques, and image consulting and more. All our instructors are experts in their field. Our city campus is conveniently located on Raymond Street and easily accessible by bus and train. Courses are offered year round and registration is easy. Just visit our website at www.middletonct. com to sign up. If you are not sure which class is right for you, please visit us, or call us to set up a free no-obligation session with your personal career counselor. Our toll free number is 1-800-464-2343.

74. What type of class does the center offer?
(A) Career development
(B) Language courses
(C) Creative writings
(D) Computer classes

75. What is mentioned about the location of the center?
(A) It has many locations in the city.
(B) It has recently moved to a new place.
(C) It is next to the city park.
(D) It is near the public transportation.

76. What does the speaker say is available at no cost?
(A) Free use of photocopiers
(B) An introductory class
(C) A meeting with a staff
(D) A textbook

Questions 77 through 79 refer to the following advertisement.

If you are looking for a place for reliable food shopping with reasonable prices, you won't have to go very far. With 15 convenient locations within the Pine City area, there is sure to be one close to your house. We sell a greater variety of products and brands that any of our competitors don't carry. We guarantee that you'll always find what you're exactly looking for. We have daily discounted products and special membership benefits for the first time users as well as our long-term loyal customers. So, what are you waiting for? Call our toll free number 1-800-555-0705 to find the store nearest to you.

77. What type of business is being advertised?
(A) A grocery store
(B) An electronic appliance
(C) A home improvement store
(D) A restaurant chain

78. How is the company different from its competitors?
(A) It opens 24 hours.
(B) It has the lowest prices.
(C) It offers free delivery.
(D) It has a large selection of goods.

79. Why does the woman say, "what are you waiting for"?
新 (A) To find out discounted products
(B) To order a special product
(C) To encourage to visit the store
(D) To be on time for a special occasion

Questions 80 through 82 refer to the following talk.

Thank you for attending today's department meeting. As the director of new product development team, I'm pleased to announce that our new line of fax machine MX-5000 has successfully passed the quality control test and is now ready for the market. Our new product team worked really hard to develop this new type of machine that has the functions of fax, printer, and scanner. We're confident that this product will rewrite the history of electronics market. Now, our market director Sean Taylor will explain how he's going to launch MX-5000. He has put together an impressive advertising campaign and will explain how he will implement it.

80. Who most likely is the speaker?
(A) A company president
(B) A marketing director
(C) A department head
(D) A sales clerk

81. What does the man mean when he says, "this product will 新 rewrite the history"?
(A) Many people participated in its development.
(B) The product will be a great success.
(C) The product has a traditional design.
(D) The product is easier to operate.

82. What will Sean Taylor discuss?
(A) A quality control standard
(B) An advertisement strategy
(C) A cost estimate for the new project
(D) An upcoming reception party

Questions 83 through 85 refer to the following introduction.

Ladies and gentlemen, it is my great pleasure to present this year's Harbor City's Awards for Civic Leadership to Melanie Tang. As the vice president of the Ferguson Accounting Associates, Ms Tang has been playing a key role in revitalizing our historic downtown city. 20 years ago, the downtown area was deteriorated by reckless development and many historical buildings were disappeared. Since then, Ms. Tang worked closely with the city planning committee and local historical societies to restore the beauty of the downtown area. She initiated many projects and some of these projects were well-known to city residents including the restoration of Buswell Mansions, and the cleaning of West-river Park. Let's give a big hand to Ms. Tang who has worked tirelessly to revitalize our city.

83. What is the purpose of the speech?
(A) To explain a new policy
(B) To introduce a new employee
(C) To give an award
(D) To select a committee member

84. Who is Ms. Tang?
(A) An executive at an accounting firm
(B) A property manager in a building
(C) A government official
(D) An award winning architect

85. What does the speaker say about the downtown area?
(A) It was completely demolished 20 years ago.
(B) Historical sites have been restored.
(C) It needs further investment from the citizens.
(D) It will accept new immigrants and settlers.

Questions 86 through 88 refer to the following talk.

Before we end today's meeting, I would like to give you an update on our employee health campaign. We have just completed the first month of our new "Making Your Way to Fitness" competition. All the participating departments did a great job of discouraging smoking habits and encouraging exercising regimens in their departments. Each point you make for not smoking one day, or walking one mile a day will be added to your department's Health Scores and the winning team will receive gift certificates for local stores, and also, one MVP member will receive one week vacation time. So, keep up the good work. Remember, you can still participate in this competition by registering online at the employee's competition corner.

86. What is the subject of the talk?
(A) A fitness program
(B) Sports equipment
(C) A technical workshop
(D) A sales competition

87. How can you add points?
(A) By working overtime
(B) By smoking less
(C) By walking as a group
(D) By keeping a good record

88. What will the winning team receive?
(A) Cash prizes
(B) Gift certificates
(C) Free airline tickets
(D) A medal of honor

Hi, Mr. Gerald. This is Donald Welch from the Sydney Office. I'm calling to confirm your attendance at the board meeting here in March. The meeting is set for March 2nd to avoid holidays of different international offices. Last week, your assistant said you weren't sure if you could attend. Has your schedule been finalized? We could plan a conference call with you if you cannot make it to the scheduled date. As you know, this annual meeting among different international branch managers provides an opportunity to unify our management policy for the future business expansion. I will send you an e-mail message with the meeting agenda. I will also send the possible meeting times for the conference call just in case. I hope to hear back from you soon.

89. What is the purpose of this message?
(A) To report the international growth
(B) To reschedule a telephone conference
(C) To confirm the attendance of a meeting
(D) To discuss the details of an e-mail message

90. What did Mr. Gerald's assistant tell Mr. Welch?
(A) Mr. Gerald's plans are uncertain.
(B) Mr. Gerald is away on a business trip.
(C) Mr. Gerald will not participate in the meeting.
(D) Mr. Gerald has already reserved a seat.

91. What does the man mean when he says, "just in case"?
新 (A) He just talked with the secretary.
(B) He will contact Mr. Gerald in person.
(C) He will send extra information for Mr. Gerald.
(D) He wants to purchase new suitcases for this trip.

Questions 92 through 94 refer to the following announcement.

Welcome to our 10th annual international banking convention. This year, we have more than 800 participants from over 40 counties to share their secrets of managing corporates and private clients. Over the next three days, we will have lectures, demonstrations, and interviews conducted by renowned experts in banking industry. And this year, we have something new. All programs and schedules of the conference can be checked electronically in any place of the conference location. You can use your own computer by using wireless Internet, or you can use the computers set up in the main hall. Now, I would like to introduce our first guest speaker, Bernardo Luna, the president of Douche Bank.

92. What kind of event are the listeners attending?
(A) A new employee orientation
(B) An international job fair
(C) A corporate board meeting
(D) A banking conference

93. According to the speaker, what will be different from last year?
(A) Some programs are available for free.
(B) Pre-registration is needed.
(C) Internet access is available.
(D) Interpretation service can be provided.

94. What will the listeners probably do next?
(A) Hear from an industry expert
(B) Sign up for an event
(C) Receive a registration form
(D) Attend the welcoming reception

新 Questions 95 through 97 refer to the following announcement and map.

Ladies and gentlemen, we are now approaching the Museum of Fine Art. We will be here for about 3 hours. During your time here, I strongly suggest everyone visit the Greek Pottery Floor and recently acquired pictures of 19th century impressionism. Cassette players for self-guided tours may be rented at the information desk. For your convenience, there is a gift shop to the left of the lobby and a cafeteria on the lower level. Don't forget to gather at the main entrance for our 3:00 departure. Now you can enjoy your time at this great museum. Please watch your step when you get off the bus.

95. Who probably is the speaker?
(A) A museum administration
(B) A tour leader
(C) A painter
(D) A sale person

96. What are the listeners encouraged to see?
(A) Greek pottery
(B) The collection of cassette players
(C) Paintings at the gift shop
(D) Floor maps at the information desk

97. Look at the graphic. Where should listeners meet at 3:00?
新 (A) 1
(B) 2
(C) 3
(D) 4

新 Questions 98 through 100 refer to the following telephone message and list.

Hello, this message is for Chris Mitchell. My name is Stella Carlson from Carlson Catering and I'm calling to double check your order for your department's picnic on September 15th. Also, you have mentioned because of unexpected guests, you wanted to increase the number of BLT sandwiches by 5 and I've notified our chef about it. However, we haven't received the details on what kind of drinks you want for the event. We have sodas, juices, teas and coffees, available in both iced and hot. Of course, for the outdoor event, cold drinks are preferred but you could have them in hot if you want. Why don't you visit our online shop at www.cartonfood.com to find details of our menu selections and give me a call back? We're open until 6 p.m. today. Thank you.

98. Why is the woman calling?
(A) To cancel an order
(B) To promote a new product
(C) To find out about the picnic location
(D) To confirm some information

99. Look at the graphic. What quantity on the original order form is no longer accurate?
新 (A) 20
(B) 8
(C) 12
(D) 15

100. What is the listener asked to do?
(A) Open the store late today
(B) Call the department head
(C) Visit the store as soon as possible
(D) Check out the website

5회

1.	(D)	2.	(B)	3.	(A)	4.	(C)	5.	(B)
6.	(B)	7.	(B)	8.	(C)	9.	(A)	10.	(A)
11.	(A)	12.	(C)	13.	(B)	14.	(A)	15.	(B)
16.	(B)	17.	(C)	18.	(A)	19.	(C)	20.	(A)
21.	(B)	22.	(C)	23.	(A)	24.	(B)	25.	(C)
26.	(C)	27.	(C)	28.	(B)	29.	(C)	30.	(C)
31.	(B)	32.	(C)	33.	(B)	34.	(A)	35.	(B)
36.	(D)	37.	(C)	38.	(A)	39.	(C)	40.	(A)
41.	(B)	42.	(A)	43.	(D)	44.	(A)	45.	(C)
46.	(D)	47.	(B)	48.	(C)	49.	(A)	50.	(D)
51.	(A)	52.	(C)	53.	(A)	54.	(C)	55.	(B)
56.	(B)	57.	(C)	58.	(C)	59.	(D)	60.	(A)
61.	(C)	62.	(D)	63.	(A)	64.	(C)	65.	(B)
66.	(C)	67.	(B)	68.	(D)	69.	(C)	70.	(C)
71.	(A)	72.	(B)	73.	(C)	74.	(C)	75.	(C)
76.	(D)	77.	(B)	78.	(C)	79.	(D)	80.	(A)
81.	(D)	82.	(C)	83.	(B)	84.	(D)	85.	(C)
86.	(D)	87.	(A)	88.	(C)	89.	(D)	90.	(C)
91.	(B)	92.	(B)	93.	(D)	94.	(D)	95.	(C)
96.	(A)	97.	(C)	98.	(D)	99.	(D)	100.	(B)

Part 1

1.
(A) Some people are walking down the hallway.
(B) Some people are exercising in a gym.
(C) Some people are shoveling the snow.
(D) Some people are wearing helmets.

2.
(A) They are pushing the carts in the warehouse.
(B) Some people are inspecting some items.
(C) People are waiting in line to pay for their purchases.
(D) Some people are shopping at an outdoor market.

3.
(A) A woman is reaching for something.
(B) The woman is looking for some blue print.
(C) Samples are being cut into small pieces.
(D) The woman is designing some fabrics.

4.
(A) The man is parking his car in the garage.
(B) The trunk of the car is being opened.
(C) A vehicle has been raised for repairs.
(D) The man is lifting a box over his shoulder.

5.
(A) They're swimming together near the ocean.
(B) They're strolling along the water's edge.
(C) Seaweeds have been left along the shore.
(D) The rocks are piled in the corner of the beach.

6.
(A) Cars are moving in both ways.
(B) Houses are bordered by a wall.
(C) White lines are being painted on the road.
(D) Cars are passing through the intersection.

Part 2

7. Who will be the new board member?
(A) We should be on board by now.
(B) Dr. Mendoza has a great chance.
(C) Let's join them at the cafeteria.

8. Where should we put the extra file folders?
(A) By the end of the day.
(B) There will be an extra charge of 10 dollars.
(C) In the supply cabinet over there.

9. You just started working here, didn't you?
(A) Yes, about a month ago.
(B) Yes, but it's already finished.
(C) Sorry, no one works at the moment.

10. Will Mr. Berkley travel by plane or train?
(A) He usually flies.
(B) He is a financial consultant.
(C) He's always in a hurry.

11. Could you close the window behind you?
(A) Sure, no problem.
(B) No, it's in front of you.
(C) We'll reopen tomorrow morning.

12. You ordered some new desks and chairs, right?
(A) We should call some maintenance staff.
(B) Yes, we can still use the old ones.
(C) Yes, we needed them for the new office.

13. Should I open the window?
(A) Yes, put it next to the door.
(B) Yes, we could use some fresh air.
(C) No, they're closed already.

14. When did the revised blueprint from the architect arrive?
(A) It came in yesterday.
(B) The architect is called Mousier Cloy.
(C) The printer will be here tomorrow.

15. How would you like your tea?
(A) I hired someone for that.
(B) With sugar, please.
(C) Coffee, or tea please.

16. What did you say your supervisor's name was?
(A) We've worked together for almost two years now.
(B) It's Melanie Taylor.
(C) Sure, I've met her before.

17. Won't you be coming to the dinner with us?
(A) Yes, I've already eaten.
(B) Yes, that was a delicious meal.
(C) No, I'm afraid I can't.

18. May I ask who's calling, please?
(A) This is Robert Kim from Pepsico.
(B) Do you want me to take your message?
(C) Sure, I'll give you a call right away.

19. Why didn't you buy the latest model?
(A) All the models are on display.
(B) Let's put them in the corner.
(C) Because it was too expensive.

20. How about hiring an outside consultant to help with the new project?
(A) That might be a better solution.
(B) He works at a consulting firm.
(C) Yes, the projection was off the target.

21. Who should I submit my manuscript to?
(A) Yes, I think it looks very good.
(B) The acquisitions editor.
(C) It's one hundred pages so far.

22. I heard you're from Japan.
(A) He's never been to Tokyo.
(B) No, all the international flights have been cancelled.
(C) Yes, from the northern part of the country.

23. We should consult a financial advisor.
(A) Okay, should I make an appointment?
(B) In our bank account.
(C) No, I didn't see the sales figures yet.

24. Excuse me, can you tell me when the next train leaves for Nanjing?
(A) The training session is set for next week.
(B) You should check the schedule board.
(C) I'm sorry, I'm too busy to go with you.

25. Don't we need protective glasses?
(A) The tables are already set for the dinner.
(B) Dr. Sorenson will give you the prescription.
(C) Yes, it's part of our safety procedures.

26. Have you finished the preparation for the party?
(A) We repaired necessary parts.
(B) Everyone will be there.
(C) I'm almost finished.

27. Is 10 a.m. flight okay or should I book you on a later one?
(A) I am not usually late for the meeting.
(B) Sorry, we're fully booked.
(C) Either would be fine.

28. What should we do if the keynote speaker can't attend the conference?
(A) At a different location.
(B) We'll have to ask someone else.
(C) Great, I'm glad you can come.

29. Please have a seat while we prepare your order.
(A) Thanks, it was delicious.
(B) Every other week is fine.
(C) Will it be ready soon?

30. You can hand in the survey results by tomorrow, can't you?
(A) To get more detailed data.
(B) Yes, the company needs more money.
(C) Actually, I'm still compiling.

31. How often do you upgrade our computer software?
(A) At a much bigger storeroom.
(B) Whenever new version is released.
(C) The technology division.

Part 3

Questions 32 through 34 refer to the following conversation.

M Hello, Greenville Construction, This is Stefan.
W Hi, the roof of my house was damaged by last night's storm and I need to someone to look at it soon. Could you come by this week?
M Ma'am. We are extremely busy today. But, I could definitely stop by at your house tomorrow if that's okay.
W Well, okay. I would also appreciate if you can let me know how much it would cost so that I can make the decision.

32. What are the speakers mainly discussing?
(A) Receiving landscaping service
(B) Repainting the house
(C) Repairing the damaged area
(D) Selling real property

33. What does the man say he can do tomorrow?
(A) Delay the payment
(B) Visit a site
(C) Listen to the forecast
(D) Meet with the architect

34. What does the woman request the man do?
(A) Send a price estimate
(B) Make a quick decision
(C) Update the construction schedule
(D) Correct the bill

Questions 35 through 37 refer to the following conversation.

M Hi, I ordered a book from Justin Lewis last week. I was wondering if it has come in yet. My name is Peter Schneider.
W Let me check it for you, Mr. Schneider. Yes, the book has arrived this morning and should be ready for you to pick up this afternoon.
M I usually get off work at four and I should be there in half an hour. What time do you close today?
W We close at five tonight and open again tomorrow at nine. You can stop by at any time during our regular hours.
M I usually finish up my work at 5:30 but I will try to be there before the store closes today.

35. What is the purpose of the call?
(A) To request directions
(B) To ask about an item
(C) To place an order
(D) To change an appointment

36. What does the woman offer to do?
(A) Replace a damaged product
(B) Change their hours
(C) Close early today
(D) Check the status of an order

37. What time does the business close today?
(A) At 4:00
(B) At 4:30
(C) At 5:00
(D) At 5:30

Questions 38 through 40 refer to the following conversation.

W Hello, could I help you find anything?
M Oh, yes. I'm looking for a new pair of hiking boots for men. Am I in the right section?
W Yes, you are and if you find anything you like, let me know. I'll help you find your size.
M Do you know if these come in different colors, like black? I really like the style, but I don't really care for these bright colors you have.
W Yes, These are good for serious hiking and everyday walking, too. We do have darker colors such as dark grey or black. Let me check the store room to see if we still have them in stock. What size are you, sir?
M I'm size ten, but I would like to try both size ten, and ten and a half.
W Why don't you look around just a bit more? I'll be right back with your shoes.

38. Where are the speakers?
(A) In a shoe store
(B) On a mountain
(C) At a paint shop
(D) At a dry cleaner

39. Why does the man say, "I don't really care for these bright colors"?
(A) The sunshine is too bright in outdoor hiking.
(B) Lighter colors tend to get dirty easily.
(C) He wants to see different colors.
(D) He wants to receive some extra discounts.

40. What does the woman offer to do?
(A) Look for a product
(B) Call another store
(C) Place a special order
(D) Change the sizes

Questions 41 through 43 refer to the following conversation.

M Hi, Kathy, Did you sign up for the occupational safety workshop on Friday?

W Yes, the memo said this class is mandatory for employees who have worked less than a year. You know I've been working only for 6 months.

M Well, apparently the engineers from the head office will demonstrate proper safety procedures to handle robotic devices and equipment in the assembly line.

W This should be very useful. I heard we're going to do some hands-on training, too. It should be much more practical than reading a manual on your own.

41. Where do the speakers most likely work?
(A) At an employment agency
(B) At a manufacturing facility
(C) At an electronic store
(D) At a trade expo

42. What is the subject of the training class?
(A) Proper procedures for safety
(B) Qualifications for line workers
(C) Efficient project management
(D) Practical application of software

43. 新 What does the woman imply when she says, "This should be very useful"?
(A) She needs to get a degree in engineering.
(B) They are trying to hire more assembly workers.
(C) The robotic devices will increase the productivity of the factory.
(D) The training will help her operate some machinery.

Questions 44 through 46 refer to the following conversation.

W Rick. Did you send out the oak table to Ms. Looney in Connecticut?

M Sorry, I couldn't. The order form I got from the sales team was incomplete. It didn't have the customer's home address. I already sent two e-mails to Ms. Looney and she hasn't replied yet.

W We need to get that order out immediately. It's been two weeks and we need to clear out the space for the new inventory soon.

M Why don't I stop by at the store this afternoon to see if I can talk the sale representative who took the order?

W Good idea. I think that is the fastest way to solve the problem.

44. What has Rick already done this week?
(A) Send some e-mails
(B) Deliver some merchandise
(C) Called the customer
(D) Compliant about customer service

45. According to the man, what was the problem?
(A) Sales agent was out of town.
(B) The product was sent to a wrong place.
(C) Some of the information was missing.
(D) The customer complained about the late delivery.

46. What will the man probably do next?
(A) Order a different product
(B) Stop by at Ms. Looney's house
(C) Clean up the space
(D) Talk to someone in charge

Questions 47 through 49 refer to the following conversation.

W I'm so glad you got the copier to work. My meeting starts in half an hour, I was afraid I wouldn't have the handouts ready in time. I'm so relived.

M Well, all I did was clearing some papers stuck in the feeder. How many copies do you have to make?

W Well, I invited 8 clients and there is Mr. Belmont and myself. So, that would be 10 copies all together I think.

M You should make some extra copies since clients sometimes bring guests along with them.

W Good idea. It's better to be safe than sorry.

47. What are the speakers mainly discussing?
(A) Ordering new office equipment
(B) Handouts for the meeting
(C) Changes in the meeting location
(D) Woman's performance at the company

48. What was the woman's problem?
(A) A presentation was delayed.
(B) An order was not processed.
(C) A machine is not working.
(D) There is a lack of supplies during the meeting.

49. What will the woman do next?
(A) Copy some documents
(B) Contact her clients
(C) Order more snacks
(D) Invite a few more guests

新 Questions 50 through 52 refer to the following conversation with three speakers.

W Hello, My name is Young-Hee Park and I'm here to take some pictures of the museum's geology exhibit for the Archelogy Today magazine. I have an appointment with Mr. Eric Richardson, the public relations manager at 10 o'clock.

M1 Yes, Ms. Park. Why don't you have a seat while I get in touch with Mr. Richardson. He's giving a short tour to some of the visitors right now.

W No problem. Actually, I am the one who got here a bit early.

M1 Hello, Mr. Richardson. Ms. Park from Archeology Today magazine is waiting to see you about the new geology exhibit on Modern Art Wing.

M2 I'm almost done. Why don't you take Ms. Park to the exhibit room so that I can meet her there? And don't forget give her the catalogs and other materials on our museum.

M1 Yes, sir. I'll do that. Ms. Park, Mr. Richardson is ready to meet you in the geology exhibit. Why don't I take you there and explain about our collection too? Follow me, please.

W Thank you.

50. Who is Mr. Richardson?
(A) A magazine editor
(B) A geologist
(C) An art donor
(D) A public relations employce

51. What is Mr. Richardson doing right now?
(A) Showing the museum around to visitors
(B) Filling out some paperwork
(C) Giving a lecture to his students
(D) Meeting with some local artists

52. What is the woman asked to do?
(A) Explore the museum on her own
(B) Receive a visitor's pass
(C) Go to the exhibit room
(D) Wait in his office

Questions 53 through 55 refer to the following conversation.

M Hello, I'd like to take the next train to Hamburg this afternoon. Are there any seats still available?

W I'm sorry. The next train is completely booked. Usually buying a ticket on short notice isn't a big problem at this time of the day but there will be a bike race in Hamburg tomorrow.

M Hmm. Are there any other options that'll get me there today, or early tomorrow morning if it's possible? I'm going to attend my cousin's wedding, so I need to be in Hamburg by noon.

W Well, there's a train leaving this evening that still has a few seats open. I'm sure you'll get there in plenty of time if you take that train. Would you like to pay for it now?

53. According to the woman, what will take place in Hamburg?
(A) A bicycle competition
(B) A film festival
(C) A professional conference
(D) A museum opening

54. Why is the man going to Hamburg?
(A) To meet with some clients
(B) To purchase some real estate
(C) To attend a family celebration
(D) To be trained for a competition

55. What does the woman recommend?
(A) Buy a monthly pass
(B) Take a later train
(C) Rent a bicycle
(D) Pay less for the same ticket

Questions 56 through 58 refer to the following conversation.

W Bill, I'm having trouble with this spreadsheet. I spent a lot of time entering all the data, but in the end the numbers came out inconsistent.

M Did you check to see what the problems are?

W I did check, but I don't understand. I know all the data is right, and the formulas look okay, but something is still not adding up right. What should I do? I need to finish this sheet to complete the financial report in the last quarter.

M Try to install the latest version of the accounting program in your computer. If that doesn't work, I'll look at it myself.

W OK, I'll try to do that.

56. What are the speakers discussing?
(A) A budget report
(B) A financial spreadsheet
(C) A computer technician
(D) A business loan

57. What seems to be the problem?
(A) The new version hasn't come out yet.
(B) The woman is not good at calculation.
(C) Some numbers don't add up correctly.
(D) An accountant gave the wrong data.

58. What does the man imply when he says, "I'll look at it myself"?
(A) He likes to work alone.
(B) He had the same problem.
(C) He knows enough to help the woman.
(D) He is not in his office right now.

Questions 59 through 61 refer to the following conversation.

W Hi, my name is Becky Elkordy. I've recently opened a new restaurant in the area and I'm visiting local businesses to drop off our menu. We specialize in Middle Eastern cuisine.

M That sounds interesting. I'm not familiar with Middle Eastern food. Can you tell me a little more about it?

W Well, we eat a lot of barbeque meat served together with homemade bread and yogurt. Each day, we serve a lunch special so you can try different dishes.

M That sounds great. I'm glad you stopped by. I planned to eat out today anyway, so I'll give your restaurant a try and eat there.

W Thank you. I'll be expecting you today, then.

59. What is the purpose of the woman's visit?
(A) To make travel arrangement
(B) To pick up a package
(C) To distribute some coupons
(D) To promote a business

60. What does the man inquire about?
(A) Information about the cuisine
(B) A company's location
(C) Payment options
(D) Business hours

61. What is the man planning to do?
(A) Try different clothes
(B) Register for a cooking class
(C) Eat at a new restaurant
(D) Look for online menus

Questions 62 through 64 refer to the following conversation.

M Hi, Cynthia. Can you help me find some sales figures for international offices? I have to finish this report for the sales team but I couldn't find necessary data.

W I'm sorry. I have a meeting with Mr. Murdoch in 10 minutes in his office. You could ask Peter to help you. He used to work at the sales team. He should know better than I do.

M I've already tried to contact him, but he's not in his office.

W Why don't you call and leave a memo with his secretary? She should be able to help you with Peter's schedule.

M I doubt she's in her office but I'll give it a try.

62. What does the man need some help with?
(A) Hire a new employee
(B) Copy some reports
(C) Extend the deadline
(D) Find some data

63. Why is the woman unable to help the man?
(A) She needs to be somewhere.
(B) She has to finish her report.
(C) She is selling some products.
(D) She is meeting with Peter.

64. What does the woman suggest the man do?
(A) Change the competition date
(B) Find someone to replace him
(C) Contact an assistant for help
(D) Leave the office early today

新 Questions 65 through 67 refer to the following conversation and ticket.

M This week has been really busy because of the sales conference, hasn't it? Do you have any plans for the weekend? I think I am going to visit my sister in Florida.

W Well, I've got a ticket for the famous Jazz band, 'Sincerity', on this Saturday night at the Grand Opera House. The problem is that my brother was supposed to drive me there, and he has an emergency meeting out of town. So I don't have a ride anymore.

M Oh, but you know, on the weekend, there's a bus to the Opera House. You can catch it on the 9th Avenue.

W That's good to know. The concert starts at eight o'clock, but VIP ticket holders are invited to a pre-reception that starts from seven and I'm so excited about meeting with some of the performers at the reception.

65. What does the woman plan to do on the weekend?
(A) Attend a conference
(B) Watch a performance
(C) Meet with family member
(D) Buy a ticket for an opera

66. What is the woman's problem?
(A) She lost her ticket.
(B) She doesn't care for arts.
(C) She has no ride.
(D) She has to work.

67. 新 Look at the graphic. When will the woman plan to arrive at the opera house?
(A) At 6:00 p.m.
(B) At 7:00 p.m.
(C) At 8:00 p.m.
(D) At 9:00 p.m.

新 Questions 68 through 70 refer to the following conversation and schedule.

W I just got an e-mail from Mr. Fredrickson. He confirmed that four clients from San Francisco will be coming on Friday to discuss the new remodeling project.

M Great. Now, I can finalize Friday's meeting. I was waiting to hear how many people would be attending before making a reservation.

W Also, they want to go back to San Francisco after the meeting and a quick lunch.

M Then, I think we should cancel the reservation at Nova restaurant and just have something light at American Bistro since it's right down the street from our office. We could save some time for the wrap-up session, too.

W Good idea. We should try our best to accommodate their opinions.

68. What is the purpose of the client's visit?
(A) To hire more staff for the project
(B) To plan a luncheon meeting
(C) To schedule a conference
(D) To discuss the building remodeling

69. Why has the man waited to make a reservation?
(A) He has to revise some reports.
(B) He was working for some other projects.
(C) He did not know how many guests are coming.
(D) He wasn't sure what food to order.

70. 新 Look at the graphic. Which scheduled time has the incorrect location?
(A) 10 a.m.
(B) 12 p.m.
(C) 1 p.m.
(D) 3 p.m.

Part 4

Questions 71 through 73 refer to the following advertisement.

For this holiday, please come to Office Dot and enjoy the great savings on new desks, chairs, tables and filing cabinets that your office needs. We also have impressive collections of accessories such as lamps, picture frames, and more. Now is the best time to give your office a new look at the lowest price of the year. But, hurry. This offer is only good for Monday through Wednesday. Office Dot is located on 250 Main Street, next to the City Park. For more detailed information, please look for the business section of today's newspaper. Office Dot, the trusted partner for your office life.

71. What do they sell?
(A) Office furniture
(B) Bedding sheets
(C) Filing folders
(D) Electronic appliance

72. What does the speaker encourage people to do?
(A) Take a holiday break
(B) Redecorate the office
(C) Enter a contest for an office remodeling
(D) Save money for the future

73. How long will the sale last?
(A) One day
(B) Two days
(C) Three days
(D) Seven days

Questions 74 through 76 refer to the following recorded message.

Hello, Mr. Fernando. My name is Allison Sanders from the accounting department of Foremost Advertising. Your name was referred to me by one of my colleagues in the creative department at our company. I heard you've been providing catering services for Ms. Townsend for more than a year and she speaks very highly of you. Our department is planning a special picnic on March 15th and wants to hire you to provide food and drinks for the event. Our department has about twenty employees and we expect thirty or so family members too. Would you give me a call to discuss the detailed menus and prices? The picnic is only a month away and I need to arrange everything as soon as possible. I'd like to talk to you before the end of this week. My direct number is 555-2134. Give me a call.

74. What is the purpose of the message?
(A) To place an advertisement
(B) To transfer to another department
(C) To ask for catering service
(D) To recommend a picnic place

75. What has been planned for March?
(A) A farewell dinner
(B) A sales promotion
(C) A company event
(D) A birthday party

76. What is the listener asked to do?
(A) Meet with the chef in person
(B) Call family members
(C) Come up with the new menu
(D) Contact the following number

Questions 77 through 79 refer to the following announcement.

Good evening ladies and gentlemen and welcome to the Baxton Symphony Orchestra's first concert of the season. We regret to inform you that our program will be starting 15 minutes later than scheduled. We apologize that our guest violinist Pamela Watson was delayed getting to the music hall because of the traffic difficulties and we'd like to give her a few more minutes to warm up. In the meantime, I encourage to read over the background information on tonight's performance including the modern Russian composer Ian Kolinsky. The program background was written by our own symphony conductor, Martin Russo and you'll find that article on page 7 of the program.

77. Where most likely is the announcement being made?
(A) In a recording studio
(B) In an orchestra concert
(C) At a bus terminal
(D) At a radio station

78. Why has there been a schedule change?
(A) The stage needs to be cleaned up.
(B) The instrument needs to be shipped.
(C) A special guest has arrived late.
(D) Seating arrangement is taking longer.

79. According to the speaker, what did Martin Russo do?
(A) He played the violin.
(B) He used to live in Russia.
(C) He conducted some interviews.
(D) He wrote an article.

Questions 80 through 82 refer to the following announcement.

Before we end today's meeting, I'd like to remind you that all computer software in our office will be updated on Friday after the regular working hours. This is a regular maintenance procedure to improve efficiency and prevent possible hacking into our system. The staff from the technical support team will be checking each computer for viruses and updating software that is officially used in the company. Your files and data won't be affected by this inspection and maintenance. However, those who use laptops for outside work, such as sales personnel and customer's service representatives, should stop by at the technical support division before Friday for an individual checkup. Call Mr. Rudy Paten in the technical division for more information. Thank you.

80. What is the purpose of this message?
(A) To inform a maintenance job
(B) To train how to use new software
(C) To purchase new equipment
(D) To hire more technicians

81. What will happen to personal files?
(A) They have to be copied beforehand.
(B) They have to be moved to a different place.
(C) They got some viruses.
(D) They won't be affected.

82. What should you do if you have a laptop?
(A) Copy your files to a desktop
(B) Replace it with a new one
(C) Visit the technical support team
(D) Leave home early on Friday

Questions 83 through 85 refer to the following announcement.

Hello and welcome to the bottling plant of the Pure Water Company. My name is Raymond Walters, and I am the great grandson of Samuel Walters, the founder of Pure Water. Let me start today's tour by showing you where the water source for our bottled water is located. If you look out the window, you'll see the southern slope of Blue Mountain. That's where we get our fresh water. The water gets piped down to our environmentally friendly reservoir and goes through a series of processes to ensure its safety and consistency. Now, let me show you how our innovative machinery works to process the natural water and make it more enjoyable and safe for our customers. Follow me, please.

83. What is the speaker introducing?
(A) A healthy menu for everyone
(B) A tour of the factory
(C) A mountain hiking trip
(D) A safety inspection

84. Why did the speaker mention Blue Mountain?
(A) Because it is where he lives
(B) Because it has beautiful scenery
(C) Because it has rather steep slopes
(D) Because it is the water source

85. What does the man imply when he says, "more enjoyable and safe"?
新
(A) The tour is interesting and enjoyable.
(B) They invest a lot on factory safety.
(C) They produce health conscious products.
(D) They have to hurry to get to the show not to be late.

Questions 86 through 88 refer to the following telephone message.

Hi, Mr. Reynolds. This is Amber Paleen from Own Your Domain. I'm calling you to inform that your contract with us to hold the domain of vertias.com and veritaseducation.com is almost over. Your current terms for both domains will be expired on the date of 31st of September. We recommend you either to call us or to log on to our website at www.ownyourdomain.com as soon as possible to keep your rights on these domains. Renewing your contract for both domains is $120 for one year and $200 for two years. Failing to do so could result in losing your valuable domains to other individuals or companies. Thank you and we'll be waiting to hear from you.

86. What is the purpose of the message?
(A) To sell a new product
(B) To advertise discounted prices
(C) To request detailed information
(D) To tell the contract term is almost finished

87. What will happen at the end of September?
(A) The ownership of domains is finished.
(B) They will launch a new product.
(C) They will send out some information.
(D) They will move it to a new place.

88. What is the listener asked to do as soon as possible?
(A) Bring in the old contract
(B) Pay $200 in advance
(C) Contact the company
(D) Purchase one more domain

Questions 89 through 91 refer to the following recorded message.

Hello, this message is for Larry Taylor. My name is Elizabeth Seong, and I'm a reporter from the Brooklyn Times. Our newspaper is planning to run an article about the local restaurants in the community. Your restaurant was recommended by the most people we surveyed last week. As the head chef and owner, you oversee all of the operations and could be able to tell us more about your restaurant's food and services. We'd love to schedule an interview with you at your restaurant. We'll be taking some pictures of your signature dishes as well. Please call me back at 555-4235 and let me know when you are available for your interview. Thank you and I'll be waiting to hear from you.

89. Why does the woman say, "Our newspaper is planning to run an article"?
新
(A) She wants him to participate in a race sponsored by the newspaper company.
(B) She wants to deliver some newspaper to his restaurant.
(C) She wants him to edit some manuscript.
(D) She wants to put his story on the paper.

90. What is the purpose of the message?
(A) To change an appointment
(B) To provide fresh ingredients
(C) To request an interview
(D) To apply for the open position

91. What does the speaker say about Mr. Taylor?
(A) He has little experience.
(B) He is in charge of the restaurant.
(C) He is publishing a new book.
(D) He has changed his job recently.

新 Questions 92 through 94 refer to the following introduction and schedule.

Good morning and welcome to the Business Management course. I am Mark Anderson and I will be your instructor in this 6 week course. Each week, we will be covering a different subject of business management. Some subjects will be familiar to you, such as managing quality and operations, which you as managers might have experienced before. Other subjects should be new to some of you such as budgeting and financing. I'm sorry to inform you that the last subject on your schedule has been changed into "Public Relations" after the feedback we've got from previous class graduates. There will be weekly reading assignments and I will also provide you with some helpful articles and magazines. However, I think you will get the most from class discussions with your classmates who can give you the real stories of the business world. That is the real value of taking this course with other business people.

92. What is the main subject of the course?
(A) Writing persuasive articles
(B) Business management
(C) Presentation skills
(D) Obtaining a job in IT industry

93. Look at the graphic. Which class subject has been revised
新 to a different one?
(A) Business Strategy
(B) Finance for managers
(C) IT and e-business
(D) Global environment

94. What does the speaker consider to be the most valuable part of this class?
(A) Various newspaper articles
(B) Lectures and presentation during the seminar
(C) Weekly homework assignment
(D) Class discussion with other people

新 Questions 95 through 97 refer to the following telephone message and chart.

Hello, Ms. Nelson. My name is Min Hee and I work in the personnel department of Sam Electronics. We have recently received a resume of Patrick Nelson applying for the position of a sales manager. And he named you as a reference. We had an interview with him yesterday and I'd like to talk to you about Patrick, especially about the projects he was in charge of. As his immediate supervisor, you should have a lot to tell about his work performance. I heard one of the accounts he handled became the most profitable one and we'd like to know how he managed the project and worked with other team members. Would you please call us back at your convenient time to 555-3345? We close at 6 p.m. today, and I'll be available all afternoon. It would take only a few minutes of your time. Thank you for your cooperation.

95. What is the purpose of this message?
(A) To hire a new employee
(B) To set up an interview time
(C) To get more information
(D) To offer a job at her company

96. What does the speaker want to know about Mr. Patrick Nelson?
(A) His professional experience
(B) His relations with managers
(C) His educational background
(D) His appearance

97. Look at the graphic. What project is Mr. Nelson involved in?
新
(A) Sam Electronics
(B) PTA Contract
(C) City Hall
(D) Ashton Project

新 Questions 98 through 100 refer to the following news report and list.

In other news, the cost of staying cool during the warm season is getting higher and higher. This summer, most of us need to think of alternative ways to keep ourselves cool. Starting next week, the electricity rates are expected to go up to almost thirty percent in some regions. So, what can you do to reduce the cost of electricity? Residents who will experience over 20% increase in electricity bill should seriously think about getting new energy efficient appliances, the industry experts insist. Other energy consultants say that most families could save up to ten percent of energy just by improving the efficiency of their home appliances. I recommend taking those plugs out when you're not watching your TVs or using your computers. We can reduce the waste of electricity by turning off all unused devices and appliances in and around the house. This is Kevin Kwan, reporting from the Energy Department of Washington, Now back to you.

98. According to the speaker, what will happen next week?
(A) The discounted prices will be available.
(B) The demand for electricity will decrease.
(C) The weather will finally get warmer.
(D) The cost of electricity will increase.

99. Look at the graphic. Residents of which region are NOT
新 recommended to purchase new equipment?
(A) Boston
(B) Quincy
(C) Cambridge
(D) Worcester

100. What does the speaker recommend that listeners do?
(A) Contact the energy provider in your community
(B) Take the plugs out of unused outlets
(C) Use a traditional way of cooling method
(D) Keep watching the news for further information

6회

1.	(D)	2.	(A)	3.	(D)	4.	(C)	5.	(B)
6.	(B)	7.	(C)	8.	(A)	9.	(C)	10.	(B)
11.	(A)	12.	(C)	13.	(C)	14.	(A)	15.	(C)
16.	(A)	17.	(C)	18.	(B)	19.	(A)	20.	(C)
21.	(A)	22.	(A)	23.	(B)	24.	(A)	25.	(C)
26.	(A)	27.	(B)	28.	(C)	29.	(B)	30.	(A)
31.	(A)	32.	(D)	33.	(C)	34.	(B)	35.	(C)
36.	(A)	37.	(D)	38.	(B)	39.	(D)	40.	(D)
41.	(C)	42.	(B)	43.	(A)	44.	(A)	45.	(D)
46.	(C)	47.	(A)	48.	(B)	49.	(D)	50.	(B)
51.	(A)	52.	(C)	53.	(B)	54.	(B)	55.	(D)
56.	(D)	57.	(B)	58.	(A)	59.	(D)	60.	(C)
61.	(B)	62.	(C)	63.	(D)	64.	(C)	65.	(C)
66.	(B)	67.	(D)	68.	(D)	69.	(B)	70.	(B)
71.	(A)	72.	(D)	73.	(C)	74.	(B)	75.	(A)
76.	(D)	77.	(C)	78.	(C)	79.	(D)	80.	(D)
81.	(B)	82.	(A)	83.	(D)	84.	(B)	85.	(A)
86.	(A)	87.	(C)	88.	(C)	89.	(B)	90.	(C)
91.	(A)	92.	(D)	93.	(B)	94.	(D)	95.	(C)
96.	(B)	97.	(A)	98.	(C)	99.	(C)	100.	(C)

Part 1

1.
(A) The man is standing on a boat.
(B) The man is catching fish with a fish net.
(C) The man is putting on sun-glasses.
(D) There are clouds in the sky.

2.
(A) The man is checking the label of an item.
(B) The man is stacking some bottles on the shelf.
(C) Some bottles are being piled in boxes.
(D) Liquid is being poured from a wine bottle.

3.
(A) The cars are moving in single file.
(B) The building is going through the renovation.
(C) The structure is being built over the bridge.
(D) The road passes through the archway.

4.
(A) The men are sitting around the table.
(B) The men are rearranging some furniture.
(C) Some people are resting on the porch.
(D) Some rugs have been rolled up in the corner.

5.
(A) Some people are shopping for clothes.
(B) Books have been organized on tables.
(C) Students are purchasing books for their examination.
(D) Some chairs have been lined up in rows.

6.
(A) Some children are seated around the fountain.
(B) Steps lead to the front of the house.
(C) They are all sitting side by side.
(D) They are holding onto the hand rail.

Part 2

7. Who approved the new floor plans for the museum?
(A) The design is due next week.
(B) The plants need to be watered.
(C) The building inspector.

8. How long is the flight to Chicago?
(A) About 11 hours.
(B) It was a long time ago.
(C) It'll depart at three o'clock.

9. Should I turn left at the first light, or the second?
(A) We turned down the first offer.
(B) Give me two of them, please.
(C) The third one, actually.

10. What's the estimate for completing the project for Asakan Group?
(A) We don't expect so.
(B) Around 3,500 Euros.
(C) Two weeks minimum.

11. The weather is great for a change.
(A) I hope it stays like this.
(B) We need to make some changes.
(C) We should stay home all day.

12. I'm afraid this manual for the new fax machine has to be rewritten.
(A) It is hard to get accustomed to manual labors.
(B) No, we only need ten of them.
(C) I can do first thing tomorrow.

13. You went to the meeting, didn't you?
(A) Yes, the fax's been fixed.
(B) I'll introduce him.
(C) Which one?

14. Why don't I give you a hand with those boxes?
(A) That would save me some time, thank you.
(B) Sure, I can give you a hand.
(C) Sorry, I've been busy all day.

15. Wasn't there a home improvement store on this street?
(A) Store it on the shelf over here.
(B) We need to repaint the house.
(C) There used to be.

16. Which candidate would be better for the vacant position in the payroll division?
(A) Probably Mr. Dawson.
(B) The blue one is cheaper.
(C) I have better qualifications.

17. We could give you an extra discount if the amount goes over 500 dollars.
(A) No, this item was not on sale.
(B) I would like to have it gift-wrapped.
(C) Really? That's good to know.

18. Why did you use this type of paper to print your resume?
(A) The deadline is due next Monday.
(B) To make it more visible.
(C) Because we need to hire someone.

19. When did you and your family move to Chicago?
(A) After I changed my job.
(B) We're ready to leave now.
(C) One daughter and a son.

20. Isn't this data in the budget report a little bit outdated?
(A) The date has been delayed.
(B) We did everything could.
(C) Yes, we have to update it soon.

21. Should we go over the report now, or after the meeting?
(A) As soon as possible.
(B) It's too far from here.
(C) It lasted almost two hours.

22. What does the new shift manager look like?
(A) He's tall and wears glasses.
(B) He likes everyone to be on time.
(C) I've never been to the head office, yet.

23. Why isn't the projector in the main hall?
(A) It's about the company profits.
(B) I think someone is using it already.
(C) It will take about two hours.

194

24. Could you inform me of the decision as soon as possible?
(A) I'll give you a call by the end of this week.
(B) No, the information was all wrong.
(C) Sure, he'll start working right away.

25. Have you already taken the tour of our factory?
(A) I didn't take the medications yet.
(B) Yes, the facts are pretty clear.
(C) Yes, I was really impressed.

26. Don't you have a meeting with the finance director?
(A) Yes, I'd better get going.
(B) No, the plane got delayed.
(C) I'm glad to hear that.

27. Do you know when the company will be relocated to a new location?
(A) No, I don't know the manager.
(B) I believe the date is set for next month.
(C) We'll be transferring to the Paris branch.

28. Would you like to see our latest product catalog?
(A) Here you are.
(B) No, it's in different categories.
(C) Do you have a copy with you?

29. Where did you learn to play the piano so well?
(A) We play a different game instead.
(B) I took lessons as a child.
(C) At the concert on the weekend.

30. Should I edit the document that Amy has written?
(A) That's what I would suggest.
(B) Yes, she is applying for the editor's position.
(C) The documentary is for all age groups.

31. Do you know if the new secretary for Mr. Patel has started yet?
(A) She'll start next Monday.
(B) She works until 5 o'clock.
(C) The place has already opened.

Part 3

Questions 32 through 34 refer to the following conversation.

M Mr. Hwang is visiting us from Bangkok office next week. We should show him around the city while he's here. Where should we take him?

W We have museums, theaters, beautiful sceneries in and around the city. How much time does he have here?

M He'll be staying here about a week but I heard he has a tight schedule.

W Why don't we put together a list of things he might enjoy and he can decide what he wants to do with his time.

32. What are the speakers discussing?
(A) Staying at a hotel
(B) Reserving a flight
(C) A special exhibit
(D) Entertaining a visitor

33. What does the woman NOT suggest?
(A) A museum
(B) A theater
(C) A restaurant
(D) A scenic place

34. What will the woman do next?
(A) Reserve tickets for the event
(B) Make a list of activities
(C) Contact Mr. Hwang
(D) Talk with the travel agency

Questions 35 through 37 refer to the following conversation.

M Hi, I'm calling because I think I left my umbrella in your restaurant at lunch today. I was sitting at one of the tables near the window.

W Yes, we actually have two umbrellas left here. Could you describe yours for me?

M It was a small black one with the brand name Shield written on the handle.

W Hold on for a second. Yes, one of the umbrellas here looks just like that.

M I could come by for it today after work. How late are you open?

W Our evening hours are from 6 to 10 and we're closing in an hour.

35. Why is the man calling the restaurant?
(A) To ask if her client is there
(B) To reserve a table by the window
(C) To ask about a missing item
(D) To request a special menu

36. What does the woman ask the man to do?
(A) Provide a description
(B) Confirm a credit card number
(C) Supply a guest list
(D) Choose a date for the event

37. According to the woman, what will happen in one hour?
(A) A manager will call back.
(B) An announcement will be made.
(C) A transaction will be approved.
(D) A business will close.

Questions 38 through 40 refer to the following conversation.

W Now that Frank has retired and Sally took maternity leave, we are two people shorter than usual. Are we planning to hire soon?

M I hope so. We're already understaffed and the contract we got yesterday with Mayhem Electronics will mean more work for everyone.

W I agree. Maybe they can move someone from the sales department over here while we're looking for a suitable person to fill Frank's position.

M That's actually a good idea. I'll call the personnel director and ask him about it right away.

38. What does the woman mean when she says, "we are two people shorter than usual"?
新
(A) Some of the employees are not as tall as the others.
(B) They have fewer employees working these days.
(C) The hours of operation have been shortened.
(D) They don't have enough money on their budget.

39. What did they get yesterday?
(A) A promotion
(B) A pay raise
(C) A transfer
(D) A contract

40. What does the man suggest as a solution?
(A) Contacting an employment agency
(B) Putting an advertisement in the paper
(C) Working overtime until the project is finished
(D) Getting help from another department

W Eugene, some of us in the office are planning to start a baseball team as a way to get some exercise after work. Would you be interested in joining?

M Well, I really enjoy baseball and I could definitely get more exercise, but I'm not sure I have time. I teach a class at the local community center after work.

W Oh, I see. Perhaps we could meet over the weekend instead. Would you be able to participate if we played on Saturday mornings?

M Absolutely. Let me know when the first practice is, and I'll be sure to come.

41. What are the speakers discussing?
(A) Volunteering in the community
(B) Changing the work shifts
(C) Organizing a sports team
(D) Buying baseball game tickets

42. 新 What does the man imply when he says, "I could definitely get more exercise"?
(A) He wants to meet other players in the team.
(B) He'd like to join the sport team.
(C) He'd rather to play other sports.
(D) He'd like to join a gym near the office.

43. What does the woman suggest?
(A) Gathering on the weekend
(B) Finding a sponsor
(C) Waiting for a special offer
(D) Participating in a competition

M Hi, Aya. How is your story about the new mayor coming along?

W I know you wanted to print it in the Sunday edition, but I've had trouble scheduling a meeting with the mayor. He seems to be so busy these days. I don't think my article will be ready in time.

M Well, keep trying until you get an interview. But, we need to send everything to the printer at least on Friday night.

W Why don't you talk to Steve? His article is almost ready I think. We should have a back-up plan in case my story doesn't go through.

M Good idea. We might have to print Steve's city budget plans instead.

44. Who most likely is the woman?
(A) A newspaper reporter
(B) A city official
(C) A technical support agent
(D) A television producer

45. What is the woman's problem?
(A) She is too busy these days.
(B) Steve's gone on a business trip.
(C) The printer needs the story sooner.
(D) She has not been able to schedule a meeting.

46. What does the man decide to do?
(A) Let go of the woman
(B) Talk to the mayor himself
(C) Print a different story
(D) Delay the printing job for Sunday

M Beth, could you help me with something? I think this photocopier is broken. The power is connected and the switch is on, but none of the keys is working. I think it's broken.

W I doubt it's broken. Don't you know about the power saving feature? When the machine is not in use, it looks like it's turned off, but it's actually saving energy.

M Wow, that's amazing. How did you figure that out? How do I turn it back on?

W You press the energy saving button at the top of the controls. I learned from Jimmy in the marketing when we were working after hours.

47. What is the man's problem?
(A) He cannot make copies.
(B) The phone connection is weak.
(C) The power is out in the whole building.
(D) He needs to save money for the future.

48. According to the woman, what is special about the equipment?
(A) It is powerful for its size.
(B) It reduces energy use.
(C) It updates software automatically.
(D) It is environmentally friendly.

49. How did the woman learn to operate the equipment?
(A) She took classes.
(B) She watched a video.
(C) She read it from an instruction.
(D) Someone told her.

W Hello, I'm from Sunrise Supermarket headquarters to conduct a survey about customer satisfaction. I was wondering if you could tell me a little about your experience in shopping here.

M1 Sure, we shop here all the time.

M2 You know it's become a really good place to shop since the owner decided to move to this new location last year.

M1 You're right. The place got bigger and cleaner.

W I see, did you shop Sunrise Supermarket when it was located on Brighton Avenue?

M1 I went there a few times but the store was so small.

M2 Yes, I didn't have a wide selection like we have here. What's so great about this new bigger location is that it offers a larger variety of items.

W Thank you, here are some discount coupons for you to use for your next visit to Sunrise Supermarket.

50. Why is the woman at the supermarket today?
(A) To meet the owner
(B) To conduct a survey
(C) To set up a display
(D) To buy some food

51. What did the owner change about the supermarket last year?
(A) The location
(B) The hours
(C) The names
(D) The manager

52. What do the men say they like about the supermarket?
(A) The low prices
(B) The store design
(C) The wide selection of products
(D) The friendly customer service

Questions 53 through 55 refer to the following conversation.

M Have you read the survey results from the last quarter? Our guests complained the most about the lightings in their rooms. They say lightings by the desk are too dark to do any actual reading.
W Yes, especially many business customers commented on that. We could put extra lamp on the desk.
M That's a good idea, but we need to get an approval from the regional office, first.
W Yes, let's put together a proposal to present at the next regional manager's meeting.

53. Where do the speakers most likely work?
(A) At a newspaper company
(B) At a hotel
(C) At an interior designer's office
(D) At a furniture store

54. What does the woman suggest?
(A) Inviting more people
(B) Buying more lamps
(C) Cleaning the facility
(D) Borrowing money from a bank

55. What does the man say their next step should be?
(A) To request extra payment
(B) To make an appointment
(C) To visit the regional office
(D) To write a proposal

Questions 56 through 58 refer to the following conversation.

W Hi. Mr. Anderson. My name is Sally Nelson and I just started working here as a sales representative. I was told to speak to you about ordering business cards.
M Yes, Ms. Nelson. Our company uses several printing suppliers but I recommend Office-Max. Their work is excellent quality. The only problem is that they're little slower than others.
W That's okay. That will be fine. I'm still in the middle of my three-week training session. So, I won't need my cards until the end of the month.
M Good. Let me give you their number then.

56. What does the woman want to order?
(A) A telephone system
(B) Desks and chairs
(C) Training manuals
(D) Business cards

57. According to the man, what is the problem with Office-Max?
(A) Its prices are expensive.
(B) It's not as fast as the others.
(C) Its products are poor quality.
(D) Its location is inconvenient.

58. What does the woman mean when she says, "That'll be fine"?
(A) She'll order from the suggested company.
(B) She thinks three weeks' training is too long.
(C) She'll use a different supplier.
(D) She'll call other places for an estimate.

Questions 59 through 61 refer to the following conversation.

W Hi, This is Christine Bell from Hollywood Film Company. I'm directing a short film, and there is a scene taking place in a library. Your library building looks ideal for its authentic looks. Could I arrange with someone to do this?
M Well. You have to get a written permission directly from our library head manager, Mark Chavez. But, I'm afraid he's out of town and won't be back this week.
W Well, our schedule is pretty tight. Is there any way that I can get in touch with him?
M I cannot give out his number without permission. But he checks on the library every afternoon before we close. If you leave your contact information, I can ask him to call you.

59. What is the woman's occupation?
(A) An assistant librarian
(B) A facility manager
(C) An architect
(D) A film director

60. What does the man say the woman has to do?
(A) Stay open late tonight
(B) Select a different location
(C) Receive a written permission
(D) Get a library card

61. What does the man offer to do for the woman?
(A) Get a permission before they close today
(B) Ask someone to call her
(C) Meet with her on Monday
(D) Give her a phone number

Questions 62 through 64 refer to the following conversation.

W What do you think about Derek Simmons who we just interviewed? I like him a lot, but he seems a bit overqualified for the position. In his last position, he managed almost 50 employees.
M Well, then how about recommending him to the position in Paris? That position needs an applicant with managing experience, right?
W That's a good idea. I heard that Paris division needs the new manager right away because they are opening up a new shopping center at the end of this month. But I wonder if Mr. Simmons is willing to relocate that soon.
M Let's give it a try. Why don't I call Mr. Simmons right away? If he's interested, then we can set up a phone interview for him.

62. What does the woman say about Derek Simmons?
(A) He applied for several positions.
(B) He doesn't like his current position.
(C) He has more experience than required.
(D) He wants to live abroad.

63. According to the woman, what is happening in the Paris office?
(A) They are hiring more staff.
(B) They are expanding its facility.
(C) They are relocating to a new location.
(D) They're opening up a shopping center.

64. What will the man probably do next?
(A) Review a resume
(B) Call the manager in Paris
(C) Speak to an applicant
(D) Arrange an interview

M	Excuse me, I saw an advertisement for your vacation homes on the beach of Cape Cod. Are any of those still available?
W	Yes, most of the big ones are taken but we still have a couple of small ones available. These houses overlook the beach and are close to the city so, very popular with young people like you.
M	That might work, but I have to ask my friends before making a decision. How many people does that house accommodate?
W	It sleeps eight comfortably and up to ten. Here, why don't you take this brochure with a map and show it to your friends?
M	Hmm. We'd like the one away from other houses. The one close to the light house would be perfect. Is this one still available?
W	Yes, and the one near the main road is also available. It's a bit far from the beach but it's really quiet. But, I recommend making up your mind quickly because these won't last long since the summer is around the corner.

65. Who most likely is the woman?
(A) A tour guide
(B) A store cashier
(C) A property manager
(D) A newspaper editor

66. What does the man ask about?
(A) The cost of renting
(B) The size of the house
(C) The availability of extra beds
(D) The proximity to the city market

67. Look at the graphic. Which location will the man probably 新 take?
(A) 1
(B) 2
(C) 3
(D) 4

新 Questions 68 through 70 refer to the following conversation and schedule.

M	Hi, Diana, this is Tom, the plant coordinator. I'm calling to schedule you for a mandatory training course on workplace safety.
W	Yes, but I'm really busy this week. The new textile machinery is being installed and I have to be here to oversee the work.
M	That's okay. We can work around your schedule. All you have to do is to take any one of the three courses within a couple of months. I'll be sending you an e-mail with the detailed schedule.
W	Okay, that sounds good. When is the next available session?
M	Well, today is already August 10th. The next available session is Wednesday at 10 a.m. at your Garner manufacturing facility. Would you be able to come?
W	I think so. I'll mark the date on my calendar.

68. What does the man want the woman to do?
(A) Apply for a job
(B) Conduct a safety inspection
(C) Deliver some equipment
(D) Attend a training session

69. What is the woman doing this week?
(A) Interviewing some applicants
(B) Supervising an installation
(C) Training new employees
(D) Taking some time off from work

70. Look at the graphic. On which date will the woman take the 新 required course?
(A) August 10th
(B) August 17th
(C) August 25th
(D) September 1st

Part 4

Questions 71 through 73 refer to the following recorded message.

Hello, this message is for Patty Martin. This is Tony from Dr. Kemble's office and I'm calling to confirm your appointment for tomorrow at 3:00 Wednesday. Because you're a new patient, we have sent you a patient information form in your mail last week. Please bring the completed form with you tomorrow. This will help you speed up your sign up process. If you want to change your appointment time, please call me back at 555-1221 by 4:30 today. Thank you and we look forward to seeing you tomorrow at three.

71. Who is the caller?
(A) A receptionist
(B) A doctor
(C) A pharmacist
(D) A patient

72. What is the purpose of the call?
(A) To make a reservation
(B) To change the prescription
(C) To inquire about a patient
(D) To remind of an appointment

73. What is the listener asked to do?
(A) Arrive a few minutes early
(B) Report an address change
(C) Bring some paperwork
(D) Change the appointment to another time

Questions 74 through 76 refer to the following advertisement.

Always envying those who play music well? Waiting for a chance to actually learn and play a musical instrument? This time, Brighten Music Store can make it happen for you. We're located on Chelsea Street next to the Huntington City Library. Our hours are from 10 a.m. to 7 p.m. Monday through Friday. And this week, we have a special event prepared for you. Our annual students' concert will be performed at 6 o'clock on March 7th, Saturday. So, come on down and enjoy the music and see how you could perform like a real musician. In addition to regular piano and keyboard lessons, we'll soon be offering organ lessons of all levels. These new music classes will start early next month. So, come and visit Brighton Music School located on 755 Chelsea Street next to the Huntington Library.

74. What is the speaker promoting?
(A) Extended hours
(B) Music classes
(C) Newly published books
(D) An innovative new instrument

75. What will happen next month?
(A) Lessons will begin.
(B) A new location will open.
(C) A performance will be held.
(D) A guest player will be invited.

76. What is located next to the advertised business?
(A) A sports arena
(B) A famous bookstore
(C) A large sculpture
(D) A public facility

Questions 77 through 79 refer to the following announcement.

Before we finish today, I have some news about the company's website. Becky Brown has spent almost two months to redesign our company's website and from now on we will use it to post announcements about company events, and other important news concerning our work at the EMC Corporation. So, when you get back to your desk after the meeting today, make sure EMC Corporation's official website is set up as the home page in your computer. That way, each morning when you come to work and turn on your computer, you'll see the important messages and news at our company. Also, if you have an announcement that you think will be interest of everyone, let Becky know so that she can post it for you.

77. What is this announcement about?
(A) An upcoming inspection
(B) Relocation to a new place
(C) An updated website
(D) A maintenance job

78. What do employees have to do?
(A) Install the new software
(B) Contact technical support staff
(C) Check the homepages on their computer
(D) Be punctual in the morning at the worksite

79. Why should employees contact Becky?
(A) To register for the online seminar
(B) To talk to the management via Internet
(C) To complain about the poor connection
(D) To submit possible announcements

Questions 80 through 82 refer to the following announcement.

Good morning and welcome to the Cape Cod Travels. On behalf of the residents of Cape Cod, I would like to welcome all of you to our beautiful beaches. On our tour of the cape, you'll be able to spot the biggest whales and dolphins traveling around the Atlantic Ocean. You'll also be able to taste robust local sea food dishes including the famous steamed lobsters. The entire tour will last about 6 hours and you'll have plenty of time to enjoy the sun on the deck and take lots of pictures. This will be a once-in-a-lifetime chance for you to experience the natural beauty at its best. Also, we'll also have a marine biologist Dr. Chris Gary will join us later to explain about local animals and plants and answer any questions you might have. Now, let's get going.

80. According to the speaker, what can you see during the tour?
(A) Other travelers
(B) Rare trees and plants
(C) Traditional architecture
(D) Some sea animals

81. What does the speaker imply when she says, "once-in-a-lifetime chance"?
(A) It will be the biggest sale of the year.
(B) They will have a great time during the tour.
(C) There will be a chance to see the natives.
(D) The guest speaker is usually hard to meet.

82. Who will the listeners meet later on?
(A) An industry expert
(B) A seafood chef
(C) A sales person
(D) A hotel manager

Questions 83 through 85 refer to the following introduction.

I'm pleased that so many of you could come to this luncheon discussion session. Today, we're joined by Angela Dunmore, the renowned landscaper, and creator of the sculpture located in our first floor lobby. As the new vice president of this company, I was compelled to make our headquarters to serve both our clients and employees better. And having more inviting environment by adding artwork throughout the building is the big step I took for that initiative. Fortunately, Ms. Dunmore has agreed to lend us some of her own paintings until she find better places for them such as museum or private houses. Ms. Dunmore is here today to talk about the subjects of her paintings and what had inspired her to do what she does now. Let us give her a warm welcome, shall we?

83. How does the speaker want to improve the company headquarters?
(A) Painting offices with diverse colors
(B) Using land around the building wisely
(C) Giving better trainings to employees
(D) Displaying more artworks

84. What has Ms. Dunmore agreed to do?
(A) Visit the company's other locations
(B) Lend some artworks
(C) Lead training classes
(D) Decorate private houses

85. What will Ms. Dunmore speak about?
(A) The inspiration for her work
(B) How she got started in her business
(C) Where she met the speaker
(D) Her favorite art pieces

Questions 86 through 88 refer to the following telephone message.

Hi Sally, this is Charlie Rydal calling from the main office in London. Thank you so much for helping me coordinate next month's conference in Buenos Aires. Although I have done many conferences before, I haven't done any in South America markets and since my Spanish ability needs some polishing, your help will be so appreciated. Could you reserve a hotel that has a large conference room and at least 60 or so single or double rooms available for the week of September 9th? We expect at least 200 participants from 50 countries. Make sure they have all the equipment and line installed in the conference hall for individual lectures and presentations. Find possible hotels and send me an e-mail with their website information. I'll check the sites myself and we can make the final decision together. If you have any questions, do not hesitate to contact me at any time. Thank you again.

86. What is the message mainly about?
(A) Arranging an international conference
(B) Cancelling a hotel reservation
(C) Inviting people over to his house
(D) Making a travel arrangement

87. What does the speaker mean when he says, "needs some polishing"?
(A) He needs some help to reserve a hotel room.
(B) He wants to fix his car right away.
(C) He cannot speak the language fluently.
(D) He wants to visit the Spain soon.

88. What information does the speaker request?
(A) How to use certain equipment
(B) The company's travel policy
(C) Possible locations for an event
(D) The price of a new product

Questions 89 through 91 refer to the following news report.

Good evening and thank you for listening to WRX evening business report, Earlier today, Steven Martinez, the president of Berkley Communications announced that his company has developed a new operating system. Mr. Martinez said that the new software program will be compatible with any kinds of computers and mobile devices in the market. The product is expected to be launched in early next month, but the customers can use the trial version of this software as early as next week by filling out a short online registration form. Mr. Martinez projects that the total sales this year will be about 20 percent higher than last year's because of this new product.

89. What is the news mainly about?
(A) A possible merger deal in the computer industry
(B) Development of a new product
(C) A company's sales figures
(D) A technical training session

90. How can customers try the new product for free?
(A) By visiting a nearby store
(B) By mailing out the request from
(C) By submitting an online form
(D) By purchasing another product

91. According to Mr. Martinez, what will most likely happen by the end of the year?
(A) Company sales will increase.
(B) Additional employees will be hired.
(C) New facility will be added to the existing one.
(D) Company cost will be reduced.

新 Questions 92 through 94 refer to the following recorded message and schedule.

Hello and thank you for calling Mohawk Paper Store, the largest provider for quality business cards, flyers, brochures and other promotional stationery items in Boston area. We have a variety of styles and sizes to effectively present your company and if we don't have in stock what you want, we are happy to place a special order. Unfortunately, we're not open right now, but you leave your name and number, we will return your call as soon as possible. Our normal business hours are 9 a.m. to 6 p.m. Monday through Friday, and from this week, we're also extending our weekend business hours by one hour. Please take advantage of this great opportunity and visit our store soon. Thank you and have a nice day.

92. What does the store sell?
(A) Shipping materials
(B) Electronic equipment
(C) Cakes and baking items
(D) Stationery products

93. What does the business do for its customers?
(A) It holds a special promotional event.
(B) It orders out of stock items.
(C) It opens on Sundays.
(D) It gives out special prices.

94. Look at the graphic. What time will the store open until on 新 Saturdays from this week?
(A) At 9:00 a.m.
(B) At 10:00 a.m.
(C) At 5:00 p.m.
(D) At 6:00 p.m.

新 Questions 95 through 97 refer to the following announcement and schedule.

Attention passengers, this is an express train to Hartsville. I'm sorry to announce that there'll be some change in today's schedule. This train will only stop at Morrow Street before it arrives at the final destination, Hartsville Station. We will not be stopping at any other stations. If you want to change trains at Sunset Road or Cypress, please exit and take the local trains. Once again, this is an express train and the next stop is Morrow Street. Please be considerate and do not put any luggage on the seat next to you or in the aisles. If you bags are too large to be put on your overhead shelf, they can be placed in the baggage areas adjacent to each door. Thank you for riding with us and please have your ticket ready for collection. Morrow Street is the next. This train will only stop at Morrow Street.

95. Who most likely is the speaker?
(A) A flight attendant
(B) A ticket agent
(C) A train conductor
(D) A travel guide

96. Look at the graphic. What should passengers going for 新 Cypress do?
(A) Take the Hartsville Express
(B) Take the Morrison Local train
(C) Change trains at Sunset Road
(D) Go to track number 11

97. Where are the passengers advised to put oversized bags?
(A) Next to the doors
(B) In the baggage cars
(C) On the seats next to yours
(D) In the aisles

新 Questions 98 through 100 refer to the following short talk and list.

Good afternoon. My name is Sandy Nelson, a sales manager from Easy Learn Corp based in Chicago. I'm honored to be part of the Annual Teachers' Conference today. I'm here to tell you more about our innovative teaching strategies. Easy Learn Corp has been producing learning tools for students who have difficulties in reading and writing. The new "Make up a Story" software can help any student make their writings into an impressive presentation of materials, books, newspapers or any kind of publication forms. It has built-in layouts, dictionaries, and a personal assistant fairy that can tailor the software to individual student needs. The usual introductory version of this program is listed in your handout. However, for today's conference participants, we offer a special 20 dollars off from the regular price for you, which is a major discount. Now, let me show you how exactly this program works.

98. Where are the listeners?
(A) At a PTA meeting
(B) At a sales training workshop
(C) At a teachers' conference
(D) In a studio for a radio program

99. What is being described?
(A) Graduation requirements
(B) New computer equipment
(C) A new software program
(D) A family counseling

100. Look at the graphic. How much will participants to today's 新 event have to pay for "Make up a Story"?
(A) 20 dollars
(B) 30 dollars
(C) 40 dollars
(D) 60 dollars

7회

1. (B)	2. (D)	3. (B)	4. (D)	5. (A)
6. (C)	7. (A)	8. (B)	9. (B)	10. (A)
11. (C)	12. (A)	13. (A)	14. (A)	15. (A)
16. (B)	17. (C)	18. (C)	19. (A)	20. (C)
21. (A)	22. (B)	23. (C)	24. (B)	25. (A)
26. (C)	27. (A)	28. (A)	29. (C)	30. (A)
31. (B)	32. (C)	33. (C)	34. (D)	35. (D)
36. (C)	37. (D)	38. (B)	39. (D)	40. (A)
41. (B)	42. (B)	43. (C)	44. (B)	45. (D)
46. (D)	47. (B)	48. (B)	49. (D)	50. (D)
51. (C)	52. (D)	53. (A)	54. (B)	55. (D)
56. (C)	57. (D)	58. (D)	59. (A)	60. (A)
61. (D)	62. (A)	63. (B)	64. (C)	65. (C)
66. (B)	67. (D)	68. (B)	69. (A)	70. (D)
71. (A)	72. (A)	73. (C)	74. (D)	75. (C)
76. (C)	77. (D)	78. (C)	79. (B)	80. (B)
81. (D)	82. (D)	83. (C)	84. (D)	85. (B)
86. (D)	87. (A)	88. (B)	89. (A)	90. (B)
91. (D)	92. (B)	93. (A)	94. (D)	95. (A)
96. (C)	97. (D)	98. (B)	99. (B)	100. (D)

Part 1

1.
(A) A girl is digging the soil.
(B) Plants are being watered.
(C) A girl is raking some leaves.
(D) Crops are being harvested.

2.
(A) Some signs are being posted on the board.
(B) Some cars are waiting in line to get some gas.
(C) The man is cleaning the windshield.
(D) A car has stopped at a service station.

3.
(A) The man is turning off the light.
(B) The man is sitting on a stool.
(C) The man is recording his performance.
(D) The man is fixing a guitar on a stage.

4.
(A) Flowers are being arranged on the table.
(B) Decorations are placed near the door.
(C) The floor is being cleaned.
(D) The lights have been turned on.

5.
(A) A ramp is leaning against the back of the truck.
(B) They are moving some chairs to the house.
(C) They are stacking some merchandise in a store.
(D) A truck is being parked near the building.

6.
(A) Water is flowing over a dam.
(B) Cars are passing through a tunnel.
(C) A bridge is suspended over water.
(D) A walkway encircles a lake.

Part 2

7. When will the market analysis for the new product be available?
(A) You can pick it up now.
(B) I'm free after three.
(C) The resort is completely empty.

8. Do you have enough pens, or would you like some more?
(A) I'm full, thank you.
(B) I'd like a few more, please.
(C) Please, leave on the next flight.

9. Where did you put my umbrella?
(A) It's going to rain today.
(B) I left it by the front door.
(C) Did you check the forecast?

10. Who was hired for the creative director's position?
(A) I haven't heard anything yet.
(B) The job needs a lot of creativity and motivation.
(C) The prices are available on the website.

11. Which of the employees would be interested in this project?
(A) The interest went up by 5 percent.
(B) You can see the projection on this chart.
(C) I think Jeremy should be.

12. This new model comes in many different colors.
(A) Do you have it in black?
(B) She's born to be a model.
(C) The delivery costs about 5 dollars.

13. What should be the next procedure?
(A) We should check the instructions again.
(B) Let's put the stamp on the letter.
(C) I think the next room is empty.

14. Why don't you call the personnel office to find out about the vacancy?
(A) The position's been already filled.
(B) Let's find out the price first.
(C) Sorry, no table is available at the moment.

15. Isn't the new vice president stopping by at our department today?
(A) She'll be here in the afternoon.
(B) Let's ship them by courier.
(C) No, the present should be purchased ahead of time.

16. Have you tried to contact Mr. Chang from Tao-Electronics?
(A) I'm afraid he didn't try his best.
(B) I already sent him two e-mails last week.
(C) The appliance store is not open today.

17. Where should I attach the candidates' photographs?
(A) I brought my own camera.
(B) Detach the end part of it.
(C) To the top of each form.

18. Do you think the board will reach the final decision soon?
(A) Yes, the next stop is the final destination.
(B) We haven't met each other yet.
(C) That's what everyone thinks.

19. You already know Mr. Armstrong, don't you?
(A) We met at a seminar last year.
(B) Yes, now is a good time.
(C) I don't know where to go.

20. Who was the man standing in the corner of the room?
(A) It wasn't that difficult.
(B) Through the back door.
(C) Someone I know.

21. You commute by car, don't you?
(A) Yes, I usually do.
(B) It takes about 30 minutes.
(C) Sure, I can give you a ride.

22. Would you like to stop for some coffee or finish the competitor analysis first?
(A) The copier is broken again.
(B) Let's take a break.
(C) The forecast said it will stop soon.

23. How can you read those small letters?
(A) I want a little bigger one.
(B) The number is 555-0057.
(C) I can't do without my glasses.

24. I just saw your briefcase in the conference room.
(A) Do you want me to brief you on the progress?
(B) So, that's where I left it.
(C) Yes, we've met before.

25. The building designs weren't due this week, were they?
(A) The deadline was extended.
(B) Yes, I build it myself.
(C) It has some fascinating features.

26. How often do we send direct mails to our loyal customers?
(A) Sales are from Monday through Wednesday.
(B) Yes, we should send them a fax right away.
(C) Let me check from our computer database.

27. Do you know where they keep the tea?
(A) In the employee lounge.
(B) Every day at 2 p.m.
(C) Thank you, but I already had some.

28. Why do we have two copies of this contract?
(A) One is for the lawyer to review.
(B) Make twenty copies in total.
(C) We can fix the machine.

29. Aren't you coming to the reception tonight?
(A) It's partly finished.
(B) No, I haven't received anything yet.
(C) Yes, are you going, too?

30. We should check the stock list before moving any boxes.
(A) I have it right here.
(B) About 50 things are listed in the paper.
(C) Moving expenses are pretty high.

31. Didn't someone reserve the conference room for the meeting?
(A) Sure, I'll have some more.
(B) I asked John to do that.
(C) We've already been there before.

Part 3

Questions 32 through 34 refer to the following conversation.

M Excuse me. Do you have any more lettuce? I don't see any here.
W Sorry, but we have run out of it. The shipment has been small because there hasn't been much rain this season.
M Hmm. I wonder what I can use for salad instead of lettuce. I already bought tomatoes and mushrooms.
W Well, these cabbages would also be good for salad. Sliced onions are also great in texture too but you might want to soak them in water to get rid of the bad smell.

32. Where does the conversation probably take place?
(A) At a farm
(B) At a restaurant
(C) At a grocery store
(D) At a post office

33. What does the woman say about the shipment?
(A) It has been delayed.
(B) It is imported from a foreign country.
(C) It has been small.
(D) It has been damaged.

34. What is the man making?
(A) A multi-grain bread
(B) A vegetable soup
(C) A fruit pie
(D) A mixed salad

Questions 35 through 37 refer to the following conversation.

M Have you heard the news? Mr. Takeshi in payroll department got into a car crash last night and he is in the state hospital right now. His wife called this morning to tell us.
W That's terrible. Is he all right?
M Not really, He'll be out of his office for a while, about two weeks in the hospital, and another week at home to get some rest.
W Why don't we pay him a visit while he is in the hospital? It would be nice for him to see someone from work.

35. Why is Mr. Takeshi out of the office?
(A) He's on a business trip.
(B) He's on a vacation.
(C) He's working in a hospital.
(D) He was in a car accident.

36. How long will Mr. Takeshi be away from work?
(A) One week
(B) Two weeks
(C) Three weeks
(D) One month

37. What does the woman suggest doing?
(A) Visiting him at his house
(B) Paying him some money
(C) Delivering him some documents
(D) Seeing him at the hospital

Questions 38 through 40 refer to the following conversation.

W Hi, I'm Hayley Johnson, the payroll manager here at H&K Pharmaceuticals.
M Nice to meet you Ms. Johnson.
W No problem. Since today is your first day at the company, I'll be setting up payroll information. Did you receive the forms I emailed you?
M Yes, Thank you for sending me the information in advance. I have them all filled out and brought them with me as instructed.
W That's great. Now, all I need is to see a form of identification that includes photo.
M Would driver's license be okay?
W Of course. After we set up the whole thing and we can log on to your computer system and start checking-in your working hours.

38. Who most likely is the man?
(A) A potential client
(B) A new employee
(C) A technical consultant
(D) A pharmacist

39. What did the woman send in advance?
(A) A meeting agenda
(B) Directions to the company
(C) Her account information
(D) Some paperwork

40. What is the man asked to show?
(A) Photo identification
(B) A revised contract
(C) A confirmation e-mail
(D) A work portfolio

Questions 41 through 43 refer to the following conversation.

M Have you read the new novel by Emily Johnson? It is such a great story.

W I agree, and I heard that the story is so popular that they are making a block-buster film out of it.

M Yes, I read that news too. So, who do you think would be the best actor for Edward's role?

W I'm not sure. I just hope the movie captures the essence of the story as real as possible. It's such a great novel.

41. What are the speakers discussing?
(A) A play
(B) A novel
(C) A lecture
(D) A concert

42. What do the speakers say about Emily Johnson?
(A) She played different roles in a movie.
(B) She published a new book.
(C) She has won prizes before.
(D) She likes many actors.

43. What do the speakers agree with?
(A) They're going to watch the movie together.
(B) They're waiting for a new novel by Emily Johnson.
(C) They both liked the story by Emily Johnson.
(D) They don't want the story to be made as a movie.

Questions 44 through 46 refer to the following conversation.

W Jack, How many of these computers do we have to work on today? It feels like we've been working for hours.

M These two are the last ones from today's work order. But tomorrow, we'll have to install programs on 40 or more of them. The entire 5th floor should be done.

W How about you start some of those while I'm working on these? If we start ahead on tomorrow's job this evening, we could save some time tomorrow.

M Normally I would, but I can't work late tonight. I will go to a concert with my wife at six and have to get off work at 5. Sorry.

44. What are the speakers doing?
(A) Delivering computers
(B) Installing software
(C) Assembling office furniture
(D) Preparing musical instruments

45. What does the woman suggest?
(A) Starting early tomorrow
(B) Taking a break
(C) Meeting with her brother
(D) Working late tonight

46. What does the man plan to do in the evening?
(A) Visit his brother from out of town
(B) Go to a company banquet
(C) Check out the inventory in the warehouse
(D) Attend a musical performance

Questions 47 through 49 refer to the following conversation.

W I've been trying to reserve a seat for the international marketing seminar next week but I keep getting an error message at the last stage. Did you already do yours?

M I did, but I didn't use online registration. I just dial the number from a promotional pamphlet they gave us. Maybe you should do that too.

W I don't have the pamphlet with me. Do you still have yours?

M I should have it in my office. Why don't I email the number to you when I get back from lunch?

47. What are the speakers discussing?
(A) Booking a flight
(B) Signing up for a lecture
(C) Shipping some items
(D) Updating a website

48. What is the problem?
(A) A phone number is not listed in the directory.
(B) A website is not working properly.
(C) The marketing team has few staff members.
(D) An e-mail address is incorrect.

49. What does the man offer to do?
(A) Register for the seminar
(B) Have the pamphlet delivered
(C) Call some clients
(D) Send the woman some information

Questions 50 through 52 refer to the following conversation.

W Kevin. Do you know it takes forever to start my computer? I don't understand why it's running so slowly. I already updated the software twice this month.

M Maybe it is time for you to get a new one. Try High-Tech Electronics on Main Street. They have the best selections and low prices. Their sales assistants are willing to answer any questions you might have. I bought mine there and I'm happy with it.

W Maybe I will. But, I need to do some research before I actually get a new one.

M They even carry used computers too. Why don't you take your old computer with you to see whether you could trade it in for a new one?

50. What is the woman's problem?
(A) Her printer was jammed.
(B) The service was too slow at a restaurant.
(C) The online connection needs to be updated.
(D) Her computer doesn't work properly.

51. What is NOT the reason the man recommend High-Tech Electronics?
(A) They have wide selections.
(B) Their prices are reasonable.
(C) They deliver for free.
(D) Their employees are kind and willing to help.

52. What does the woman mean when she says, "I need to do some research"?
(A) She majored in science research before.
(B) She needs to find some discount information.
(C) She wants to learn more about computer software.
(D) She needs more information before making a purchase.

W Michael, Andrew, new shipment has arrived from Hong Kong. Can you handle it for me?

M1 Yes, Ms. Hatcher. I'm supposed to store it in the warehouse Aisle B, shelf 30, but the shelf is already with boxes.

M2 Oh, those boxes were supposed to be loaded on the truck and be sent out today, but shipping date was changed at the last minute.

W When is the new shipping date?

M2 Now we're not sending them out until tomorrow.

M1 Oh, then we have to get a new assignment for today's shipment from the management.

W Why don't I call the warehouse supervisor and find the new space?

M1 Thank you. I don't see much free space on the shelves in this area.

M2 Meanwhile, I'll cover it and make sure it is safe.

53. Where do the speakers most likely work?
(A) In a warehouse
(B) In a shopping center
(C) At a real estate agency
(D) At a moving company

54. What is the cause of the problem?
(A) A store closed earlier than usual.
(B) A shipping date was delayed.
(C) A package was heavier than expected.
(D) A customer complaint was filed.

55. What does the woman say she will do?
(A) Call the customer about the delay
(B) Label some boxes
(C) Check the database for information
(D) Talk to a supervisor

Questions 56 through 58 refer to the following conversation.

W Thank you for coming. Our company has not been too happy with our current shipping company and we're trying to find a new one.

M Well, I'm happy to give you more information on our company and services. I'm sure you'll find our rates are all very competitive, especially the international ones.

W We produce fresh flowers especially the rare and exotic ones such as peony or magnolia for the special occasions. We need them to be delivered to many locations domestically and internationally. Do you think you company is equipped to handle these kinds of shipment?

M Yes, we have plenty of experience with fresh and fragile shipment. Now, can we talk about your budget and standard charges? Then, we can start drafting a contract.

56. Where does the man work?
(A) A manufacturing facility
(B) An airline company
(C) A shipping company
(D) A travel agency

57. What does the man mean when he says, "you'll find our rates are all very competitive"?
(A) They are the fastest growing company.
(B) They're providing faster services.
(C) They can accommodate large orders.
(D) Their prices are lower than other companies'.

58. What will the speakers probably do next?
(A) Deliver some merchandise
(B) Look for more suppliers
(C) Arrange shipping schedules
(D) Discuss a business contract

Questions 59 through 61 refer to the following conversation.

M Hi, Dennis. Can you help me join the conference call? I've never done it and I've got one scheduled in 30 minutes.

W Sure, It's not too bad. First, all the callers have to call a special number at a given time and enter a common access code. Do you have all the numbers with you?

M They should be written in the e-mail I got from the committee. Let me go and check that out again.

W Once you have those numbers, you are all set to start the conference call.

59. Why is the man concerned?
(A) He's trying something new.
(B) He has to talk to the company president.
(C) He forgot about an appointment.
(D) He forgot to send a reply.

60. What does the man ask the woman to do?
(A) Help with a telephone call
(B) Check some calculations
(C) Make a reservation
(D) Prepare some report

61. Why is the man going to check his e-mail again?
(A) It needs to be printed out.
(B) It needs to be replied soon.
(C) It was sent to a wrong person.
(D) It contains some information.

新 Questions 62 through 64 refer to the following conversation and map.

M Ms. Bingham. I just received the new safety permit from the regional inspector issued for our factory. Do you want me to hang it behind the receptionist counter?

W Actually, no. The rule has changed this year. Now, the permit has to be within the two meters of the main entrance to the factory floor. We should put it on the wall right next to the main door.

M Okay, but we still have some time. The old one doesn't expire until Friday. So, I will put up a new one on next Monday.

W Thanks. I really appreciate that.

62. Where do the speakers work?
(A) At a production facility
(B) At a medical clinic
(C) At a restaurant
(D) At a government agency

63. Look at the graphic. Which location should the document 新 be posted?
(A) 1
(B) 2
(C) 3
(D) 4

64. According to the man, what will occur on Friday?
(A) A facility will shut down.
(B) New employees will start.
(C) A permit will expire.
(D) An inspector will visit.

M	How may I help you?
W	Yes, My doctor recommended I change my diet to include more protein in it. I am a vegetarian. I don't eat meat but I think I can drink milk. Milk does have a lot of protein, right?
M	Of course, milk is a good source of protein and calcium. Come this way. We have a lot of options to choose from.
W	You're right. There are many kinds. Hmm. I have to watch out my weight too. My doctor also warned me about having too much of fried and sugary food. This one has more than 5 grams of it.
M	In that case, I would suggest non-fat milk and you can add nuts or grains for more vitamins and minerals.
W	Thank you. You've been a great help.

65. Why is the woman looking for a certain product?
(A) She wants to open up a grocery store.
(B) She's allergic to a particular ingredient.
(C) She wants to change her diet to a healthier one.
(D) She's looking for a specific brand of food.

66. Look at the graphic. Which of the ingredients does the 新 woman express concern about?
(A) Protein
(B) Fat
(C) Sugar
(D) Sodium

67. What does the man suggest that the woman do?
(A) Try one of new products
(B) Consult her doctor first
(C) Go to another store
(D) Purchase a different one

W	I'd like to look at some rental spaces that you have listed on your website. Is the one on 1200 Mason Boulevard still available?
M	Well, I'm afraid that one is taken this morning. But I could show you more properties near that building. They're not as cheap as the one you saw, but some of them are quite affordable.
W	Well, I'm planning to open up my boutique shop on May First and I need at least one month to prepare everything.
M	We should hurry then. Why don't you stop by my office tomorrow and I'll show you around the one you might be interested in?
W	As long as it's close to the Mason Boulevard, I'm fine with it. My biggest concern is the rent. I don't want to pay any more than I really have to.
M	I'm going to send you a link to show available properties on and close to Mason Boulevard. I would recommend the one near the Longwood Station. It has the lowest rent for now.

68. What does the woman want to rent?
(A) A storage space
(B) An office unit
(C) Some furniture
(D) A direction to a place

69. What can be inferred about her business?
(A) She's opening a new store.
(B) She's borrowing money from a bank.
(C) She's moving into a new location.
(D) She's importing products from overseas.

70. Look at the graphic. Which unit will the woman likely see
新 today?
(A) Unit 1
(B) Unit 2
(C) Unit 3
(D) Unit 4

Part 4

Questions 71 through 73 refer to the following recorded message.

Hello, this message is for Tim Sanders. I'm calling about having wood flooring installed in my shop. I run a small hair salon in Bayside Mall and I'd like to change the flooring to wooden one. Could you give me a price estimate for this job? You were recommended to me by a friend of mine. You did some work for her a few years ago and she was very happy with the quality of work. I did the rough measuring of the store and if you call me back I can give the information so that you can prepare an estimate. Or, we can set up an appointment so that you can come over see the shop for yourself. My name is Emily and my number is 555-2482 and I'll be waiting for your call, thank you.

71. What type of business does Tim Sanders probably work for?
(A) A flooring company
(B) A cleaning service company
(C) An accounting firm
(D) A moving company

72. What information does the speaker want?
(A) The cost of a job
(B) The location of a business
(C) The time of completion date
(D) The availability of a product

73. What did the speaker's colleagues say about the business?
(A) It is conveniently located.
(B) It only takes large scale orders.
(C) It does high-quality job.
(D) It gives discounts for new customers.

Questions 74 through 76 refer to the following telephone message.

Hi, Mr. Phillips. I'm calling from CVS Pharmacy. You came yesterday and dropped off a prescription for your medication. You've asked to deliver the medicines to your house when it's ready, but there has been a problem. The prescription form you gave us was missing the signature of the doctor. We've called your doctor, Dr. Lee and he will be faxing a new form today. But unfortunately, your medication won't be delivered this morning like we have promised. It should be ready late this afternoon because some information should be verified. We're sorry for the delay and if you have any questions, please call us back. Otherwise, your medicine will be delivered to your house by the end of today. Thank you.

74. What did Mr. Phillips request?
(A) Contact number of the doctor
(B) An appointment to see a doctor
(C) Information about prescription cost
(D) Delivery of some medicine

75. Why is there a delay?
(A) A medication is out of stock.
(B) An address was incomplete.
(C) An autograph was missing.
(D) A doctor was out of office.

TEST 07

76. Why does the man say, "Some information should be verified"?
(A) They need to receive the payment information.
(B) They have to fix the fax machine.
(C) They have to check the prescription again.
(D) They have to find out the correct address.

Questions 77 through 79 refer to the following talk.

Welcome aboard on our international mountain travel bus. We're ready to start our trip to Vancouver. We'll be traveling about 4 hours before we cross the US-Canadian borders. Today's weather is supposed to be sunny all day and we should be able to enjoy spectacular views of the mountain on the way. From time to time, I'll stop the bus to point out the famous landmarks of the area. Before we depart, I suggest everyone check to make sure you have your passports and other travel documents. It would be a shame to find out later on that you don't have the proper IDs and documents and go back on your own. If you have done that, then we're ready to start another exciting day.

77. Where does this talk take place?
(A) On a mountain
(B) In Vancouver
(C) Near the boarders
(D) On a bus

78. According to the speaker, what will the listeners do later in the day?
(A) Climb the mountain trail
(B) Visit the local stores
(C) Cross the international border
(D) Transfer to trains in Canada

79. What does the speaker ask the listeners to do?
(A) Take out their tickets
(B) Check out some documents
(C) Have some snack
(D) Look at the maps

Questions 80 through 82 refer to the following advertisement.

Are you looking for a healthy and balanced life? Are you tired of juggling between your work and family? Now, you can have it all. Kundalini Yoga, the most powerful and fastest acting yoga known to the world will help you manage your life better. The trail blazing course for beginners has been specially designed and produced by Guru Khalsha, PhD. Dr. Khasha is a teacher, and an author of 20 books on health and self-management. Now, you have the chance to learn the basics of Kundalini Yoga through the convenient online training sessions. We started the live online broadcasting on basic yoga steps from last week. To find updated schedules and information on group discounts, please call 1-800-555-1285. Now, find peace in your life.

80. What does the woman imply when she says, "Now, you can have it all"?
(A) People can buy the product today.
(B) The exercise can help you balance your life.
(C) The yoga will help you lose weight.
(D) People can meet the expert they've been waiting for.

81. What has recently been available for customers?
(A) Autographed books
(B) Discount coupons
(C) Tickets to a live performance
(D) An online course

82. What do you have to do to get more information about the business?
(A) Visit the website
(B) Contact the store manager
(C) Stop by at the nearest location
(D) Call the following number

Questions 83 through 85 refer to the following news report.

In local news, Sun Valley will soon become a national park. On Monday, the government finally put this popular gathering place on its list of the country's protected areas. The Bureau of National Parks said this place was chosen as an ecological reserve because of its unique settings that has both recreational and scientific values. Sun Valley was one of the few places in the nation that has rare wild plants and trees that are nearly extinct in other parts of the country. Some residents however, said they were disappointed by the decision because it will increase the traffic and noise and make it difficult for local residents to enjoy the site. We will have more news after the short weather update.

83. What is the report about?
(A) Local history
(B) Gardening tips
(C) A new national park
(D) The discovery of rare plants

84. According to the speaker, what does Sun Valley have?
(A) Historic architecture
(B) Natural caves
(C) Unusual animals
(D) Unique plants

85. What do some people expect will happen?
(A) New plants and trees will be studied.
(B) The local traffic will be increased.
(C) The business in the area will be benefited from the decision.
(D) Some environment could be damaged.

Questions 86 through 88 refer to the following recorded message.

Welcome. You have reached the maintenance office of Beacon Electronics Service Center. Customer satisfaction is our number one goal. I'm afraid our office is currently closed. Our regular business hours are from Monday through Friday from 9 a.m. to 9 p.m. For frequently asked questions concerning operating your equipment, please log on to www.beaconelectrnoics.com. If you're experiencing a maintenance problem that requires immediate attention, please call our after-hour operators at 555-2394. For routine maintenance, please leave a detailed message after the recording including your name and contact number, and we will reply as soon as the office opens in the morning. Thank you for using Beacon Electronics, the number one manufacturer of reliable home electronics.

86. What is the purpose of the message?
(A) To receive customer feedback
(B) To complain about the product quality
(C) To inform customers about upcoming holidays
(D) To give information on office operations

87. What should listeners do if they need immediate help?
(A) Contact another number
(B) Leave a message after the tone
(C) Visit the emergency location
(D) Call again the next morning

88. What information should the listener provide?
(A) A registration number
(B) A name and a number
(C) The name of the store
(D) An insurance policy

Questions 89 through 91 refer to the following talk.

Well, I have an announcement before we move on to the next item on the agenda. The product design team has passed a real challenge on to us in the packaging engineering. They need a packaging for a new line of lamps that have a large decorative glass shade. Of course, it is very important to protect the glass components of the lamps, but it is also important to design the packaging that is cost-effective and visually appealing. I'll be distributing the sheet that has a drawing with the dimensions of the lamps. So review them and we'll get together this afternoon to discuss the packaging designs. I'm looking forward to hearing some fresh ideas from you guys.

89. Who most likely is the speaker?
(A) An engineer
(B) A sales agent
(C) An accounting officer
(D) A graphic designer

90. What is the talk mainly about?
(A) Boosting product sales
(B) Designing a package
(C) Drawing a new building plan
(D) Developing an advertising campaign

91. 新 What does the man imply when he says, "I'm looking forward to hearing some fresh ideas"?
(A) Employees should save some money.
(B) Employees should purchase fresh ingredients.
(C) Employees should produce new lamps.
(D) Employees should come up with new designs.

Questions 92 through 94 refer to the following talk.

Thank you all for coming on such a short notice. The sales and marketing division just informed me that the completion date for our website redesign has been moved up to next Friday. We only have about ten days before the deadline. I know this could be a bit of stress for some of you, but the management thinks that having the workable website before introducing a new line of products will be necessary. It is my job to make sure this project is finished on time with quality work. Let me know if you have any questions or concerns on your assignment. This project is our top priority over all other projects. So, if you've completed your part and have extra time, please contact my assistant Ms. Eunice at extension 857. There are still many sections that need help. Let us work together to make it a success.

92. What is the purpose of the talk?
(A) To introduce a new product
(B) To announce a change in the deadline
(C) To explain new company procedures
(D) To accept applications for a sales job

93. What is the speaker responsible for?
(A) Developing the company's website
(B) Answering customer questions
(C) Promoting company's new products
(D) Consulting with company executives

94. What should the listeners do if they have time available?
(A) Call him immediately
(B) Fill out the request form
(C) Check the website for any errors
(D) Request additional work

新 Questions 95 through 97 refer to the following announcement and map.

The city of Boston would like to inform residents of the upcoming marathon competition. This Monday, April 12th will be our 10th Boston Marathon Competition organized by the Boston Athletic Association. The traffic will be closed in many parts of the city, so we encourage you to check your travel routes before you leave home this morning. Athletes as well as citizens will leave Union Street Start Line at 10 o'clock a.m. sharp. The first winner will arrive at the finish line at Boylston Street in a little over 2 hours after the competition starts. However, the road blocks will last about 8 hours until most participants have passed the major roads including Central Street and Washington Street. For more information, please, contact BAA's office at 617-222-8473 or visit their website at www.baa.com.

95. What is this announcement about?
(A) An upcoming event
(B) A travel destination
(C) A design competition
(D) Rush hour traffic

96. 新 Look at the graphic. Where will the participants finish their race?
(A) 1
(B) 2
(C) 3
(D) 4

97. What should people with questions do?
(A) Visit the office
(B) Call the marathon manager
(C) Send an e-mail to BAA's office
(D) Contact the relevant agency

新 Questions 98 through 100 refer to the following announcement and list.

Good morning ladies and gentlemen, and welcome to the association of accountants' annual conference. I just want to make a few announcements before the morning schedule begins. Please note that the New Age Software demonstration session which was scheduled to be held in one of the conference rooms has been moved to the lobby hall to accommodate more people. Also, tickets are still available for tomorrow night's banquet. It starts at 7 in the banquet hall and the feature presenter is Mr. Marvin Klein, the author of "My life's accounts". Mr. Klein plans to have a book signing after the presentation. If you haven't purchased your ticket yet, please stop by at the registration desk set up next to the main entrance.

98. Where most likely is the announcement being made?
(A) At a musical performance
(B) At a professional conference
(C) At a software demonstration
(D) At a retirement banquet

99. 新 Look at the graphic. Which room is no longer used at today's programs?
(A) Banquet hall
(B) Conference Room B
(C) Conference Room C
(D) Dining hall

100. Where can you buy tickets for tomorrow night's event?
(A) In the banquet hall
(B) At the book signing
(C) At the product demonstration
(D) At the registration desk

1.	(D)	2.	(B)	3.	(D)	4.	(B)	5.	(C)
6.	(C)	7.	(A)	8.	(B)	9.	(A)	10.	(C)
11.	(B)	12.	(A)	13.	(A)	14.	(C)	15.	(A)
16.	(C)	17.	(B)	18.	(B)	19.	(A)	20.	(B)
21.	(A)	22.	(C)	23.	(B)	24.	(C)	25.	(A)
26.	(A)	27.	(B)	28.	(C)	29.	(B)	30.	(A)
31.	(C)	32.	(C)	33.	(D)	34.	(D)	35.	(A)
36.	(D)	37.	(A)	38.	(D)	39.	(B)	40.	(D)
41.	(A)	42.	(C)	43.	(D)	44.	(A)	45.	(C)
46.	(B)	47.	(A)	48.	(D)	49.	(B)	50.	(C)
51.	(B)	52.	(C)	53.	(A)	54.	(C)	55.	(D)
56.	(C)	57.	(B)	58.	(D)	59.	(D)	60.	(D)
61.	(A)	62.	(C)	63.	(B)	64.	(D)	65.	(B)
66.	(C)	67.	(B)	68.	(C)	69.	(C)	70.	(D)
71.	(A)	72.	(C)	73.	(D)	74.	(C)	75.	(A)
76.	(D)	77.	(C)	78.	(B)	79.	(D)	80.	(C)
81.	(B)	82.	(D)	83.	(C)	84.	(C)	85.	(D)
86.	(B)	87.	(C)	88.	(D)	89.	(D)	90.	(B)
91.	(C)	92.	(A)	93.	(C)	94.	(C)	95.	(D)
96.	(D)	97.	(C)	98.	(C)	99.	(D)	100.	(A)

Part 1

1.
(A) The man is walking in his office.
(B) The man is writing on the board.
(C) The man is signing his name.
(D) The man is working at his desk.

2.
(A) They are taking photographs in the office.
(B) They are facing the opposite directions.
(C) The woman is handing some papers to the man.
(D) The man is making some notes on a piece of paper.

3.
(A) A vehicle is driving through the country road.
(B) Stonewalls are standing along the street.
(C) Trees have been planted around a house.
(D) Tracks have been left on the ground.

4.
(A) The man is scrubbing the floor.
(B) Leaves are being raked into a pile.
(C) The man is trimming tree branches.
(D) Trees are being planted in a garden.

5.
(A) The woman is pushing some buttons.
(B) The woman is reaching into her bag.
(C) A machine is located against the wall.
(D) The food is being served at a restaurant.

6.
(A) The building is being demolished.
(B) The construction has not been finished.
(C) The structure has multiple levels.
(D) There are no railings on the balconies.

Part 2

7. When is the safety inspection this month?
(A) Friday morning.
(B) At the main factory floor.
(C) Next month's budget.

8. Excuse me, can you help me find my seat?
(A) Thanks, but I'd rather stay here.
(B) Certainly, please follow me.
(C) How long would it take to finish?

9. Would you like anything from our dessert menu?
(A) I'll just have some coffee.
(B) The bakery doesn't open until 10.
(C) Yes, I'd like to see him in a black suit.

10. Do you know any pharmacies around here?
(A) No, we've never met before.
(B) The doctor gave me this prescription.
(C) There's one on Emerson Street.

11. Did you proofread the manuscript from George Sampson?
(A) We don't have enough proof for now.
(B) Yes, I made some corrections too.
(C) Yes, George has published two books.

12. Isn't that your umbrella in the corner?
(A) Mine was broken.
(B) It's not raining outside.
(C) The forecast will be on in 5 minutes.

13. What construction project are you involved in?
(A) We're building a recreation center.
(B) I didn't read the instructions.
(C) The projected budget is 5 million dollars.

14. Did you make it to the Valarie's party last night?
(A) Sorry, we didn't have enough supplies.
(B) Actually, tomorrow is better for me.
(C) No, the traffic was really bad.

15. Weren't you at the international job fair last month?
(A) Yes, were you too?
(B) I was transferred to that department.
(C) No, the offering prices were too low.

16. Where is the national conference being held this year?
(A) From August 2nd through August 5th.
(B) To introduce a new line of products.
(C) They're still considering some options.

17. The attendant was just here, wasn't he?
(A) I think the address was wrong.
(B) No, he left an hour ago.
(C) Yes, It's just the right size.

18. Why didn't we order new printer for the sales team?
(A) We should make at least twenty copies.
(B) We couldn't get the manager's approval.
(C) The employees are getting trainings.

19. You went to the lecture, didn't you?
(A) You mean the one Mr. Bean gave?
(B) Yes, put it over here.
(C) The weather is awesome.

20. Why are the applications on Mr. Kim's desk?
(A) He doesn't like the applicant.
(B) He wants to review them one more time.
(C) The position needs much experience.

21. Do you know who's in charge of recording the actual performance?
(A) I think I am.
(B) You could put it on your credit card.
(C) Maria Sanchez gave an excellent speech.

22. How do you fill the printer when it's out of paper?
(A) It's temporarily out of service.
(B) We should call the technician right away.
(C) It goes in the drawer on the bottom.

23. The fax machine isn't working any more.
(A) Can you send it by faster delivery?
(B) I thought it was fixed last week.
(C) Do you like working here so far?

208

24. How many people are expected to show up at the training seminar?
(A) They are showing it every two hours.
(B) For the next 6 to 8 months.
(C) Everyone from the sales division.

25. Would you like me to show you how to set up the new accounting program?
(A) Thanks, I'm having trouble with it.
(B) The software has a good reputation.
(C) Yes, that's a great team.

26. The apartment will be available in July.
(A) Is it for sale or for lease?
(B) They moved in recently.
(C) I'll just take a small part.

27. Couldn't we reschedule our meeting for tomorrow?
(A) Please bring your briefcase.
(B) Actually, I'll be visiting the Milan office.
(C) How did the meeting go?

28. Would you like to go to the cafeteria, or do you want to go out for lunch?
(A) Yes, the lunch was delicious.
(B) That place is known to be famous.
(C) Actually, I brought some sandwiches.

29. Has Mr. Wills been notified of the promotion?
(A) We didn't know each other then.
(B) I told him in person at the morning meeting.
(C) Yes, we have updated the program.

30. Are you busy with your work now, or can you help me move these boxes?
(A) I'll be done in a few minutes.
(B) Let's order some more supplies today.
(C) The shipment got delayed at the port.

31. We have introduced a new line of women's wear this month, haven't we?
(A) Next month is our 20th anniversary.
(B) Yes, the introduction was brief but efficient.
(C) Yes, and we are expecting high sales.

Part 3

Questions 32 through 34 refer to the following conversation.

M   Hi, Jill. How's your apartment search going?
W   Well, I've been looking all over the places, but the rents for the ones close to downtown are just too high.
M   Some of my friends had some luck in finding reasonably priced apartment through the Internet. There's a few websites I could recommend. Maybe you should try to check them out.
W   My lease will expire at the end of this month. I'm ready to do anything.

32. What are the speakers discussing?
(A) Looking for a job
(B) Designing a website
(C) Finding a place to live
(D) Maintaining a personal relationship

33. What problem does the woman mention?
(A) Unfriendly landlord
(B) Small space
(C) Long commute
(D) High prices

34. What will the woman most likely do next?
(A) Talk to a leasing agent
(B) Call the man's friends
(C) Hire some professional help
(D) Consult some websites

新 Questions 35 through 37 refer to the following conversation with three speakers.

W1   Hello, Is this Office Master? My name is Marianne and I'd like to talk to Mr. Richard Ford. He is supposed give me more information about the business cards I'm planning to order for the next month's event.
W2   I'm sorry, but Mr. Ford has already left for the day. He works only until 4 on Friday. Could I help you with anything?
W1   I really need to finalize the design. Otherwise I won't be able to hand out my cards during the trade show in two weeks.
W2   In that case, do you want me to refer you to another consultant to help you choose what you want? Mr. Stevens has been working at our firm for a long time and he is available at the moment.
W1   Yes, please.
W2   Hold on for a moment.
M   Hello, this is Patrick Stevens. I heard you need some help choosing the right design for your card.
W1   Yes, I've looked at the samples on your website and picked up three of my favorites, but I can't narrow it down any more.
M   You've done great. Why don't we go through the ones you choose and then we start from there? Can you read the model number of each design you choose?

35. What does Marianne want to discuss with Mr. Ford?
(A) The details of an order
(B) The designs of a catalog
(C) A schedule change
(D) Upcoming business meetings

36. Why is Mr. Ford unavailable at this time?
(A) He's out of town.
(B) He has a doctor's appointment.
(C) He's helping other customers.
(D) He has left work for the day.

37. What does the man ask Marianne to do?
(A) Provide information on her preferences
(B) Look at the product brochures
(C) Modify the design to show the company logo
(D) Pay for the business cards she ordered

Questions 38 through 40 refer to the following conversation.

M   Hey, Cindy. Would you like to see a concert on Saturday at a civic center? A local band is giving a charity concert for the Children's Cancer Foundation.
W   That sounds a lot of fun, but my cousin is visiting me from out of state and I have to spend the weekend with her.
M   Why don't we invite your cousin too? Nobody can really say no to a night of music and fun. Do you want me to check whether they still have tickets?
W   Thanks, could you do that for me? I'll call my cousin and see if she's interested.

38. What are the speakers discussing?
(A) Reservation for a hotel
(B) Donation to a charity
(C) A famous performer
(D) Plan for the weekend

39. Who is the woman scheduled to meet?
(A) A band member
(B) A relative
(C) An overseas sales associate
(D) A travel agent

40. What does the man offer to find out?
(A) Arrival time of a plane
(B) Location of the concert
(C) Price for a trip
(D) Ticket availability

Questions 41 through 43 refer to the following conversation.

M Hi, I ordered a pair of glasses last week and they haven't arrived yet. My name is David Morris.
W Yes, Mr. Morris. I'm afraid the particular model you have ordered is currently out of stock and will take another two weeks to have them shipped from overseas.
M Really? I need those glasses as soon as possible. Do you have any other products similar to the ones I have ordered?
W Let me check our online database to give you better suggestions.
M I also want to find out whether there would be an extra charge.

41. What is the purpose of the call?
(A) To check the status of his order
(B) To order more products
(C) To find out prices of new glasses
(D) To get an accurate estimate of a job

42. What is the problem with the product?
(A) Its price has increased.
(B) It has been shipped to a wrong place.
(C) It's unavailable at the moment.
(D) They offer special prices online.

43. What will the woman do next?
(A) Order glasses for him
(B) Cancel the previous order
(C) Send out the shipment
(D) Log on to a computer

Questions 44 through 46 refer to the following conversation.

M Michelle, I'd like to leave for the airport as soon as the meeting is over. How about we grab a cab in front of the office around 3:00?
W We'll arrive way too early if we leave then. Our flight doesn't depart until 7.
M Yes, but we'll avoid rush hour traffic. The traffic will be worse today because of the unexpected rain.
W But if the weather gets much worse, the flight might be delayed, too. Why don't I check the online weather information to make sure nothing out of the ordinary happens today?

44. Where does this conversation take place?
(A) At an office
(B) At the airport
(C) At a taxi stand
(D) At a bus terminal

45. Why does the man want to leave early?
(A) He likes to get on the plane early.
(B) He doesn't like to hurry at the last minute.
(C) He's afraid the traffic will be bad.
(D) He wants to try a new way to the airport.

46. What will the woman do next?
(A) Check the airline information
(B) Log on to the Internet
(C) Contact a travel agency
(D) Change the flight schedule

Questions 47 through 49 refer to the following conversation.

W Hello, I bought this book because it had a 30% discount tag on it. When I got home, I realized that I've been overcharged. So, I'm back today with my receipt to clear things up.
M Oh, I'm sorry about that. We had a problem with our cash registers yesterday. Let me refund you the difference now.
W By the way, I noticed that a new café section of the store is finally open. I've been looking forward to it. The pastries smell really good.
M Actually, we offer a free cup of coffee to celebrate the opening of a café.
W Really? I should go and check it out right now.

47. Why does the woman say, "I'm back today with my receipt to clear things up"?
(A) She wants to obtain a refund.
(B) She's here to purchase new books.
(C) She's already talked with the manager.
(D) She is complaining about the product quality.

48. What does the woman notice while she is in the store?
(A) Merchandize has been rearranged.
(B) Only a few cashiers are on duty.
(C) The store is unusually crowded.
(D) A new section of the store has opened.

49. What is being offered today?
(A) A signed copy of a best-selling book
(B) A free beverage for all customers
(C) A discount coupon for a future purchase
(D) A complimentary piece of cake

新 Questions 50 through 52 refer to the following conversation with three speakers.

M1 Elizabeth, Ray, I wanted to talk to you about the cycling tour of the city that our bike shop is leading this month. How is it coming along?
M2 Yes, I'm almost done with flight and hotel arrangement of the tour.
M1 I noticed you adjusted the tour itinerary by removing the visit to the community park.
W Yes, the park is just too far away. It takes about 30 minutes to bike there, so there wouldn't be enough time to see everything.
M1 I understand your point. But I think it's important that our customers here at the bike shop get to know the places in the city that are good for cycling.
W Well, we could make flyers that include detailed directions on how to get to the park on the new path and hand them out here in the shop. That way, people could go by themselves on another day if they want to.
M1 Or, we could change the path to include the park. Ray, I want you to find out how much time is left before we finalize the plan.
M2 Yes, I'll do that.

50. Where most likely do the speakers work?
(A) At a community park
(B) At a gift shop
(C) At a bicycle store
(D) At a travel agency

51. Why did the woman change a plan?
(A) A tour guide is unavailable.
(B) A location is too far.
(C) The facility is closed.
(D) The admission fee is too expensive.

52. What does the woman suggest?
(A) Talking to some customers
(B) Finding a new employee
(C) Providing a handout
(D) Changing the bikes

Questions 53 through 55 refer to the following conversation.

> **W** Good morning, James. The supervisor at the construction site just called. He said he needs the updated building plan before he orders any supplies.
> **M** Yes, we just finished revising the plan this morning but I'll be in another meeting for the rest of the morning. So, I was thinking about taking it to the site myself and show him after lunch.
> **W** Well, I think the supervisor needs to look at it before then. Why don't you give it to me and I'd be happy to deliver it to him this morning? You can have a conversation with him through the phone later on.
> **M** Will you do that for me? Thank you.

53. What message does the woman give the man?
(A) A document is needed.
(B) A supervisor is not available.
(C) The construction is behind schedule.
(D) A meeting has to be held.

54. What was recently updated?
(A) A contact list
(B) Budget figures
(C) A building plan
(D) Construction equipment

55. What does the woman offer?
(A) She would call the supervisor.
(B) She would write the report.
(C) She would postpone the construction.
(D) She would make a delivery.

Questions 56 through 58 refer to the following conversation.

> **W** I'm looking forward to moving into our new bookstore. It's right in the middle of the shopping district, so the location is fantastic. We will have so much more customers.
> **M** Right, but I just hope we get everything packed before the movers come tomorrow. We've only packed half of the books and we also need to take apart all these shelves today.
> **W** Haven't you heard? We just have to pack books because they wouldn't know how to organize them. But, everything else including bookshelves will be handled by movers.
> **M** Well, that's good news. I would be so relieved when everything is over and when the new store opens up next week.
> **W** Me too, let's hope for the best.

56. What does woman imply when she says, "We will have so much more customers"?
(A) Customers will like the new book.
(B) The discount sale will take place soon.
(C) The relocation will help the business.
(D) The woman likes to shop at his store.

57. What is the man concerned about?
(A) Reducing operating costs
(B) Completing the work in time
(C) Ordering new books for business
(D) Hiring maintenance staff

58. What will happen next week?
(A) A new manager will come.
(B) Customers can order products.
(C) New furniture will be delivered.
(D) A new store will open.

Questions 59 through 61 refer to the following conversation.

> **W** Hello, My name is Tammy and I'm calling from Summerset Public Library to ask if your business would consider making a donation to our renovation project.
> **M** Oh, yes. I heard news about it the other day. The library needs a new reading room for children, right?
> **W** That is correct. Our community has a growing number of children and we don't have any place to accommodate them. We already collected some books from last month's charity events but we don't have enough funding to add a new reading room to our facility.
> **M** I think it's important to support community projects. Where should I send a check?

59. What is the purpose of the call?
(A) To attract more customers
(B) To promote an upcoming event
(C) To offer an cost estimate
(D) To raise money for a project

60. What would the library like to do?
(A) Survey its members
(B) Hold special workshops
(C) Buy more books
(D) Expand its facility

61. What does the man mean when he says, "it's important to support the community projects"?
(A) He will donate some money for a cause.
(B) He used to work at the library.
(C) He has children of his own.
(D) He will write a book about the story.

Questions 62 through 64 refer to the following conversation.

> **W** Did you hear the news? Our company and TXA Electronics are discussing a merger. I just talk to Mr. Morales about it.
> **M** Yes, I heard it at the manager's meeting yesterday. Later this week, they are going to officially announce the results of the merger negotiation.
> **W** Wow. I didn't know our company and TXA have any common interests. I wonder our jobs would be affected by this deal. I've been working here only for about a year.
> **M** Don't worry. At the manager's meeting, the same topic was brought up. Our jobs would probably be the same. The only major change is that our department will be in charge of training employees from TXA on our manufacturing procedure.

62. What is the conversation mainly about?
(A) Launching a new product
(B) A training schedule
(C) A possible business deal
(D) An employee evaluation

63. What will happen later this week?
(A) A procedure will be reviewed.
(B) A public announcement will be made.
(C) They will be moving into a new building.
(D) New employees will be hired.

64. What new task might the speakers be responsible for?
(A) Negotiating contract terms
(B) Making production manuals
(C) Arranging press conferences
(D) Holding training sessions

TEST 08

M Alice, I lost my mobile phone on the train yesterday and I need a new one as soon as possible. Can you recommend a store where I can get a dependable one?

W Try the Ericsson Store on Boylston Avenue. It's a bit far from the office, but they carry all the latest lines and the prices are quite affordable.

M Oh, I think that's the place where I bought my computer before. I don't remember exactly where the store is located.

W It's not that difficult. Just go down Highway 95 until you see the Mayhem Shopping center, then get off the next exit. The store should be on your right once you make a left onto the Boylston Avenue.

65. What does the man want to purchase?
(A) A television set
(B) A cellular phone
(C) A briefcase
(D) A phone card

66. Why does the woman recommend Ericsson Store?
(A) It carries on the products from major manufacturers.
(B) It is close to the office.
(C) The prices are reasonable.
(D) The staff members are dependable.

67. 新 Look at the graphic. Which exit should the man take to get to Ericsson Store?
(A) Exit 11
(B) Exit 12
(C) Exit 13
(D) Exit 14

M Hi Sally, this is Martin, your editor for *World Business Magazine*. Can we talk now?

W Sure, I have a minute.

M Great. Would you be able to increase the word count for your "Smart Money" article to 3,000 words? Our readers are very much interested in your investment strategy.

W OK, there's plenty to cover on the topic. But I have another article due that same day.

M Yes, I saw that on your assignment chart. Here's what I'm going to do. Let's extend the deadline for your other assignment by a week. You should be able to focus on the "Money" article.

W Thanks. I really appreciate it. By the way, I've been compiling some ideas for pieces to write. I'll send them to you later today for some feedback.

68. What does the man ask the woman to do?
(A) Purchase the newspaper subscription
(B) Make arrangements for a meeting
(C) Increase the length of an article
(D) Correct a mistake in a document

69. 新 Look at the graphic. Which article's deadline will be changed?
(A) The Presidential Candidates
(B) Smart Money
(C) Nature Walk in New Zealand
(D) TECH Gizmo

70. What does the woman say she will give to the man?
(A) An itinerary
(B) Customer survey results
(C) Notes from a meeting
(D) Ideas for future articles

Part 4

Questions 71 through 73 refer to the following advertisement.

Tired of using your old vacuum cleaner? Try new Euro-Speed, ES-200 vacuum cleaner! The ES-200 is light weight and easy to handle. It has more power than any other hand-held vacuum cleaners in the market and will clean faster than you could imagine. Recently featured in the new product section on Quality Appliance Magazine, the ES-200 is the hottest item on the market. And if you call today, you'll receive 20% savings from the retail price. So, call 555-2343 right now and get your own Euro-Speed today.

71. What is being advertised?
(A) A cleaning device
(B) Magazine subscription
(C) Office supplies
(D) A ticket outlet

72. Where was the product recently featured?
(A) In a newspaper
(B) In a promotional flyer
(C) In a professional magazine
(D) In a company newsletter

73. What is offered today?
(A) Extra dust bags
(B) Free deliver service
(C) Personal consultation
(D) A discounted price

Questions 74 through 76 refer to the following announcement.

Attention passengers, the blue line train to DuPont Circle will be delayed for 30 minutes due to unexpected railway condition changes. We recommend the passengers take the red line train from this station, and transfer to the blue line at East river Station. Be sure to pick up your free transfer voucher at the customer service desk here before you board the red line. The customer service desk is located on the basement 1 and can be reached from any exits in the station. Again, the blue line train for DuPont Circle will be 30 minutes late. We're sorry for your inconvenience.

74. Why is this announcement being made?
(A) Passengers cannot find right trains.
(B) Special promotion is being announced.
(C) Some transportation will be delayed for a while.
(D) A maintenance job will be conducted.

75. What should listeners do at East river Street Station?
(A) Change trains
(B) Receive special vouchers
(C) Exit the station
(D) Find the conductor

76. Why are the listeners asked to go to the customer service desk?
(A) To get a map of train lines
(B) To pick up their luggage
(C) To buy tickets to the next destination
(D) To receive a transfer coupon

Questions 77 through 79 refer to the following talk.

Welcome everyone to our special banquet this evening honoring Mr. Doug Hanson. As you know Doug Hanson made a great impact on our organization. During 25 years of his service at our company, he served many positions and helped many employees. Especially for the last 5 years as the accounting executive director, he did a lot to cut unnecessary cost for the organization and return the profits to its rightful owners, shareholders, employees and customers. Although we will miss him a lot, he'll be very busy after his retirement. I know personally he will be looking forward to pursuing his other interests including painting and photographing. And starting next month, he will also help Max Publishing as a part time consultant. So, join me and congratulate Doug on his successful career and more successful future life.

77. Where is this speech probably being given?
(A) At a product demonstration
(B) At a shareholders' meeting
(C) At a retirement dinner
(D) At a customer appreciation banquet

78. What has Doug done for the last 5 years?
(A) He increased the company sales.
(B) He reduced the expenses.
(C) He consulted many clients.
(D) He developed a new program.

79. What will Doug Hanson do next month?
(A) Travel around the world
(B) Come back and visit his colleagues
(C) Run his own business
(D) Start a part-time job

Questions 80 through 82 refer to the following talk.

Good morning and welcome to the first of four training sessions for our company's new database system. This software was designed by the Tokyo branch of our Information Technology Department. As sales staff, you must know the importance of accurate data management to socialize and manage your customers. You'll get to do this and much more after one month of training. Today, after the general introduction, we'll learn data entry procedures. Later on, we'll learn to sort them out in a customized way to help you, and make impressive printouts with it. If you experience any difficulties during or after the class, please contact the technology help center, or send an e-mail to our department. Now let's begin.

80. What does the speaker indicate about the software?
(A) It's been introduced to the market before.
(B) It does not have any difficult functions.
(C) It was developed by an overseas office.
(D) Customers would be interested in buying it.

81. What will the listeners learn to do first today?
(A) Communicate with each other
(B) Enter the data into the system
(C) Mail the letters to customers
(D) Sort the information into different groups

82. According to the speaker, what should listeners do if they have problems?
(A) Call the man
(B) Refer to the manual
(C) Check the website
(D) Contact the help center

Questions 83 through 85 refer to the following telephone message.

Hi Mary, this is Jenna from the Harrisburg Community Book Club. It is Monday at 5 o'clock. I'm calling to let you know that we had to reschedule this week's book club meeting. Something came up at my house. So, rather than meeting at my house on Thursday, we'll be meeting at Michelle's house on Friday at 7:00 p.m., our regular time. Sorry for the confusion. Just to remind you that we will be talking about "A light in September" by John Faulkner. If you can't make it on the new date, please call Michelle so that she will know how many people she can expect at the meeting. I hope to see you there. Good Bye.

83. What is the purpose of this telephone message?
(A) To inquire about the food order
(B) To suggest a new book for the meeting
(C) To notify a member of a change
(D) To introduce a new member to the club

84. 新 What does the woman mean when she says, "sorry for the confusion"?
(A) She's sorry to change the book of the discussion.
(B) She was confused about the direction she got before.
(C) She had to change the venue because of her personal reason.
(D) She's late for the meeting and wants to make up for it.

85. What can be inferred about John Faulkner?
(A) He is a new member.
(B) He will be at the meeting.
(C) He has a house in the area.
(D) He writes stories.

Questions 86 through 88 refer to the following telephone message.

Hi, Mr. Norris, this is Miki Ayako from Creative Advertising. You recently completed one of our firm's online surveys. Based on your responses and demography, we're inviting you to take part in a focus group discussion. Our firm is preparing an advertising campaign to promote a new product from a famous automobile company. We'd like to show you three different commercials on a new product and get your reactions to them. The session will take about an hour and you'll be getting 100 dollar worth of gift certificate that can be used in any local stores and departments in the area. We value your feedback. Please call me back by Friday at 555-2353 to let me know you're interested.

86. What type of company does the speaker work for?
(A) A news station
(B) An advertising company
(C) An automobile manufacturer
(D) A certified dealership

87. Why is the speaker contacting Mr. Norris?
(A) To encourage him to buy a new product
(B) To offer him a special deal
(C) To ask him to participate in a discussion
(D) To provide him with more information about the meeting

88. What is Mr. Norris asked to do by Friday?
(A) Submit a payment
(B) Visit a website
(C) Mail a registration form
(D) Return a phone call

Questions 89 through 91 refer to the following advertisement.

Bestville Apartment Complex is known for its quite and scenic location under the hills of Blue Mountain where hikers are dreaming of going. Now, in addition to the charming surroundings at the park, a limited number of furnished units have been updated with brand new high-tech home appliances – a flat screen TV, a refrigerator, a washer and a drier. These new updated units are available for rent starting this March. You'll love living in Bestville Apartment Complex where all residents have free access to our swimming pool and spa center. You can also bring in your guests with a minimum fee. To schedule a tour, call 555-3245.

89. Where does the speaker say Bestville Complex is located?
(A) In a downtown neighborhood
(B) Close to a shopping mall
(C) Next to a public transportation
(D) Near a famous mountain

90. What does the man imply when he says, "These new updated units are available"?
(A) They have just built a new apartment complex.
(B) Some units have been remodeled.
(C) They are selling appliances at the lowest prices.
(D) Some information was printed incorrectly.

91. According to the speaker, what is free for all residents of Bestville Complex?
(A) A storage space
(B) Free Internet access
(C) A swimming facility
(D) Parking spaces

新 Questions 92 through 94 refer to the following talk and schedule.

Thank you for coming. I wanted to meet with you to talk about your next assignment. Four of you will form a project team for The Grill W restaurant. The client has hired our architectural firm to remodel their first floor main hall before the start of the next tour season. Grill W has many international tourists and they want the main hall to have the atmosphere of more traditional western steak house. I already put together the intended timelines of work involved. Let me give you the copies of schedule now. However, please note that after talking with the owner of the restaurant, we've decided that the time for carpeting and vinyl flooring should be shortened by one day. This way, we can still have three days for clean-up. We will go through the timelines together. So if you have any questions or concerns, let me know. Let's do our best to deliver the quality service and meet the client's deadline at the same time.

92. Where does the speaker work?
(A) An architectural firm
(B) A restaurant
(C) A tourist center
(D) A convention center

93. What is the speaker mainly discussing?
(A) Hosting a big scale banquet
(B) Organizing an international convention
(C) Renovating a property
(D) Relocating to a new facility

94. Look at the graphic. How long will the duration for Carpets & Vinyl floor?
(A) Two days
(B) Three days
(C) Four days
(D) Five days

新 Questions 95 through 97 refer to the following talk and list.

Thank you all for coming to today's demonstration. I'm so glad to be a part of the 2012 Job Fair for local businesses. My name is Stanley and the program I'm going to show you today is our newest product "M-Pro" series and I will help your company or agency to manage your applicants' database more efficiently than ever. It has sorting options for all levels including regions, ages, and language abilities. It also has online features that will search and match other applicants who have similar qualifications and skills and how much they're getting paid. Especially, you're managing a number of applicants such as more than 500, M-Pro Intensive would really be helpful. Through this innovative software, you can evaluate your applicant's more efficiently and objectively. Before we begin, I'd like to recommend you to keep the copy of our flyer to get a 10% discount on purchasing any of the M-pro series.

95. Where would you hear this message?
(A) At a new employees' workshop
(B) In a language classroom
(C) At a press conference
(D) At a local job fair

96. What is the purpose of the talk?
(A) To inform participants of a closing
(B) To sort people into different groups
(C) To warn employees about a possible danger
(D) To show the features of a product

97. Look at the graphic. How much would a participant with a flyer pay for M-Pro Intensive?
(A) $ 60.00
(B) $ 80.00
(C) $ 90.00
(D) $ 100.00

新 Questions 98 through 100 refer to the following excerpt from a meeting and chart.

Now let's move on. I reviewed our quarterly sales figures yesterday and I'm happy to report that our sales increased dramatically compared to those of the previous year. Sales of most of the frozen food in the supermarket have continued to be strong, but it's the sales of the veggie platter, fish and seafood dinners that have led the sales drive. Particularly, the newly introduced product showed the most growth in the same period and indicated how much it was loved by healthy conscious women and men in their 20s and 30s. I think the trend to choose healthy menus over traditional high calorie dishes will continue. Because they proved to be so popular, we're planning to offer healthy dessert lines, such as fruit sherbet or yogurt to our customers. We want to test customers' interest before we start the new line. So next week, we'll begin doing some market research by using online surveys through our website.

98. What did the speaker review yesterday?
(A) Product samples
(B) An advertising proposal
(C) Some sales data
(D) A new website

99. Look at the graphic. Which item was most loved by health conscious customers?
(A) Yogurt and Sherbet
(B) Fish fillet
(C) Meat dish
(D) Veggie platter

100. What is the purpose of the survey?
(A) To determine customer interest in new products
(B) To identify the market for frozen food
(C) To find the best way to attract new customers
(D) To ask about the recent sales experience

214

1.	(B)	2.	(D)	3.	(D)	4.	(C)	5.	(A)
6.	(D)	7.	(B)	8.	(A)	9.	(A)	10.	(B)
11.	(B)	12.	(A)	13.	(B)	14.	(A)	15.	(C)
16.	(A)	17.	(C)	18.	(A)	19.	(B)	20.	(A)
21.	(C)	22.	(A)	23.	(A)	24.	(B)	25.	(C)
26.	(A)	27.	(B)	28.	(C)	29.	(A)	30.	(C)
31.	(C)	32.	(D)	33.	(A)	34.	(C)	35.	(B)
36.	(D)	37.	(C)	38.	(D)	39.	(B)	40.	(C)
41.	(C)	42.	(A)	43.	(D)	44.	(D)	45.	(C)
46.	(B)	47.	(D)	48.	(C)	49.	(D)	50.	(A)
51.	(C)	52.	(D)	53.	(C)	54.	(A)	55.	(D)
56.	(A)	57.	(D)	58.	(C)	59.	(B)	60.	(C)
61.	(A)	62.	(B)	63.	(C)	64.	(C)	65.	(D)
66.	(C)	67.	(B)	68.	(B)	69.	(C)	70.	(A)
71.	(D)	72.	(C)	73.	(A)	74.	(C)	75.	(D)
76.	(D)	77.	(A)	78.	(C)	79.	(D)	80.	(A)
81.	(C)	82.	(D)	83.	(C)	84.	(B)	85.	(D)
86.	(C)	87.	(D)	88.	(B)	89.	(D)	90.	(D)
91.	(A)	92.	(C)	93.	(D)	94.	(D)	95.	(D)
96.	(B)	97.	(D)	98.	(C)	99.	(D)	100.	(A)

Part 1

1. (A) The road is being improved.
   (B) The man is pushing a wheelbarrow.
   (C) The man is moving some bricks.
   (D) The lumbers have been stacked on the ground.

2. (A) Travelers are waiting to check into a hotel.
   (B) Passengers are lining up to board a plane.
   (C) The woman is pulling her luggage up the stairs.
   (D) Some people are standing next to the luggage.

3. (A) Construction vehicles are approaching the site.
   (B) A road is being resurfaced.
   (C) A hole is being covered with plastic sheets.
   (D) Pipes have been placed in a trench.

4. (A) The men are sitting next to each other.
   (B) The men are facing each other.
   (C) One man is leaning over the table.
   (D) One man is dictating a letter to the other.

5. (A) Bicycles have been secured to metal posts.
   (B) Bicycles are being parked near a building.
   (C) Bushes have been trimmed in a garden.
   (D) Tires have been discarded from the bicycles.

6. (A) They are stacking papers into a pile.
   (B) They are organizing meeting schedules.
   (C) They are participating in a sport competition.
   (D) Some people have turned away from the windows.

Part 2

7. Who is supposed to participate in the marketing seminar?
   (A) It was Ms. Santos' idea.
   (B) Anyone who's interested.
   (C) The registration fee is free.

8. Why wasn't this report sent to Mr. Hwang?
   (A) It needs to be reviewed first.
   (B) Because the reporter isn't here yet.
   (C) Sure, I could send it to him.

9. When did contractors get here?
   (A) Early this morning.
   (B) Sign at the bottom of the page.
   (C) It will take about a week.

10. What's in those boxes we have received today?
    (A) Let's put them in different boxes.
    (B) New office supplies we had ordered.
    (C) You should send them right away.

11. I'd like to cancel my reservation, please.
    (A) Sorry, we don't have any tables available.
    (B) May I have your name, please?
    (C) Sure, the number is 555-1212.

12. Do you know where the orientation is being held?
    (A) Sure, follow me.
    (B) It'll be finished in an hour.
    (C) Yes, let's organize a party.

13. Would you like to take this yourself, or do you want it to be delivered?
    (A) I can't take the bus.
    (B) I'll pick it up later on.
    (C) There will be some delivery charge.

14. This is the key to the stockroom, isn't it?
    (A) No, use the one with a blue tag.
    (B) No, the sales are over now.
    (C) Yes, let's put them in the stockroom.

15. Who's supporting this charity function?
    (A) The machine is malfunctioning.
    (B) It will be held in the Marriot Hotel.
    (C) Georgia Foundation is.

16. Have all the guests arrived yet?
    (A) They're waiting in the other room.
    (B) My guess is as good as yours.
    (C) There is a musical performance in the theater.

17. The show begins at 8 o'clock, doesn't it?
    (A) He's a great performer.
    (B) We should take the next flight.
    (C) The time should be on the ticket.

18. How often do you attend the company's professional seminars?
    (A) Whenever I have time.
    (B) About the sales projection.
    (C) I'd love to participate.

19. Which company should we select to provide food for our company event?
    (A) We have a variety of selections.
    (B) The Loretta Catering did a good job before.
    (C) It'll be held next Sunday.

20. Haven't you read that novel before?
    (A) Yes, but I liked it so much I'm reading it again.
    (B) No, I've never met him before.
    (C) It was the best movie I've ever seen.

21. Is the convenience store on Main Street open 24 hours a day?
    (A) When would be convenient for you?
    (B) No, we have to make the reservation in advance.
    (C) Yes, but it closes on some holidays.

22. I just found out that our flight has been delayed.
    (A) For how long?
    (B) No, I couldn't find it.
    (C) Let's meet at the lobby.

23. Why weren't you at the budget meeting for the board?
    (A) There was an emergency at the Omaha branch.
    (B) The meeting was held at the main conference room.
    (C) Sure, I'll look over the figures one more time.

24. Haven't you booked your flight to Milwaukee yet?
(A) Yes, the airport has been changed.
(B) Actually, I just did it.
(C) It was announced just yesterday.

25. Have you contacted the insurance agency, or do you want me to call them?
(A) No, I didn't like the terms in the contract.
(B) Did you use the right number?
(C) I already had a talk with them.

26. Why don't we use an electric screwdriver to assemble the table?
(A) I have one in my toolbox.
(B) I prefer to go alone.
(C) The appliance should be stored in the back.

27. Could you hand out conference materials to the participants waiting at the registration?
(A) There will be 50 dollar fee.
(B) I'm afraid I won't be able to.
(C) Thanks, but I already have one.

28. We should check the inventory before we order more merchandise.
(A) Yes, the technician will be here soon.
(B) We have a fully equipped facility.
(C) I'll have it done right away.

29. There's no more paper in the supply cabinet.
(A) Maria is in charge of keeping it stocked.
(B) Who used the last ink cartridge?
(C) I read it in the newspaper this morning.

30. Why don't we start on the marketing project today?
(A) The market doesn't open on the weekends.
(B) I think she is the new project leader.
(C) Actually, the budget analysis needs to be done first.

31. Didn't Amy Peterson do a great job of representing our firm at the convention?
(A) I didn't get the job I wanted.
(B) Yes, let's register for the seminar right away.
(C) Yes, she is an effective presenter.

Part 3

Questions 32 through 34 refer to the following conversation.

M Jennifer, I need you to reschedule my 10 o'clock client to another time. I have to see someone at the hospital.
W Sure, Dr. Bernard. What time do you want me to change it to? Would 2 o'clock in the afternoon be good for you?
M Actually, I should be able to be back to the office by 2, so let's make that appointment at 3. I need some time to review Ms. Harrison's file before I see her.
W OK, sir. I'll ask her to come at 3.

32. What does the man ask the woman to do?
(A) Check the flight schedule
(B) Reserve a seat at a restaurant
(C) Go to see a doctor at the hospital
(D) Change the appointment time

33. What will the man do tomorrow morning at 10 a.m.?
(A) Visit a hospital
(B) Meet a client
(C) Wait in the lobby
(D) Go over some file

34. When will the man be back to the office?
(A) At 12:00 p.m.
(B) At 1:00 p.m.
(C) At 2:00 p.m.
(D) At 3:00 p.m.

Questions 35 through 37 refer to the following conversation.

M I just read an e-mail from the customer who complained about our restaurant's slow service. Although she was happy with food quality and atmosphere, she said she wouldn't recommend our place.
W I got similar comments from other customers when they leave the restaurant. Maybe we should hire more staff during the dinner serving time.
M That's actually a very good idea. But we will need to come up with a proposal requesting more staff.
W Let's get together this afternoon to finish the report. We can make the formal request to the general manager tomorrow.

35. Where do the speakers most likely work?
(A) At a post office
(B) At a restaurant
(C) At an employment agency
(D) At a marketing firm

36. What does the woman suggest?
(A) Find a reliable supplier
(B) Improve food quality
(C) Change serving staff
(D) Hire more people

37. What are they going to do this afternoon?
(A) Talk to more customers
(B) Change dinner schedules
(C) Write some documents
(D) Meet with the general manager

Questions 38 through 40 refer to the following conversation.

W Hello, I'm calling about the ad I saw in the newspaper about your interior design classes. Can you tell me more about your classes?
M Of course, I'd be glad to. First semester starts in 2 weeks and you have to take 2 required courses and 3 selective courses. We offer a professional diploma once you finish the one year full time classes.
W Oh. Do you have any evening classes? I work full time as a maintenance crew at an apartment complex.
M Well, we offer part-time evening classes, but it would take longer to get the diploma. If you give me your address, I'll send you a brochure and an application.
W Thank you. I really appreciate it. I also would like to know whether you offer any kind of scholarship.

38. Why is the woman calling?
(A) To ask for a discount
(B) To change the interior of her house
(C) To subscribe a newspaper
(D) To inquire about a class

39. What is the woman concerned about?
(A) The cost of tuition
(B) Class hours
(C) Housing options
(D) Professional experience

40. What does the man offer to do?
(A) Find a job for her
(B) Give her a scholarship
(C) Send the woman some information
(D) Accept the woman's application

M Hi, Lydia. You've been to Milan before, right? How did you like the place?

W I was there recently for an international conference and I loved it. The food, people, and atmosphere, everything was great.

M Next month I'm traveling to Milan to meet some important clients. Do you have any suggestions about what to see when I'm there?

W There are lots of places I could recommend. It depends on how much time you have. How long will you be there?

M I'll be there for a week, but I'll only have a one day that I'm not seeing clients. I won't have much time.

W In that case, I think you should try a group bus tour. It's an excellent way to see all the major landmarks in the city in a short amount of time.

M Good idea. Do you have more information about it; like how much it costs, and what time it starts?

W If you check the Official Italy Tourism Board, I'm sure you'll find all the information you need.

41. What will the man do in Milan next month?
(A) Attend a conference
(B) Visit corporate headquarters
(C) Meet with some clients
(D) Purchase some products

42. What does the woman ask the man about?
(A) The length of his stay
(B) The topic of his presentation
(C) The cost of his tickets
(D) The name of his clients

43. What does the woman recommend?
(A) Getting a group discount
(B) Visiting a museum
(C) Meeting with local residents
(D) Taking a bus tour

Questions 44 through 46 refer to the following conversation.

M Hi, Ms. Young. Sorry I couldn't come to this morning's meeting. Can you fill me in?

W Sure, on Monday, the inspectors are coming to conduct a routine safety test on the assembly line. So, you and other machine operators won't have to work on the factory floor that day.

M Oh, okay. Should we work somewhere else on Monday then?

W Yes, we are going to assign you all day to help the layout of the new plant in Grover City. They need some input from the workers like you who have actually used the machinery.

44. What does the man apologize for?
(A) Not passing the test
(B) Forgetting the delivery
(C) Not participating in the training
(D) Missing a meeting

45. What will happen at the factory on Monday?
(A) Some employees will be evaluated.
(B) The policies will be changed.
(C) An inspection will be conducted.
(D) A demonstration will be given.

46. What is the man asked to provide in Grover City?
(A) Move some machinery
(B) Give some opinion
(C) Lay off some staff
(D) Train some employees

Questions 47 through 49 refer to the following conversation.

M Hi, my name is Chris Park. I talked to someone at your hotel about a week ago to make a reservation. I'm calling to make sure the reservation I made was correct.

W Yes, Mr. Park. Could you give me your reference number if possible?

M Yes, it's 74459. I specifically asked for a room with the ocean view. Can you check on it while you're at it?

W Yes, one moment please. Here you are. Two nights and three days from August 10th through 13th under the name of Chris Park. Your reservation has been confirmed, sir.

47. Why is the man calling?
(A) He wants to reserve a room.
(B) He wants to stay in a different room.
(C) He wants to change the date of arrival.
(D) He wants to confirm a reservation.

48. What does the woman ask the man to do?
(A) To give his home address
(B) To tell his name in full
(C) To provide her with some number
(D) To explain the reason for his visit

49. What can be inferred about the man?
(A) He stayed at this hotel before.
(B) He lost his reservation number.
(C) He will arrive on a different date.
(D) He likes to stay in a room with a view.

Questions 50 through 52 refer to the following conversation.

M Hi, is this the personnel office? I just read an e-mail about the training courses that the new employees are required to take. Where can I get the schedule for these classes?

W Well, the classes are online. You can take them whenever you want. Because their classes are required ones, you can take them during your work hours.

M Great, my manager suggests that I take a business writing class. How do I register for that one?

W Well, just visit our company website and click on the work skills training tab. It will give an overview of the courses and registration processes.

50. What are the speakers discussing?
(A) Training classes
(B) Hiring procedure
(C) Performance evaluation
(D) Efficient communication

51. What does the woman imply when she says, "you can take them during your work hours"?
新
(A) The company will pay for the registration.
(B) The man has changed his work hours.
(C) Classes are work-related topics.
(D) The work schedules are too tight these days.

52. What does the woman suggest the man do?
(A) Speak with the supervisor
(B) Visit the personnel office
(C) Update the software
(D) Refer to the online site

TEST 09

新 Questions 53 through 55 refer to the following conversation with three speakers.

M   I really appreciate your meeting with me today. Ms. Oliver and Ms. Langston, I'm sure you'll want to use Aquaria's environmentally friendly cleaning supplies for your hotel once I tell you about them.

W1 Thanks for coming. We're looking forward to your presentation.

W2 We haven't purchased your cleaning products before because they're quite costly.

W1 We have over 400 rooms in this hotel. So we try to be careful about how much we spend on cleaning supplies.

M   I understand. The Aquaria product line costs a little more than others, but it will save you money in many other ways. For example, our carpet cleaner is very gentle, so it won't cause fading.

W2 Replacing the carpets is the big expense for our budget in the long run.

W1 It's true. Alright, can you give us a demonstration of your products?

M   Of course, why don't you wear these gloves and aprons first to be safe just in case?

53. What kind of products are the speakers discussing?
(A) Office equipment
(B) Healthy food
(C) Cleaning supplies
(D) Kitchen supplies

54. Why has the Aquaria products never been used before?
(A) They're rather expensive.
(B) They are complicated to use.
(C) They're not environmentally friendly.
(D) Their products relatively new in the industry.

55. What is the man asked to do?
(A) Clean up the alley of the hotel
(B) Cancel the previous orders
(C) Move some furniture to the side
(D) Give a product demonstration

Questions 56 through 58 refer to the following conversation.

W   These flower arrangements are beautiful. But, you only have two sets on display. Do you have more in the back? I need at least eight arrangements for my dinner party.

M   Well, these are all we have right now, but we can create them for you if you want. When do you need them?

W   I'm planning a farewell party for my colleague. The party will start tomorrow night, so we need the flowers around three in the afternoon. Do you deliver?

M   Yes, delivery will be free, and we can bring you them early tomorrow afternoon. But, because we're creating them on such a short notice, we have to treat them as a special order and add 5% to your total cost. Would that be okay?

W   I guess I have no choice. Please make sure they're delivered in time.

56. What does the woman want the man to do?
(A) Provide flower arrangements
(B) Change the display in the store
(C) Plan a dinner party for her
(D) Cancel her order for tomorrow

57. When is the event taking place?
(A) Tonight
(B) Tomorrow morning
(C) Tomorrow afternoon
(D) Tomorrow evening

58. What does the man mean when he says, "we have to treat them as a special order"?
新
(A) Special decorations will be made.
(B) There will be a delivery charge.
(C) They have to make them in a rush.
(D) The sales price has gone up.

Questions 59 through 61 refer to the following conversation.

W   Frank, did you hear Mr. Thomson is leaving by the end of this month?

M   Yes, I did. I heard he wants to travel around world and write historic novels. He said he's always dreaming about doing just that. You know, he's been a lawyer in our firm for almost 35 years. I think he's looking forward to some changes.

W   Good for him. But I think many of us will miss him a lot. He's one of the best attorneys in our law firm, you know. Is there going to be a party for him?

M   Yes, we're planning a reception for him in the conference room on this Friday. I hope everyone could join us.

W   I might be late because of some contract negotiations but I'm sure to be there.

59. Why is Mr. Thomson leaving his position?
(A) To teach at a university
(B) To pursue other interests
(C) To start his own business
(D) To transfer to an overseas division

60. Where does Mr. Thomson most likely work?
(A) At an employment agency
(B) At a travel agency
(C) At a law firm
(D) At a publishing firm

61. What will take place on Friday?
(A) An office party
(B) A job interview
(C) A press conference
(D) An awards ceremony

Questions 62 through 64 refer to the following conversation and schedule.

M   Gee. I can't wait until the repaving work on the southbound highway is over. The detour of the city construction route takes almost 30 minutes longer than my usual commute to work.

W   Yes, I'm having the same problem with you. However, the yesterday's newspaper said the construction might take longer than expected because of the unexpected storm.

M   Well, they need to speed up, otherwise there will be complaints from many citizens like us. Did the article say when it could be finished?

W   Well, I read from the city website that the design was finalized on April 15th as scheduled, but the deadline for the next task has to be pushed back by 10 days. But the completion date will be the same on September 1st.

M   That's good to know. I'm glad the construction will be over before the winter comes.

62. What is under construction?
(A) A tunnel
(B) A highway
(C) A parking garage
(D) An office building

63. Why has the construction schedule been changed?
(A) There are not enough workers.
(B) They didn't have enough money.
(C) The weather has been bad.
(D) They couldn't get permission from the authorities.

64. Look at the graphic. Which task has to be extended?
新 (A) Approval
(B) Design
(C) Demolition
(D) Final completion

新 Questions 65 through 67 refer to the following conversation and menu.

W　Busy Bee's Café. How may I help you?
M　Hi, I'm calling from Eagle Software Systems. I'm planning a luncheon meeting for my department. Can you take a reservation for around 20 people?
W　Of course, sir. What date do you have in mind? We're sometimes booked up depending on days.
M　Well, I'm thinking about next Tuesday at 1 o'clock.
W　Yes, we're available for 20 people on that day.
M　Also, some of employees don't eat meat. Do you have vegetarian menus?
W　Of course. In fact, our vegetarian menus are pretty popular among vegetarians and regular customers in the area. We were even named the area's best vegetarian eatery by the City Food.
M　That's good to know.
W　As you can see on our menu, some items will have the word "healthy" in their names. Those meals don't have any meats in them.

65. What type of event is the man organizing?
(A) A dealers' meeting
(B) A client lunch
(C) A retirement party
(D) A department luncheon

66. What does the woman mention about the café?
(A) Cancellations require 24 hours' notice.
(B) The menu changes seasonally.
(C) It received recognition from local diners.
(D) It has many rooms to accommodate different sizes of groups.

67. Look at the graphic. What menu item does not contain
新 meat?
(A) The sampler
(B) The soup
(C) The salad
(D) The sandwich

新 Questions 68 through 70 refer to the following conversation and map.

W　Hi, I was looking through your company's website and saw the rental units listed inside the Hillside shopping mall which is scheduled to reopen in a few months. I'm interested in opening a hair salon there.
M　Yes, we have several spaces left. The first floor ones would be perfect because of the foot traffic. There will be a skin-care shop in the mall so it would be helpful.
W　Yes, I've looked at the floor plan of the shopping mall online. As you mentioned, I want the location with lots of foot traffic, hopefully near an elevator or an escalator.
M　Well, there will be also a lot of people near the exit area, but if you prefer the one near the escalator, we can accommodate that. Would you like to look at it first?
W　That would be great. I'm going away for a trade show for the weekend, so I'd like to look at it before I leave. Can I come by this afternoon?

68. Why is the woman calling?
(A) To finalize a renovation project
(B) To inquire about the property
(C) To confirm a delivery address
(D) To attend a professional conference

69. What type of business does the woman want to open?
(A) A family restaurant
(B) A skin-care shop
(C) A hair salon
(D) An art supply store

70. Look at the graphic. Which location will the woman probably
新 take?
(A) 1
(B) 2
(C) 3
(D) 4

Part 4

Questions 71 through 73 refer to the following recorded message.

Hello, you have reached the Delta Engineering employee's weather hot line. Due to heavy rain and flooding, the office will be closed today. If you are able to, please work at home. You may enter our company's official website and register your working hours through our online payroll system. We expect the office to be open during regular business hours. For further information and notification, please check our automated messages through the day. Thank you.

71. Who is this message intended for?
(A) People who have technical problems
(B) The weather forecasters
(C) The morning commuters
(D) The company's employees

72. What caused the office closure?
(A) Updates on equipment
(B) Inspection on the facility
(C) Weather conditions
(D) Maintenance job

73. What are the listeners asked to do?
(A) Work using online system
(B) Come to work after lunch
(C) Enter another password
(D) Record the automated message

Questions 74 through 76 refer to the following announcement.

May I have your attention to an urgent message, please? A white sedan license number XG356 is currently blocking the exit out of the parking lot on level 2. If you are the owner of the vehicle, please come to the parking lot on level 2 and remove your car immediately. Otherwise, it will be towed at your expense. Also, a blue truck with license number TY3759 is parking at a handicapped area without a permit. Parking spaces for the handicapped should be kept vacant for their proper use. Please move your car to one of the designated areas for visitor. The visitors' parking spaces at our building are available at the south corner of each level and they are clearly marked with yellow colors. Thank you for your cooperation.

74. Who probably is making the announcement?
(A) A building resident
(B) A traffic officer
(C) A property manager
(D) An auto technician

75. What is said about the sedan?
(A) Its headlights are on.
(B) It has parked on level 1.
(C) The driver does not have handicapped permit.
(D) It is blocking the entrance.

76. Where should a visitor to the building park?
(A) In any of the spaces on level 2
(B) In front of the exit
(C) In vacant spaces
(D) In the color marked area

Questions 77 through 79 refer to the following announcement.

Attention, all employees. This is a reminder that assembly lines 11 and 12 will shut down at 3 o'clock in the afternoon so that some of the machinery be replaced with new equipment. This is a part of regular maintenance procedures to ensure safety operation. Employees regularly work on these lines will instead review operating guidelines for the new equipment with our training manager, Douglas Xing. Mr. Xing will meet you at the meeting room three, located next to the company cafeteria at 3:00 p.m. Again, assembly lines 11 and 12 will be shut down tomorrow afternoon. For more information, contact the security office.

77. Where most likely is the announcement being made?
(A) In a factory
(B) In an electronics store
(C) In an employment agency
(D) In a park

78. What will happen at three o'clock?
(A) The work will begin at the factory.
(B) The factory will be closed for the day.
(C) Some machines will be turned off.
(D) Some videos will be shown.

79. Who is Douglas Xing?
(A) A factory supervisor
(B) A personnel officer
(C) A line worker
(D) A training manager

Questions 80 through 82 refer to the following telephone message.

Good morning, Ms. Allen. This is Maria from Butterfly Floral Shop. One of our drivers stopped by at your place to deliver a bouquet of flowers this morning, but nobody was available to receive them. We can try to deliver them again later today, but we need to know someone will be at your house. If not, you can pick up your bouquet at our shop, or arrange another delivery time within two days. As you can see, fresh flowers bouquets are made just for you and do not have a long shelf time. Please call us at Butterfly Flowers at 555-2473. We will close at 5 o'clock today and will open tomorrow morning at 9 a.m. Thank you and have a nice day.

80. According to the message, what happened today?
(A) A delivery was attempted.
(B) An order was received.
(C) Someone from the flower shop called.
(D) A party has been arranged.

81. 新 What does woman mean when she says, "do not have a long shelf time"?
(A) They have to wait for a long time to buy the flowers.
(B) The address was incorrectly recorded.
(C) The flowers are perishable products.
(D) The flowers are not selling well these days.

82. What will happen at 9 a.m. tomorrow?
(A) A deliver person will visit again.
(B) The flowers will be discarded.
(C) New order should be made.
(D) A store will open.

Questions 83 through 85 refer to the following talk.

Attention ladies and gentlemen. As we end our conference, I'm proudly introducing our final presenter, Dr. Elizabeth Lorain. Ms. Lorain's presentation today is about the latest advancement in alternative energy. Specifically, she will talk about the recent development in alternative fuels using corns and other grains. I should note that Dr. Lorain has worked at the Ministry of Commerce planning the energy policies for the whole country. She was also recently invited to join an international panel of scientists and researchers to work on this topic. She is one of a few females selected to serve at this committee. Now, Ms. Lorain will speak on the Future of Energy World and will gladly answer any questions later on. Let us welcome Ms. Lorain with a round of applause.

83. Where is this talk probably taking place?
(A) In a power plant
(B) In a government agency
(C) In an auditorium
(D) In a radio station

84. What is the topic of Ms. Lorain's talk?
(A) Fuel prices
(B) Alternative energy
(C) Financial planning
(D) Developing countries

85. What has Ms. Lorain recently been invited to do?
(A) To design a new generation automobile
(B) To call for a professional meeting
(C) To ask questions to a panel of scientists
(D) To conduct research with other members

Questions 86 through 88 refer to the following advertisement.

Looking for an affordable business space in a hurry? We have the place for you. Construction will soon be completed on Downtown Office Complex. Designed by award winning Bingham Creative Architectural firm, the building will surely win an award of its own. The complex features spacious office space fully furnished with desks, computer, and other office equipment. We have an impressive lobby and waiting area, meeting rooms of different sizes, and underground parking spaces, all for free when you sign the leasing contract with us. The building is conveniently located near the restaurant and shopping district. But only a number of units are left now. So act fast and grab this unique opportunity. To review the inside of the different units, visit our online photo gallery at www.downtownoffice.com.

86. What is being advertised?
(A) A stationery store
(B) A suburban property
(C) An office space
(D) An equipment rental

87. What is said about Bingham Creative?
(A) It only designs office buildings.
(B) It provides free utilities for tenants.
(C) It is hiring new employees.
(D) It has won awards before.

88. 新 What does the woman imply when she says, "act fast and grab this unique opportunity"?
(A) The building is famous for its unique design.
(B) The units could sell out quickly.
(C) The deadline is getting closer.
(D) The discount amount is much bigger than ever.

Questions 89 through 91 refer to the following talk.

Now before we finish, I'd like to tell you about the significant change that will affect everyone at this company. We've been using traditional paper-based payroll cards and the payroll department had to calculate individual employee's pay check by hand. But, starting next month, we will use a new online system that would enable us to calculate and track our work records more accurately and efficiently. All you have to do is to log on to your computer when you start your work in the morning. You'll all be receiving a memo that explains the procedure of registering for you own database system. We'll also set up some training classes soon for those who need help with the new system. Details about training classes and how to enroll for them will be included in the e-mail you'll get.

89. What is the main purpose of this talk?
(A) To reserve a seat in the training class
(B) To describe the process of getting a raise
(C) To clarify a change in work hours
(D) To announce a new payroll system

90. Why does the man say, "to calculate and track our work records more accurately and efficiently"?
(A) To pay for the price of new software
(B) To encourage employees to work harder
(C) To introduce a new online tutorial link
(D) To emphasize the merits of new software

91. How can the listeners get more information?
(A) By reading a memo
(B) By visiting the website
(C) By stopping by at the payroll office
(D) By looking over the program manual

Questions 92 through 94 refer to the following excerpt from a meeting.

Thank you for coming. Before we start today's meeting, first I would like to congratulate us all on accomplishing the goal of increasing sales by over 5% last month. This is mainly due to the popularity of our newly launched women's line of summer dresses, Easy Breeze. However, we need to build on this success and prepare for the winter season. I've been looking into an exciting line of leather and fur coats from a young designer Michael Yamaguchi. These leathers are not actually animal skins but rather synthetically manufactured fabrics that have remarkable similarity with real animal skins, and will be loved by both fashion leaders and animal lovers. Now, you are going to see some of Yamaguchi's new designs for the next season and are asked to give me feedbacks on how we should incorporate them into our lines.

92. What type of business does the speaker probably work for?
(A) A travel agency
(B) An environmentalists' group
(C) An apparel company
(D) A financial institute

93. What's the main purpose of the meeting?
(A) To train new employees
(B) To expand into an overseas market
(C) To review next year's budget
(D) To discuss new products

94. What are the employees asked to do?
(A) Taste different food samples
(B) Meet employees from overseas branches
(C) Contact possible designers for the next season
(D) Provide opinions on some designs

Questions 95 through 97 refer to the following speech and chart.

First, I am happy to announce that our sales for the new Alley's makeup box have increased by thirty percent in the southern region, while profits are up by almost eighteen percent. This is mainly due to our new colorful cosmetic lines targeting women who are sensitive to fashion trends. We have teamed up with leading fashion designers to predict new trendy colors and come up with this year's must-have lipsticks and eye colors. In March of this year, the new pastel line of new lip and cheek colors was launched and made a biggest sales increase the following month. The new line of products appealed to the fashion-forward women in their twenties and early thirties. We especially thanked the employees who developed and maintained a close relationship with the fashion world. To recognize their effort and encourage continuous dedication, next month all employees will receive a ten percent bonus in their paychecks. I hope we can celebrate this success and continue to endeavor to make Alley's Cosmetics better.

95. What is the purpose of this speech?
(A) To welcome new staff
(B) To present awards to employees
(C) To expand into overseas markets
(D) To report successful sales results

96. Look at the graphic. Which month did the new pastel line of products make a huge increase in sales?
(A) March
(B) April
(C) May
(D) June

97. What will happen next week?
(A) The company will open another branch.
(B) Some employees will get promotions.
(C) They will meet foreign visitors.
(D) Employees will receive bonuses.

Questions 98 through 100 refer to the following announcement and map.

Now, let me tell you one more thing before we close today's meeting. I know parking has been a problem for the last few months after we hire more doctors and nurses to get ready for the next year's expansion. So, management made an agreement with Marshall Shopping Center on Maple Avenue to lease some of their parking spaces in their lot. Unfortunately, the spaces won't be available until May when they coordinate their schedules with their employees. So, in the meantime, I recommend you to use public transportation for those who have problems finding parking spaces. Also, we're trying to arrange the shuttle buses from the corner of Ridgeway Street and Parkway Street to the hospital on an hourly basis. If you want to find out detailed bus routes and schedules, please stop by at the information desk.

98. What is the purpose of the announcement?
(A) To welcome new employees
(B) To inform new security policies
(C) To address some employee concerns
(D) To solicit new clients

99. What will become available to employees in May?
(A) Flexible working hours
(B) Transportation to the bus stations
(C) New business offices
(D) Additional parking spaces

100. Look at the graphic. Which number shows where shuttle buses are supposed to stop?
(A) 1
(B) 2
(C) 3
(D) 4

10회

1.	(B)	2.	(B)	3.	(C)	4.	(D)	5.	(B)
6.	(D)	7.	(C)	8.	(B)	9.	(A)	10.	(A)
11.	(C)	12.	(B)	13.	(C)	14.	(A)	15.	(A)
16.	(C)	17.	(A)	18.	(C)	19.	(B)	20.	(B)
21.	(B)	22.	(C)	23.	(B)	24.	(A)	25.	(C)
26.	(C)	27.	(C)	28.	(B)	29.	(C)	30.	(A)
31.	(C)	32.	(B)	33.	(D)	34.	(D)	35.	(B)
36.	(D)	37.	(C)	38.	(B)	39.	(D)	40.	(C)
41.	(B)	42.	(A)	43.	(D)	44.	(A)	45.	(D)
46.	(D)	47.	(D)	48.	(C)	49.	(D)	50.	(C)
51.	(A)	52.	(D)	53.	(D)	54.	(C)	55.	(A)
56.	(A)	57.	(B)	58.	(D)	59.	(B)	60.	(D)
61.	(A)	62.	(C)	63.	(A)	64.	(C)	65.	(C)
66.	(C)	67.	(B)	68.	(B)	69.	(C)	70.	(B)
71.	(D)	72.	(C)	73.	(A)	74.	(A)	75.	(C)
76.	(C)	77.	(A)	78.	(D)	79.	(B)	80.	(C)
81.	(A)	82.	(B)	83.	(B)	84.	(D)	85.	(A)
86.	(D)	87.	(C)	88.	(A)	89.	(B)	90.	(D)
91.	(C)	92.	(C)	93.	(A)	94.	(C)	95.	(A)
96.	(B)	97.	(D)	98.	(C)	99.	(D)	100.	(A)

Part 1

1. (A) A machine is being fixed by a technician.
(B) He's positioning a paper on the glass.
(C) He's holding the lid of a machine open.
(D) A stack of papers has been set on the shelf.

2. (A) They're reading some newspapers.
(B) They're reviewing some information.
(C) They're delivering a presentation at a meeting.
(D) They're sitting in the front rows of the room.

3. (A) The furniture is being scrubbed.
(B) The door is being opened.
(C) The chairs have been pushed in.
(D) The table is currently being used.

4. (A) They're emptying some bottles.
(B) They're mixing some cement.
(C) A truck is driving into a construction site.
(D) Some dirt has been piled on the ground.

5. (A) People are crossing over the fence.
(B) Some people have opened their umbrellas.
(C) A crowd of people are gathered at the station.
(D) The lines are being repainted on the road.

6. (A) Grass is being mowed in the lawn.
(B) Some trees are growing higher than the building.
(C) A clock is being hung on the wall.
(D) Columns support the front of the building.

Part 2

7. How often do you work out at the gym?
(A) I don't work on the weekends.
(B) Let's go out for dinner.
(C) At least twice a week.

8. Do you think the committee will approve our budget proposal?
(A) We have to select a new member.
(B) I sure hope so. We did our best.
(C) The price was too expensive.

9. Have you read the new book by Michael Winters?
(A) Yes, but I like his first one more.
(B) No, we haven't met each other yet.
(C) Sure, I could lend you one.

10. Do we have extra packaging materials?
(A) We have to order some more.
(B) The machine is broken.
(C) You have to pay extra amount.

11. How do I get to the mail room?
(A) You could send it by express.
(B) We should get there by three.
(C) It's in the basement.

12. Could I borrow something to write with?
(A) We don't have enough funding.
(B) How about a pencil?
(C) I don't wear one today.

13. You can have meals in the train's dining car.
(A) The training has been delayed for an hour.
(B) It was really delicious.
(C) That's something convenient.

14. Weren't you able to sleep on the plane?
(A) Only for a few hours.
(B) No, I used different settings.
(C) Anybody can do it.

15. Who is responsible for recycling used office supplies or equipment?
(A) Jeremy usually takes care of them.
(B) The computer should arrive by tomorrow.
(C) This mail should be sent to the office manager.

16. You updated the training manual for new employees, didn't you?
(A) The train leaves in an hour.
(B) Yes, the launching show is next week.
(C) Yes, I made some changes.

17. What kind of experience do you have in sales?
(A) I've been selling electronic appliances for 5 years.
(B) The sale starts next Monday.
(C) It was a great experience.

18. Will the employees be moving to the new office in July or August?
(A) The moving expenses are too high.
(B) I think the current payment should be sustained.
(C) Mr. Gonzales should know about it.

19. Where can I find more information about the company's product lines?
(A) Let's just wait here.
(B) Check their website.
(C) Actually, I've never been there.

20. Murdock Media has a cafeteria in its building.
(A) What criteria have they applied to?
(B) I heard its food is really great.
(C) We should ask more employees to participate.

21. Mr. Torres, should this letter be forwarded to the president?
(A) No, the presentation is tomorrow.
(B) Yes, can you do that for me?
(C) Sure, let's make copies.

22. Do you want to share a taxi to the airport?
(A) The schedule is posted on the Internet.
(B) Yes, let's meet at the airport.
(C) I already have a ride, thank you.

23. When will we receive the specifications for the new color printer?
(A) It only makes black and white copies.
(B) We should be hearing from the supplier soon.
(C) In almost any electronics store in the country.

24. The directory should be in the filing cabinet.
(A) Is it in the top drawer?
(B) The files should be put away.
(C) Yes, the director wants to see you.

25. Why did you buy tickets so far in advance?
(A) They have two counters.
(B) It's right after the performance.
(C) They usually sell out quickly.

26. Do you know why the library is closed?
(A) Close to the train station.
(B) We need to return books by today.
(C) They've changed their hours.

27. Haven't you been introduced?
(A) No, I didn't send it yet.
(B) The launching show is tomorrow.
(C) To a few people.

28. What is the new administrative assistant like?
(A) I don't need any assistance.
(B) She's open and approachable.
(C) What time would be better for her?

29. Who do you think should be in charge of Henderson project?
(A) We need a new projector.
(B) The company should be relocated.
(C) That's for the board to decide.

30. Would Mr. Tao prefer to see me today, or later in the week?
(A) Wednesday would be the best.
(B) She might be late today.
(C) The product demonstration is tomorrow.

31. Why don't you check the settings of this alarm system?
(A) Let's set it aside for later.
(B) You can adjust the volume with it.
(C) Can you show me how?

Part 3

Questions 32 through 34 refer to the following conversation.

W You have reached Dr. Cunningham's office. How may I help you?
M Hi, this is Norman Craig. I made an appointment to see Dr. Cunningham at 10:30 on Friday morning. I don't think I can make it because I've been assigned to an emergency project in Asia. I'd like to cancel my appointment.
W Sure, would you like me to set up another time for you, say next week or the week after?
M Actually, I'm not sure how long this project will take. Why don't I give you a call back once I come back home and know more about my schedule?

32. Why did the man call?
(A) To find out when the doctor is available
(B) To cancel an appointment
(C) To report an emergency
(D) To take a special exam

33. What does the woman offer to do for the caller?
(A) Contact the doctor for him
(B) Review some medical record
(C) Assign him to a different project
(D) Reschedule his appointment

34. Why does the man decide to call her back later?
(A) He needs to wait for a call from his company.
(B) He needs directions to the doctor's office.
(C) He wants to stay in Asia longer.
(D) He does not know when he will be free.

Questions 35 through 37 refer to the following conversation.

M Did you hear that Ms. Long has been promoted to the director of overseas marketing?
W Yes, I did. The public relations department will miss her a lot. Do you think she will hire any new staff members?
M She told me that her new department is expanding following the increase in overseas sales. So, she will be hiring at least three new employees and a manager.
W Then, I should call my friend, Elliot. He has always wanted to work in the international marketing and he is also fluent in German and French.

35. What is stated about Ms. Long?
(A) She is looking for a job overseas.
(B) She has been recently promoted.
(C) She has traveled overseas a lot.
(D) She is moving into a new house.

36. What will Ms. Long need to do?
(A) Make a presentation to the board
(B) Train new staff
(C) Work for public relations
(D) Hire new employees

37. What does the woman say about her friend Elliot?
(A) He is a marketing expert.
(B) He has a lot of experience.
(C) He will be interested in the job.
(D) He is from France.

Questions 38 through 40 refer to the following conversation.

W Jeffrey, I ordered a new television for the reception area, and when I opened up the box there was no remote control inside.
M Hmm. That's odd. Wasn't there a list of contents included in the box? Why don't you take a look at it?
W I did, the list says the remote should be included. I guess I have to call the store's service center. Do you think they're still open?
M The store closes at six but I think their service center is open for another hour.
W Good, then I should be able to call them by seven.

38. According to the speakers, what is the problem with the television?
(A) The product is broken.
(B) The shipment is incomplete.
(C) The order was sent to a wrong place.
(D) The wrong computer model was sent.

39. What does the man recommend doing?
(A) Buying another remote control
(B) Complaining to the manager
(C) Finding a receipt
(D) Checking the list

40. What time does the store close?
(A) At 1 o'clock
(B) At 5 o'clock
(C) At 6 o'clock
(D) At 7 o'clock

W1　Nick, a new shipment of shoes came in, so I have to put price tags on them, but I don't think we have any more tags.

M　Oh, I thought we have them in stock in the storage room. Hold on. Let me check with someone. Sheela, don't we have extra price tags in the storage space?

W2　Oh, I thought I told you about it. We used up the last pack last week.

M　I will place a supply order this afternoon including boxes and wrapping papers. I'll add price tags to the list.

W2　If we order them this afternoon, they should arrive by tomorrow at the earliest.

W1　That might be too late. We really should have them ready today. Could you go to the office supply store on the Main Street right away and purchase some? We need at least 100 of them.

M　No problem. But next time, we should do regular inventory check on our supplies.

41.　What problem are they talking about?
(A) Their business received customer complaints.
(B) Their business is out of supplies.
(C) A shipment of merchandise has been delayed.
(D) Some employees are not available for consultation.

42.　What does the man say he will do this afternoon?
(A) Place an order
(B) Meet with a supervisor
(C) Update a database
(D) Call up a technician

43.　What is the man asked to do immediately?
(A) Create an inventory list
(B) Update the work schedule
(C) Unpack some boxes
(D) Go to a store

Questions 44 through 46 refer to the following conversation.

W　Michael, I haven't seen Mr. Gonzales this morning. Is he in yet? I have to talk to him about the applicant we're planning to interview tomorrow morning.

M　Actually, Mr. Gonzales is on a business trip this week. You know there is a sales conference in Tokyo.

W　Oh, you're right. I forgot about that. But, I was hoping to talk to him about this particular candidate, Ms. Margaret Summit. She said she used to work with Mr. Gonzales in Spain office. I want to verify a few things with him.

M　Well, he said he'd call before lunch. I'll tell him you stopped by and asked him to call you. He won't have much time, but I guess a few questions should be fine.

44.　Why does the woman want to talk to Mr. Gonzales?
(A) To inquire about his former colleague
(B) To confirm the time of an interview
(C) To introduce him to new employees
(D) To invite him to a sales conference

45.　What will the woman do tomorrow morning?
(A) Accept a job offer
(B) Meet with Mr. Gonzales
(C) Arrange a travel plan
(D) Interview an applicant

46.　What does the man offer to do?
(A) Give Mr. Gonzales' number
(B) Stop by at the woman's office
(C) Email the information
(D) Have someone call her

Questions 47 through 49 refer to the following conversation.

W　Peter, you know the guest speaker, Raymond Adams I invited for our seminar? His session has already finished but his flight won't leave until Saturday. I was wondering if a few of us can take him out while he's in town.

M　That's a good idea. Maybe we should show him something traditional, such as Korean museum, or a folk village?

W　Actually, I was thinking about a casual and relaxed dinner. He told me he has other plans for Friday afternoon. He's meeting his business partner to discuss a possible project. So, we should plan something for Friday night.

M　Then, how about a dinner at the Tower Restaurant? They serve a diverse international cuisine and it has a great view of the whole city.

47.　What are the speakers discussing?
(A) Attending a seminar
(B) Trying food from other countries
(C) Scheduling a flight
(D) Entertaining a visitor

48.　What does the Raymond Adams plan to do Friday afternoon?
(A) Attend a lecture
(B) Visit his relatives
(C) Meet with his partner
(D) Plan for the next trip

49.　What will the speakers probably do on Friday evening?
(A) Visit an art museum
(B) Attend a theatric performance
(C) Have a business meeting
(D) Eat at a restaurant

Questions 50 through 52 refer to the following conversation.

M　Hi, Ms. Park. This is Richard O'Neal from Sprint Mobile Telephone Services. We have noticed that you haven't paid your bill for the last two months. Do you have any problems using our service?

W　I don't? That is strange. Wait. Now that you mentioned it, I haven't received any bills. Do you have the correct address? I recently moved to a new place.

M　Our record shows that your mailing address is 255 Coolidge Street. Is this correct, ma'am?

W　No, that is an old address. I thought I called everyone and updated it, but I must have forgotten. Let me give it to you now.

M　Normally, there should be an extra fee for the late payment. But I'm going to waive the charge this time since you haven't even received any bills.

W　Thank you.

50.　What does the man imply when he says, "Do you have any problems using our service"?
新
(A) He wants to change his mobile phone service.
(B) His company recently moved into a new place.
(C) He thinks she might not be satisfied with his company.
(D) He has the same problem before.

51.　What has recently happened to the woman?
(A) She relocated to a new place.
(B) She got promoted at her company.
(C) She found a better company to do business with.
(D) She misplaced her phone and lost track of it.

52.　What does the man offer to do?
(A) Meet the woman in person
(B) Send another bill to the address
(C) Provide a special coupon for her
(D) Waiver some fees

M1 I can't believe the London Convention is next week.

W I know, it should be great with all those big name speakers and industry experts. Are we all set for the transportation?

M2 Well, the plane tickets are already taken care of and you arranged the rental car while we're there. Right, Greg?

M1 Uh-oh. I completely forgot to make the reservation. I've been so caught up with the preparation of my workshop.

M2 All right. We only have a few days before we leave. It might be difficult to get a car now.

W Let's not get stressed out about it. There must be shuttle bus services to and from the hotel. Let's talk to the hotel receptionist.

53. What are the speakers mainly discussing?
(A) Ways to reduce a travel budget
(B) Possible locations for a conference
(C) Whom they should take to the event
(D) Plans for an upcoming business trip

54. What problem do the speakers have?
(A) Their business cards didn't arrive.
(B) The reservation was made on the wrong date.
(C) The transportation arrangements are not complete.
(D) Some of the conference materials are not ready.

55. What does the woman suggest they do?
(A) Contact a hotel
(B) Cancel the order
(C) Postpone a decision
(D) Reserve an extra space

Questions 56 through 58 refer to the following conversation.

W Hey Sean. I heard you got a new job. Congratulations. What will you be doing at this company?

M I'll be managing the evening shifts at a famous Thai restaurant. My hours are pretty late. But, you know me. I don't mind working late as long as the pay is competitive.

W I remember you told me you didn't get that job a few months ago. Is this a different restaurant?

M No, it's the same one. You're right, I had an interview with them two months ago but they told they decided on another candidate. I guess that didn't work out since they called me last week and offered me the job.

W Well, it's a good thing they offered you the position. Congratulations!

56. What are the speakers discussing?
(A) Starting new employment
(B) Relocating to a new place
(C) Interviewing potential employees
(D) Scheduling a lunch appointment

57. What does the man mean when he says, "I don't mind working late as long as the pay is competitive"?
(A) He used to work at the competitor's company.
(B) He wants to receive a high salary.
(C) He doesn't like to work overtime.
(D) His work hours are pretty flexible.

58. When was the man's interview?
(A) Yesterday
(B) Last week
(C) Two weeks ago
(D) Two months ago

Questions 59 through 61 refer to the following conversation.

M Hi, Megan. I'm just starting the safety test for this new bottling machine. Do you have a minute to look over the test procedure?

W I'm sorry, Bill. I have to finish entering these data from Dr. Kyle's research project.

M I heard that the report is pretty extensive and needs a lot of attention. When is the final deadline?

W I'm meeting with Dr. Kyle tomorrow to discuss the results of the research and the format for the report. The report should be done by Wednesday since Dr. Kyle wants to look it over before he presents it at the board meeting on Friday.

M Well, good luck with it. I guess I'll have to find someone to help me with my test.

59. What does the man ask the woman to do?
(A) Wear safety gears
(B) Check a procedure
(C) Find some data
(D) Hire some temporary workers

60. Why is the woman unable to help?
(A) She is conducting an experiment.
(B) She is delivering a speech at the meeting.
(C) She is packing some materials.
(D) She needs to complete a data entry.

61. What does the woman say she will do tomorrow?
(A) Meet with a researcher
(B) Give presentation in front of the board
(C) Help the man with the test
(D) Begin writing a new report

新 Questions 62 through 64 refer to the following conversation and list.

M Excuse me, I need to buy a new printer. I'm interested in these two models and I want to know the difference between them.

W Certainly, sir. PX-70 is our newest model. It prints very fast and has an excellent color resolution. It also has scanning, copying, and faxing capability. The PX-40 and PX-50 are the last year's model. They're a bit slower and do not have a faxing feature, but we're willing to give you some discount on these models.

M Well, normally I would prefer a faster model but right now I'd like to get a discounted one because my budget is pretty tight. I'd like to get the one of these in white. But I don't see any boxed one on the shelf.

W There should be some in the stockroom. Let me get one for you. I'll meet you at the checkout counter later.

M Thank you.

62. What are the speakers talking about?
(A) Latest news from a magazine
(B) Price estimate for a job
(C) Features of two products
(D) Standards of quality control

63. Look at the graphic. Which model will the man be likely to purchase?
(A) PX 40
(B) PX 50
(C) PX 70
(D) Wait for a new model

64. What will the woman probably do next?
(A) She will talk with the manager.
(B) She will demonstrate the printer.
(C) She will find a box of product from a stockroom.
(D) She will receive the payment from the man.

225

TEST 10

M	Customer Service, Barry speaking. How may I help you?
W	Hi, I bought an office chair from you store and I was about to assemble it, but I don't' think I have all of the parts I need.
M	Oh, I'm sorry to hear that. Do you know what you're missing?
W	Well, I bought a standard office chair. I have four short nails and all of the long nails, but I don't have the small tool I'm supposed to use to assemble the chair.
M	No, problem. We have some replacement parts and tools here at the store. I can have the delivery person drop it off at your place. How does it sound?
W	Actually, I'm having lunch near your store. Why don't I stop by in the afternoon?

65. Where does the man most likely work?
(A) At a local restaurant
(B) At a shipping company
(C) At a furniture store
(D) At an assembly factory

66. Look at the graphic. What is the woman missing?
新 (A) Part A
(B) Part B
(C) Part C
(D) Assembly instructions

67. What does the man offer to do?
(A) Cancel the original order
(B) Arrange a delivery
(C) Provide some assembly instructions
(D) Take the woman to the store

M	Ms. Jackson. I'm writing an article for Next Auto Trend magazine on a new motorcycle your company is about to introduce. Everyone loved your concept vehicle that was introduced last January.
W	Yes, we have high hopes for the CF-2000.
M	The CF-2000 was originally scheduled on March 5th, but I understand there has been a problem with the production?
W	No, production is going just fine. We've had some problems with the global marketing firm. Apparently, getting feedback from potential global customers took longer than we thought, so we had some delays in the research phase of the schedule. But, everything was settled now.
M	I see. So when can customers expect to see your new model?
W	Well, the production for the first shipment will be complete on May first and the global sales will begin on the fifteenth of May.

68. What business does the woman work for?
(A) A magazine publisher
(B) A vehicle manufacturer
(C) An advertising firm
(D) A professional research center

69. Why has there been some delay?
(A) They had to modify the initial prototypes.
(B) The research costed more than expected.
(C) Communicating in global environment was difficult.
(D) Some machinery in the factory malfunctioned.

70. Look at the graphic. Which date is no longer accurate?
新 (A) Feb 15th
(B) April 1st
(C) May 1st
(D) May 15th

Part 4

Questions 71 through 73 refer to the following announcement.

Attention visitors! Right now is 4 o'clock. The special exhibit rooms in the Bronx Museum will be closing in 10 minutes. The museum café and gift shop will remain open for another hour from now. If you have checked your coats or bags when you entered, please be sure to collect them before you leave. Remember that the new exhibit from East Asia, "The Mystery of Ming Dynasty" will be opening next month. You can pick up a discounted coupon for this exhibit as you're leaving the museum today. Once again, the museum will be closing in 10.

71. What is the main purpose of this announcement?
(A) To encourage people to visit an exhibit
(B) To introduce a gift idea
(C) To inform extended hours
(D) To announce a closing time

72. When will the gift shop in the museum close?
(A) At 4:00
(B) At 4:10
(C) At 5:00
(D) At 5:10

73. What will happen next month?
(A) A new exhibit will be held.
(B) A coat room will be added.
(C) Online registration service will begin.
(D) A section will be closed for renovation.

Questions 74 through 76 refer to the following announcement.

Attention employees, please remember that this is the last week you'll be able to enter the assembly plant without a photo identification. If you haven't received your photo ID yet, please go to the security office on the first floor to get yours. Starting next Monday, all employees need to scan their badge at the main entrance in order to unlock the door. If you don't have your ID with you, you'll need to call your department to clear your ID. As before, guests must register at the front entrance to receive a temporary ID cards. If you have any questions about the new policy, please speak with the security officer, Richard Smith at extension 855. Thank you and have a nice day.

74. What is this announcement about?
(A) A change in security practice
(B) An ordering procedure for new equipment
(C) A plan to evaluate factory's employees
(D) A schedule for the regular inspection

75. According to the announcement, why should some employees go to the security office?
(A) To pick up an instruction booklet
(B) To register the new program
(C) To get an identification badge
(D) To receive orientation materials

76. What does the man imply when he says, "call your department to clear your ID"?
新 (A) Call an emergency hot line for information.
(B) The department store is out of inventory.
(C) You cannot access the building without an ID.
(D) Employees should keep their IDs at their offices.

Questions 77 through 79 refer to the following talk.

Thank you for purchasing the Cyber 2000 digital camera and watching this introductory DVD. My name is Anne and I'll give you a step by step introduction on how to use this equipment and get the best quality picture. There are many functions built in this camera to capture the images and motions of all kinds. We'll go through them one at a time and you'll learn how to use each function. But, before I start, I strongly recommend you to register your camera online at www.cyber2000.com for future services and benefits. And you'll also find all the information you are about to see in your Cyber2000 easy-to-carry handbook. Now, let us start the first step by turning your camera on and pushing the power button on the upper right-hand corner.

77. What is the purpose of this talk?
(A) To introduce an instruction video
(B) To promote a new product
(C) To change the order she had placed
(D) To welcome a group of new employees

78. What will the listeners be reviewing?
(A) Detailed terms of a contract
(B) Specific images they have gathered
(C) Many helpful online sites
(D) Various functions of a camera

79. What are the listeners asked to do?
(A) Carry the handbook all the time
(B) Sign up at the online site
(C) Explore the functions on their own
(D) Send the images to their company

Questions 80 through 82 refer to the following speech.

As the president of ENE & Associates, it is my great pleasure to announce this year's recipient of the outstanding employee awards, Ms. Sheila Wilson. During the last year alone, Sheila helped the company to gain six new major advertising accounts, including the Virgin airline and Teps Cola. This is mainly due to her creativity and effective communication skills with both clients and her team mates. Under Ms. Wilson's leadership, her team made some of the most creative and innovative campaigns in our company's history. Those advertisements not only satisfied the customers, but helped a lot to increase our clients' sales and public images. Now, before we invite Sheila up to the stage, we'd like to show you a short video highlighting some of her most successful campaigns she had worked on. So sit back and enjoy the show.

80. What is the purpose of the speech?
(A) To welcome new employees
(B) To inform a schedule change
(C) To present an employee award
(D) To report company's successful year

81. What kind of company does the speaker probably work for?
(A) An advertising agency
(B) An airline company
(C) A soft drinks company
(D) An accounting firm

82. What does the woman imply when she says, "helped a lot to increase our clients' sales"?
(A) They used to work at the clients' companies.
(B) The commercials for the clients were effective.
(C) Creativity is the most important factor in the advertisement.
(D) Ms. Wilson will become an executive of this company soon.

Questions 83 through 85 refer to the following advertisement.

If your company is planning a large meeting or picnic? Well, Stewards Food specializes in catering for corporate events. Whether it is a picnic with employees and their families, business luncheon with international clients, or an award ceremony with hundreds of participants, we offer a wide variety of healthy and delicious food and excellent services. Visit our website to check our sample menus that our chefs made from their special recipes and pictures of the events we had helped. And if you like to receive a price estimate for your event, simply click on the customer service link online and fill out the estimate request form. Once the form has been submitted, our staff will contact within 2 business days. So, schedule your next special event with Stewards Food.

83. What type of event does Stewards Food specialize in?
(A) Outdoor events
(B) Corporate functions
(C) International business
(D) Family celebrations

84. What is available on the Stewards Food's website?
(A) Chef's contact information
(B) Pictures of the service staff
(C) Price estimates for various functions
(D) Sample menus for the event

85. According to the advertisement, how can listeners request a price estimate?
(A) By linking to a website
(B) By calling a catering specialist
(C) By sending the request form by fax
(D) By contacting the person in charge

Questions 86 through 88 refer to the following telephone message.

Hi, Amy, thank you for agreeing to create the next month's book display. As you know, the theme is organic life. I just called to let you know that I need a list of books or magazines you might want to use in the display. You're more than welcomed to use any of the books, posters, or other promotional materials in the store to look the display more attractive. But, when you use the books, be sure you keep a record of everything you use in display. That way, we'll know where all our merchandise items are and answer questions our customers might have on the display. I'll be visiting other branches tomorrow, but feel free to call contact me at anytime to my mobile phone. Thank you.

86. Where does the caller probably work?
(A) At a print shop
(B) At an art gallery
(C) At a publishing company
(D) At a bookstore

87. What is the message concerned about?
(A) Ordering more products
(B) Handling customer complaints
(C) Setting up a new display
(D) Writing an article for the next month's issue

88. What does the caller ask Amy to do?
(A) Keep a detailed record
(B) Locate a missing item
(C) Create a work schedule
(D) Contact customers for an input

Questions 89 through 91 refer to the following talk.

Good morning. My name is Julia Anderson and I'm a sales manager for World Computers Incorporated. I'm thrilled to be at your regional auto maker's annual convention and to have the chance to tell you more about our newest product. The new XW-2000 notebook computer was launched less than a month ago and getting rave reviews. This new computer has an unlimited capacity of hard space and twice the maximum speed of the exiting line and will work smoothly when your auto sales persons use them as a promotional tool. The outer appearance can be customized to individual preference and it has more than 12 hours of battery life and this is much longer than any other product on the market. And today, we offer conference participants a special 30 day trial coupon with no extra cost. Please ask me after the presentation.

89. Where are the listeners?
(A) At a technical training
(B) At an auto maker's conference
(C) On an assembly floor
(D) At an annual sales seminar

90. What is the purpose of the talk?
(A) To explain today's schedule
(B) To inform changes in the program
(C) To get a discount coupon for an item
(D) To promote new electronic equipment

91. What does the woman mean when she says, "The outer appearance can be customized"?
(A) Customers buy products solely depend on its appearance.
(B) There will be extra charges for changing the outer designs.
(C) The products could look different from one another.
(D) The company is the only one which offers this kind of premium service.

Questions 92 through 94 refer to the following talk.

This is Satomi Jones, the host of "Up to Date", your favorite show that deals with issues in the business world. We have an exciting program ready for you today. Professor Mark Planko, a research psychologist at Fordham University will talk about "Peer Pressure" as a marketing technique. You probably noticed that some of the commercials that force you to buy something say that everyone else is doing it. It may not sound appealing at first. But Professor Planko will tell you that this is the oldest technique in the world of business and is still used by thousands of marketers. Professor Planko has just published a research study that explains how powerful this technique is and how it's been used in the real world today. He will share the results of his study with us after the commercial break.

92. Who is Mark Planko?
(A) A radio show host
(B) A news reporter
(C) A psychologist
(D) A company executive

93. What will be the main subject of the program?
(A) An advertising technique
(B) A new radio program
(C) New writing technique
(D) New product campaign

94. What did Mark Planko do recently?
(A) He launched a new product.
(B) He got an award for his advertisement.
(C) He published some research.
(D) He traveled around the world.

新 Questions 95 through 97 refer to the following excerpt from a meeting and chart.

The first item on our agenda is the results of our customer survey. As you may know, we have surveyed 25,000 customers from 18 restaurant locations including the new Brooklyn branch that just opened last month. As you can see, we're doing well for the most part and customers are extremely happy with the price value of our food. However, there's one area that's definitely lacking. So, for the rest of the meeting, I'd like to address the area with lowest rating. Our operation manager, Mathew Bones will be compiling a detailed analysis and writing up a report to review our process and also calculate the exact time to make a certain food and deliver it to the customer's table. That will help us to improve our procedure and boost customer satisfaction.

95. What kind of business does the speaker work for?
(A) A restaurant chain
(B) A marketing research firm
(C) A cleaning service
(D) An assembly factory

96. Look at the graphic. What does the speaker want to discuss
新 with the listeners?
(A) Quality
(B) Customer service
(C) Price
(D) Atmosphere

97. What will Mr. Bones do?
(A) Survey the customers again
(B) Calculate where the money is leaking
(C) Locate an unprofitable branch
(D) Create a detailed report

新 Questions 98 through 100 refer to the following news report and chart.

And now, Radio Max's business report, the main story of the day is the possible acquisition of Starlight Magazine by Sunnydale Corporation. Right now, in the daily newspaper market, Daily Globe has the number one subscription rate in the region. But Sunnydale has been looking for a chance to help increase its market share and expand into the creative market of the publishing industry. The two companies completed the final terms of the agreement yesterday after months of negotiations. The new Sunnydale will have 37% of the market share once the deal is finalized next month. Jack Johnson, a reporter from our station, attended this morning's press conference at Sunnydale's headquarters building. He had an opportunity to ask a few questions to the president. Jack is on the line right now to tell us about what he learned.

98. Look at the graphic. Which company will have the biggest
新 market share next month?
(A) Newswide
(B) Daily Globe
(C) Sunnydale
(D) Starlight Magazine

99. Who is Jack Johnson?
(A) A company executive
(B) A newspaper editor
(C) A mayor of the city
(D) A radio reporter

100. What event took place this morning?
(A) A news conference was held.
(B) A merger contract was signed.
(C) The president made a special announcement.
(D) They moved into a new headquarters building.

books.english.co.kr

실전 모의고사 3

LISTENING (PART I ~ IV)

NO.	ANSWER	NO.	ANSWER	NO.	ANSWER	NO.	ANSWER	NO.	ANSWER
	A B C D		A B C D		A B C D		A B C D		A B C D
1	Ⓐ Ⓑ Ⓒ Ⓓ	21	Ⓐ Ⓑ Ⓒ Ⓓ	41	Ⓐ Ⓑ Ⓒ Ⓓ	61	Ⓐ Ⓑ Ⓒ Ⓓ	81	Ⓐ Ⓑ Ⓒ Ⓓ
2	Ⓐ Ⓑ Ⓒ Ⓓ	22	Ⓐ Ⓑ Ⓒ Ⓓ	42	Ⓐ Ⓑ Ⓒ Ⓓ	62	Ⓐ Ⓑ Ⓒ Ⓓ	82	Ⓐ Ⓑ Ⓒ Ⓓ
3	Ⓐ Ⓑ Ⓒ Ⓓ	23	Ⓐ Ⓑ Ⓒ Ⓓ	43	Ⓐ Ⓑ Ⓒ Ⓓ	63	Ⓐ Ⓑ Ⓒ Ⓓ	83	Ⓐ Ⓑ Ⓒ Ⓓ
4	Ⓐ Ⓑ Ⓒ Ⓓ	24	Ⓐ Ⓑ Ⓒ Ⓓ	44	Ⓐ Ⓑ Ⓒ Ⓓ	64	Ⓐ Ⓑ Ⓒ Ⓓ	84	Ⓐ Ⓑ Ⓒ Ⓓ
5	Ⓐ Ⓑ Ⓒ Ⓓ	25	Ⓐ Ⓑ Ⓒ Ⓓ	45	Ⓐ Ⓑ Ⓒ Ⓓ	65	Ⓐ Ⓑ Ⓒ Ⓓ	85	Ⓐ Ⓑ Ⓒ Ⓓ
6	Ⓐ Ⓑ Ⓒ Ⓓ	26	Ⓐ Ⓑ Ⓒ Ⓓ	46	Ⓐ Ⓑ Ⓒ Ⓓ	66	Ⓐ Ⓑ Ⓒ Ⓓ	86	Ⓐ Ⓑ Ⓒ Ⓓ
7	Ⓐ Ⓑ Ⓒ Ⓓ	27	Ⓐ Ⓑ Ⓒ Ⓓ	47	Ⓐ Ⓑ Ⓒ Ⓓ	67	Ⓐ Ⓑ Ⓒ Ⓓ	87	Ⓐ Ⓑ Ⓒ Ⓓ
8	Ⓐ Ⓑ Ⓒ Ⓓ	28	Ⓐ Ⓑ Ⓒ Ⓓ	48	Ⓐ Ⓑ Ⓒ Ⓓ	68	Ⓐ Ⓑ Ⓒ Ⓓ	88	Ⓐ Ⓑ Ⓒ Ⓓ
9	Ⓐ Ⓑ Ⓒ Ⓓ	29	Ⓐ Ⓑ Ⓒ Ⓓ	49	Ⓐ Ⓑ Ⓒ Ⓓ	69	Ⓐ Ⓑ Ⓒ Ⓓ	89	Ⓐ Ⓑ Ⓒ Ⓓ
10	Ⓐ Ⓑ Ⓒ Ⓓ	30	Ⓐ Ⓑ Ⓒ Ⓓ	50	Ⓐ Ⓑ Ⓒ Ⓓ	70	Ⓐ Ⓑ Ⓒ Ⓓ	90	Ⓐ Ⓑ Ⓒ Ⓓ
11	Ⓐ Ⓑ Ⓒ Ⓓ	31	Ⓐ Ⓑ Ⓒ Ⓓ	51	Ⓐ Ⓑ Ⓒ Ⓓ	71	Ⓐ Ⓑ Ⓒ Ⓓ	91	Ⓐ Ⓑ Ⓒ Ⓓ
12	Ⓐ Ⓑ Ⓒ Ⓓ	32	Ⓐ Ⓑ Ⓒ Ⓓ	52	Ⓐ Ⓑ Ⓒ Ⓓ	72	Ⓐ Ⓑ Ⓒ Ⓓ	92	Ⓐ Ⓑ Ⓒ Ⓓ
13	Ⓐ Ⓑ Ⓒ Ⓓ	33	Ⓐ Ⓑ Ⓒ Ⓓ	53	Ⓐ Ⓑ Ⓒ Ⓓ	73	Ⓐ Ⓑ Ⓒ Ⓓ	93	Ⓐ Ⓑ Ⓒ Ⓓ
14	Ⓐ Ⓑ Ⓒ Ⓓ	34	Ⓐ Ⓑ Ⓒ Ⓓ	54	Ⓐ Ⓑ Ⓒ Ⓓ	74	Ⓐ Ⓑ Ⓒ Ⓓ	94	Ⓐ Ⓑ Ⓒ Ⓓ
15	Ⓐ Ⓑ Ⓒ Ⓓ	35	Ⓐ Ⓑ Ⓒ Ⓓ	55	Ⓐ Ⓑ Ⓒ Ⓓ	75	Ⓐ Ⓑ Ⓒ Ⓓ	95	Ⓐ Ⓑ Ⓒ Ⓓ
16	Ⓐ Ⓑ Ⓒ Ⓓ	36	Ⓐ Ⓑ Ⓒ Ⓓ	56	Ⓐ Ⓑ Ⓒ Ⓓ	76	Ⓐ Ⓑ Ⓒ Ⓓ	96	Ⓐ Ⓑ Ⓒ Ⓓ
17	Ⓐ Ⓑ Ⓒ Ⓓ	37	Ⓐ Ⓑ Ⓒ Ⓓ	57	Ⓐ Ⓑ Ⓒ Ⓓ	77	Ⓐ Ⓑ Ⓒ Ⓓ	97	Ⓐ Ⓑ Ⓒ Ⓓ
18	Ⓐ Ⓑ Ⓒ Ⓓ	38	Ⓐ Ⓑ Ⓒ Ⓓ	58	Ⓐ Ⓑ Ⓒ Ⓓ	78	Ⓐ Ⓑ Ⓒ Ⓓ	98	Ⓐ Ⓑ Ⓒ Ⓓ
19	Ⓐ Ⓑ Ⓒ Ⓓ	39	Ⓐ Ⓑ Ⓒ Ⓓ	59	Ⓐ Ⓑ Ⓒ Ⓓ	79	Ⓐ Ⓑ Ⓒ Ⓓ	99	Ⓐ Ⓑ Ⓒ Ⓓ
20	Ⓐ Ⓑ Ⓒ Ⓓ	40	Ⓐ Ⓑ Ⓒ Ⓓ	60	Ⓐ Ⓑ Ⓒ Ⓓ	80	Ⓐ Ⓑ Ⓒ Ⓓ	100	Ⓐ Ⓑ Ⓒ Ⓓ

실전 모의고사 4

LISTENING (PART I ~ IV)

NO.	ANSWER	NO.	ANSWER	NO.	ANSWER	NO.	ANSWER	NO.	ANSWER
	A B C D		A B C D		A B C D		A B C D		A B C D
1	Ⓐ Ⓑ Ⓒ Ⓓ	21	Ⓐ Ⓑ Ⓒ Ⓓ	41	Ⓐ Ⓑ Ⓒ Ⓓ	61	Ⓐ Ⓑ Ⓒ Ⓓ	81	Ⓐ Ⓑ Ⓒ Ⓓ
2	Ⓐ Ⓑ Ⓒ Ⓓ	22	Ⓐ Ⓑ Ⓒ Ⓓ	42	Ⓐ Ⓑ Ⓒ Ⓓ	62	Ⓐ Ⓑ Ⓒ Ⓓ	82	Ⓐ Ⓑ Ⓒ Ⓓ
3	Ⓐ Ⓑ Ⓒ Ⓓ	23	Ⓐ Ⓑ Ⓒ Ⓓ	43	Ⓐ Ⓑ Ⓒ Ⓓ	63	Ⓐ Ⓑ Ⓒ Ⓓ	83	Ⓐ Ⓑ Ⓒ Ⓓ
4	Ⓐ Ⓑ Ⓒ Ⓓ	24	Ⓐ Ⓑ Ⓒ Ⓓ	44	Ⓐ Ⓑ Ⓒ Ⓓ	64	Ⓐ Ⓑ Ⓒ Ⓓ	84	Ⓐ Ⓑ Ⓒ Ⓓ
5	Ⓐ Ⓑ Ⓒ Ⓓ	25	Ⓐ Ⓑ Ⓒ Ⓓ	45	Ⓐ Ⓑ Ⓒ Ⓓ	65	Ⓐ Ⓑ Ⓒ Ⓓ	85	Ⓐ Ⓑ Ⓒ Ⓓ
6	Ⓐ Ⓑ Ⓒ Ⓓ	26	Ⓐ Ⓑ Ⓒ Ⓓ	46	Ⓐ Ⓑ Ⓒ Ⓓ	66	Ⓐ Ⓑ Ⓒ Ⓓ	86	Ⓐ Ⓑ Ⓒ Ⓓ
7	Ⓐ Ⓑ Ⓒ Ⓓ	27	Ⓐ Ⓑ Ⓒ Ⓓ	47	Ⓐ Ⓑ Ⓒ Ⓓ	67	Ⓐ Ⓑ Ⓒ Ⓓ	87	Ⓐ Ⓑ Ⓒ Ⓓ
8	Ⓐ Ⓑ Ⓒ Ⓓ	28	Ⓐ Ⓑ Ⓒ Ⓓ	48	Ⓐ Ⓑ Ⓒ Ⓓ	68	Ⓐ Ⓑ Ⓒ Ⓓ	88	Ⓐ Ⓑ Ⓒ Ⓓ
9	Ⓐ Ⓑ Ⓒ Ⓓ	29	Ⓐ Ⓑ Ⓒ Ⓓ	49	Ⓐ Ⓑ Ⓒ Ⓓ	69	Ⓐ Ⓑ Ⓒ Ⓓ	89	Ⓐ Ⓑ Ⓒ Ⓓ
10	Ⓐ Ⓑ Ⓒ Ⓓ	30	Ⓐ Ⓑ Ⓒ Ⓓ	50	Ⓐ Ⓑ Ⓒ Ⓓ	70	Ⓐ Ⓑ Ⓒ Ⓓ	90	Ⓐ Ⓑ Ⓒ Ⓓ
11	Ⓐ Ⓑ Ⓒ Ⓓ	31	Ⓐ Ⓑ Ⓒ Ⓓ	51	Ⓐ Ⓑ Ⓒ Ⓓ	71	Ⓐ Ⓑ Ⓒ Ⓓ	91	Ⓐ Ⓑ Ⓒ Ⓓ
12	Ⓐ Ⓑ Ⓒ Ⓓ	32	Ⓐ Ⓑ Ⓒ Ⓓ	52	Ⓐ Ⓑ Ⓒ Ⓓ	72	Ⓐ Ⓑ Ⓒ Ⓓ	92	Ⓐ Ⓑ Ⓒ Ⓓ
13	Ⓐ Ⓑ Ⓒ Ⓓ	33	Ⓐ Ⓑ Ⓒ Ⓓ	53	Ⓐ Ⓑ Ⓒ Ⓓ	73	Ⓐ Ⓑ Ⓒ Ⓓ	93	Ⓐ Ⓑ Ⓒ Ⓓ
14	Ⓐ Ⓑ Ⓒ Ⓓ	34	Ⓐ Ⓑ Ⓒ Ⓓ	54	Ⓐ Ⓑ Ⓒ Ⓓ	74	Ⓐ Ⓑ Ⓒ Ⓓ	94	Ⓐ Ⓑ Ⓒ Ⓓ
15	Ⓐ Ⓑ Ⓒ Ⓓ	35	Ⓐ Ⓑ Ⓒ Ⓓ	55	Ⓐ Ⓑ Ⓒ Ⓓ	75	Ⓐ Ⓑ Ⓒ Ⓓ	95	Ⓐ Ⓑ Ⓒ Ⓓ
16	Ⓐ Ⓑ Ⓒ Ⓓ	36	Ⓐ Ⓑ Ⓒ Ⓓ	56	Ⓐ Ⓑ Ⓒ Ⓓ	76	Ⓐ Ⓑ Ⓒ Ⓓ	96	Ⓐ Ⓑ Ⓒ Ⓓ
17	Ⓐ Ⓑ Ⓒ Ⓓ	37	Ⓐ Ⓑ Ⓒ Ⓓ	57	Ⓐ Ⓑ Ⓒ Ⓓ	77	Ⓐ Ⓑ Ⓒ Ⓓ	97	Ⓐ Ⓑ Ⓒ Ⓓ
18	Ⓐ Ⓑ Ⓒ Ⓓ	38	Ⓐ Ⓑ Ⓒ Ⓓ	58	Ⓐ Ⓑ Ⓒ Ⓓ	78	Ⓐ Ⓑ Ⓒ Ⓓ	98	Ⓐ Ⓑ Ⓒ Ⓓ
19	Ⓐ Ⓑ Ⓒ Ⓓ	39	Ⓐ Ⓑ Ⓒ Ⓓ	59	Ⓐ Ⓑ Ⓒ Ⓓ	79	Ⓐ Ⓑ Ⓒ Ⓓ	99	Ⓐ Ⓑ Ⓒ Ⓓ
20	Ⓐ Ⓑ Ⓒ Ⓓ	40	Ⓐ Ⓑ Ⓒ Ⓓ	60	Ⓐ Ⓑ Ⓒ Ⓓ	80	Ⓐ Ⓑ Ⓒ Ⓓ	100	Ⓐ Ⓑ Ⓒ Ⓓ

books.english.co.kr

books.english.co.kr

No.

성명 한글 영자

실전 모의고사 8

LISTENING (PART I~IV)

No.

성명 한글 영자

실전 모의고사 7

LISTENING (PART I~IV)

books.english.co.kr

books.english.co.kr

점수변환표

Raw Score	Listening	Reading	Raw Score	Listening	Reading
100	495	495	74	350	320
99	495	490~495	73	345	315
98	495	485	72	340	310
97	495	475~480	71	335	310
96	495	465~470	70	330	305
95	485~495	455~460	69	320	300
94	480	440~450	68	315	285~290
93	470~475	435~440	67	305~310	280
92	465	425~430	66	300	275
91	460	415~420	65	295	270
90	445~455	410	64	290	265
89	440~445	405	63	285	260
88	440	395~400	62	280	255
87	430~435	395	61	275	250
86	425	390	60	270	245
85	420	385	59	265	240
84	410	380	58	260	225~230
83	405	375	57	250~255	220
82	400	370	56	245	215
81	395	365	55	240	210
80	390	360	54	235	205
79	385	345~350	53	230	200
78	380	340	52	225	195
77	365~375	335	51	220	190
76	360	330	50	215	185
75	355	325